Literacy, Language and Reading in Nineteenth-Century Ireland

The Society for the Study of Nineteenth-Century Ireland

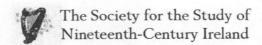

The Society for the Study of Nineteenth-Century Ireland

The purpose of the Society is to promote research into nineteenth-century Ireland, and membership is open to scholars both from Ireland and other countries. The Society welcomes members from a wide range of disciplines: literature, history, economics, geography, sociology, anthropology, theology, women's studies, fine arts, etc. It thus seeks to foster an inter-disciplinary approach to nineteenth-century Irish studies.

Series editors: Laurence M. Geary & Ciara Breathnach

Literacy, Language and Reading in Nineteenth-Century Ireland

EDITED BY REBECCA ANNE BARR,
SARAH-ANNE BUCKLEY AND
MUIREANN O'CINNEIDE

LIVERPOOL UNIVERSITY PRESS

First published 2019 by
Liverpool University Press
4 Cambridge Street
Liverpool
L69 7ZU

This paperback edition first published 2022

British Library Cataloguing-in-Publication data
A British Library CIP record is available

ISBN 978-1-78694-208-1 cased
ISBN 978-1-80085-472-7 paperback

Typeset by Carnegie Book Production, Lancaster
Printed and bound by CPI Group (UK) Ltd, Croydon CR0 4YY

Contents

List of Figures and Tables vii

Acknowledgements ix

Contributors xi

Introduction 1
Rebecca Anne Barr, Sarah-Anne Buckley and Muireann O'Cinneide

Section 1: Literacy and Bilingualism

1. Varieties of Literacy in Nineteenth-Century Ireland: Gender, Religion and Language 15
Niall Ó Ciosáin

2. Douglas Hyde (1860–1949): The Adolescent Behind the Diarist 28
Máire Nic an Bhaird and Liam Mac Mathúna

Section 2: Periodicals and Their Readers

3. The *Nation*, History, and the Making of National Citizens 53
James Quinn

4. Watchmen to the House of Israel? Irish Methodism and the Religious Press 66
Nicola Morris

5. The *Dublin Penny Journal* and Alternative Histories 87
Elizabeth Tilley

Section 3: Translation, Transmission and Transnational Literacies

6. Room with a View: Reading Ireland in the Irish College Old Library, Paris *c*.1870–1900 107
Darragh Gannon

7. 'May God Bless You and All at Home': Mid-Nineteenth Century Irish Views on Italy through the Letters of Albert Delahoyde, 1860–1870 126
Florry O'Driscoll

8. 'Good Translations' or 'Mental Dram-Drinking'? Translation and Literacy in Nineteenth-Century Ireland 139
Michèle Milan

Section 4: Visual Literacies

9. From Dublin to Dehra Dun: Language, Translation and the Mapping of Ireland and India 159
Nessa Cronin

10. Reading the Hand: Palmistry, Graphology and Alternative Literacies 176
Stephanie Rains

Select Bibliography 191

Index 207

Figures and Tables

Figure 1.1:	Female literacy index 1841	21
Figure 2.1:	Hyde's first diary spanning the period 1874–76 (NLI MS G 1036) (Reproduced with kind permission of the National Library of Ireland)	29
Figure 2.2:	Bessie Hyde's name inside front cover of Hyde's first diary (NLI MS G 1036) (Reproduced with kind permission of the National Library of Ireland)	33
Figure 2.3:	Diary entries from 1876 showing the improvement in Hyde's Irish language written skills (NLI MS G 1036) (Reproduced with kind permission of the National Library of Ireland)	38–39
Figure 2.4:	Arthur Hyde's hunting notes, displaying the family interest in recording and tabulating their hunting achievements (NLI MS 17,775) (Reproduced with kind permission of the National Library of Ireland)	41
Figure 2.5:	Sketch of Douglas Hyde in Arthur Hyde's diary, subsequently signed in Irish, Dúbhglas de hÍde (NLI MS 17,775) (Reproduced with kind permission of the National Library of Ireland)	43
Figure 2.6:	Arthur Hyde's sketches of guns and boats in his diary (NLI MS 17,775) (Reproduced with kind permission of the National Library of Ireland)	44
Figure 2.7:	Hyde's sketches of alcohol are dispersed through this diary (NLI MS G 1036) (Reproduced with kind permission of the National Library of Ireland)	49
Figure 5.1:	*Dublin Penny Journal* (1 September 1832), p. 76 (Courtesy James Hardiman Library, National University of Ireland, Galway)	93

Figure 5.2: *Dublin Penny Journal* (2 March 1833), p. 282 (Courtesy James Hardiman Library, National University of Ireland, Galway) 94
Figure 5.3.1: *Dublin Penny Journal* (14 July 1832), p. 1 (Courtesy James Hardiman Library, National University of Ireland, Galway) 97
Figure 5.3.2: G.N. Wright, *Ireland Illustrated* (London: H. Fisher, Son, and Jackson, 1831), p. 22 (Courtesy James Hardiman Library, National University of Ireland, Galway) 98
Figure 5.4: *The Irish Penny Journal* (15 August 1840), p. 1 (Courtesy James Hardiman Library, National University of Ireland, Galway) 102

Table 1.1: Female reading index by province 22
Table 1.2: Female reading index by religion 22

Acknowledgements

The editors wish to thank the Society for the Study of Nineteenth-Century Ireland, and all the participants in the SSNCI June 2015 conference on Literacy in Nineteenth-Century Ireland at the Moore Institute, National University of Ireland (NUI), Galway, from which the impetus for this volume emerged. The conference received funding from the NUI Galway School of Humanities for which we are grateful. This publication has been assisted by the NUI Galway Grant in Aid of Publication.

We wish to thank the series editors, Ciara Breathnach and Laurence Geary, and the President of the SSNCI, Ciaran O'Neill, for their guidance and support. We also want to thank Alison Welsby of Liverpool University Press who has been both patient and kind throughout the process.

Rebecca Anne Barr, Sarah-Anne Buckley and Muireann O'Cinneide
September 2018

Contributors

Rebecca Anne Barr is lecturer in English Literature at the National University of Ireland, Galway. Her research focuses on fictional form, masculinity, and sexuality in the eighteenth-century novel. With Sylvie Kleiman-Lafon and Sophie Vasset, she is co-editor of *Bellies, Bowels and Entrails in the Eighteenth Century* (Manchester University Press, 2018) and co-editor with Sean Brady and Jane McGaughey of *Ireland and Masculinities in History* (Palgrave, 2019).

Sarah-Anne Buckley is lecturer in History at the National University of Ireland, Galway. Her research centres on the history of childhood and youth. Author of *The Cruelty Man: Child Welfare, the NSPCC and the State in Ireland, 1889–1956* (Manchester University Press, 2013), she is president of the Women's History Association of Ireland, chair of the Irish History Student's Association and co-director of the Irish Centre for the Histories of Labour and Class at NUI Galway.

Nessa Cronin is lecturer in Irish Studies at the Centre for Irish Studies and associate director of the Moore Institute at the National University of Ireland, Galway. Her research lies at the intersection between cartography, colonialism and culture, and she has recently co-edited a special issue of *The Irish Review*, 'Embodied Geographies of the Nation' (2018).

Darragh Gannon is research fellow to the AHRC-funded 'A Global History of Irish Revolution, 1916–1923' at Queen's University Belfast. His research interests include the Irish revolution, museum and material culture, and global history, more broadly. In 2014 he was awarded a research fellowship to the Irish College, Paris, Old Library and Archives, by the Centre Culturel Irlandais.

Liam Mac Mathúna, emeritus professor of Irish at University College Dublin, is editor of *Éigse: A Journal of Irish Studies*, published by the National

University of Ireland. He is currently researching the life and work of Douglas Hyde, together with Máire Nic an Bhaird, Maynooth University.

Michèle Milan works in the area of translation history. Her publications include: 'Found in Translation: Franco-Irish Translation Relationships in Nineteenth-Century Ireland', PhD thesis, available at: http://doras.dcu.ie/17753/. Michèle worked as a postdoctoral researcher with Anne O'Connor (NUI Galway) on a one-year project examining translation in nineteenth-century Ireland. Since 2014, she has also directed her research towards studying the intersections between travel, translation and transnationalism in the Irish context.

Nicola Morris is a lecturer in Modern History at the University of Chester. Her publications include '"A Solid and United Phalanx?" The Protestant Churches and the Ulster Covenant 1912–2012', in John Wolffe (ed.), *Irish Religious Conflict in Comparative Perspective: Catholics, Protestants and Muslims* (Basingstoke: Palgrave Macmillan, 2014) and 'A rara avis: Jeremiah Jordan, Methodist and Nationalist', in Ciaran O'Neill (ed.), *Irish Elites in the Nineteenth Century* (Dublin: Four Courts Press, 2013).

Máire Nic an Bhaird is a lecturer in Irish Language and Literature in Maynooth University. Her main current area of research is the life and work of Douglas Hyde, Ireland's first president. She has several publications and has also presented this research on national and international television and radio programmes. She is a partner in the European Commission funded Horizon 2020 project *AgroCycle*.

Muireann O'Cinneide is lecturer in English at the National University of Ireland, Galway. She works on nineteenth-century women's travel writing and conflict narratives. She is the author of *Aristocratic Women and the Literary Nation, 1832–1868* (Basingstoke: Palgrave Macmillan, 2008); editor of two volumes in Pickering and Chatto's *Selected Works of Margaret Oliphant*, and co-editor with Tina O'Toole and Gillian McIntosh of *Women Writing War: Ireland, 1880–1922* (Dublin: UCD Press, 2016).

Niall Ó Ciosáin is senior lecturer in History at the National University of Ireland, Galway. He is the author of *Ireland in Official Print Culture 1800–50* (Oxford University Press, 2014) and *Print and Popular Culture in Ireland 1750–1850* (Macmillan: 1997), and is currently writing a book about publishing and reading in the Celtic languages in the eighteenth and nineteenth centuries.

Florry O'Driscoll completed his PhD at the National University of Ireland, Galway in 2018. His thesis is entitled 'Irish Soldiers in Risorgimento Italy and Civil War America: Nineteenth-Century Irish Nation-Building in Transnational and Comparative Perspective'. He works as an independent scholar, and his research interests are wide and varied, from Ancient History to the Modern Era.

James Quinn is managing editor of the Royal Irish Academy's *Dictionary of Irish Biography*. He has written widely on various aspects of Irish nationalism and historiography. His publications include *Soul on Fire: a Life of Thomas Russell* (Dublin: Irish Academic Press, 2002), *John Mitchel* (Dublin: UCD Press, 2008), and *Young Ireland and the Writing of Irish History* (Dublin: UCD Press, 2015).

Stephanie Rains is senior lecturer in Media Studies at Maynooth University. She published *Commodity Culture and Social Class in Dublin, 1850–1916* (Dublin: Irish Academic Press, 2010), has published articles in *Irish Studies Review, Media History* and *Irish University Review*, and is now working towards a book on twentieth-century Irish advertising and consumer culture.

Elizabeth Tilley is lecturer in English at the National University of Ireland, Galway, where she teaches Victorian literature and book history. She has published on Irish periodicals and Victorian fiction. In 2018 Broadview Press published her new critical edition of Sheridan LeFanu's *In a Glass Darkly*. At present, she is preparing a monograph on the history of nineteenth-century Irish periodicals.

Introduction

Rebecca Anne Barr, Sarah-Anne Buckley
and Muireann O'Cinneide

Nineteenth-century Ireland has long been cited as an instance of a 'literacy transition'.[1] From an apparently predominantly illiterate populace whose lack of reading and writing competencies was quantified by the 1841 census, literacy in Ireland increased dramatically within a century: the catalyst – or product – of seismic educational, political and linguistic changes. Yet the processes, and the full cultural significance, of this transition remain somewhat unclear – as does its implications for broader questions of how nineteenth-century Irish readers engaged with text and language. This volume of essays seeks to contribute to the understanding of how literacy, in its various forms and languages, functioned in nineteenth-century Ireland, and how reading and writing allowed an increasingly literate Irish populace to participate in print communities at home and abroad. In general, discussions of literacy in nineteenth-century Ireland have tended to position themselves in relation to developments in education and state institutions, a trend that has problematic repercussions, as we discuss below. As Mary E. Daly and Eugenio F. Biagini highlight in the introduction to *The Cambridge Social History of Modern Ireland*, a focus on people rather than institutions is to be welcomed. Moreover, they argue that 'Irish history is best understood in a wider European and indeed global context' rather than as an insular exception.[2] Writing of nineteenth-century Ireland, Ciarán

1 Harvey J. Graff, *The Legacies of Literacy: Continuities and Contradictions in Western Culture* (Bloomington: Indiana University Press, 1991), p. 337.

2 Eugenio F. Biagini and Mary E. Daly, 'Editors' Introduction', in Biagini and Daly (eds), *The Cambridge Social History of Modern Ireland* (Cambridge: Cambridge University Press, 2017), pp. 1–4, p. 3. See also Mary Daly and David Dickson (eds), *The Origins of Popular Literacy in Ireland: Language Change and Educational Development 1700–1920* (Dublin: Trinity College Dublin, 1990). Note also Peter K. Fallon's *Printing, Literacy, and Education in Eighteenth-Century Ireland: Why the Irish Speak English* (Lewiston, NY: Edwin Mellen Press, 2005).

O'Neill has stated that 'the expansion of literacy has been read as a product of colonially-motivated mass schooling [...] a colonial imposition aimed at eliminating both a "real" Irish culture and the Irish language', and thus it 'has become difficult to separate the literacy debate from the educational and the colonial'.[3] These long-held assumptions have been challenged by scholars such as Nicholas Wolf, whose *An Irish Speaking Island* has illuminated the complex landscape of literacy in Ireland, complicating the sense of linguistic displacement and colonial dominance from the eighteenth to the nineteenth century. Wolf's work attempts to extricate the languages of Ireland from an over-determined nationalist narrative in which the 'forces for Anglicization' attack and marginalise the indigenous language: a narrative in which 'the primary feature' of Irish is 'its endangerment and political extinction' and in which literacy features as an agent of colonisation.[4] In contrast, Wolf emphasises the linguistic diversity of the island, the large number, vibrancy and diversity of the Irish-speaking population across the nineteenth century. Literacy, then, is not simply a set of skills or competencies, but a contested and politically charged prism through which to examine Ireland's history.

Political issues are exacerbated by the opacity of meaning used when defining literacy itself. As Niall Ó Ciosáin notes in his essay in this volume, the apparently straightforward binary of literate and illiterate is more complicated than it initially appears. The spectrum of what might be thought of as 'literacy skills' can be gleaned by the categories of the 1851 Irish census: 'reading and writing', 'reading only', and neither reading nor writing.[5] The multiple categories provide a more nuanced sense of the capacities of the population in contrast to English counterparts, providing a tantalising sense of a demographic (often female) whose lack of writing skills have rendered them historically obscure. The census returns also enumerated the linguistic capacities of the population, bilingual or monoglot, in an Ireland with two co-existing and at times competing languages. This demands that this apparently uncomplicated notion of 'literacy' be unpacked, contextualised and analysed more fully.

The boundaries between reading, writing and literacy are often assumed and thus rather poorly defined – in academic discourse as well as in lived experience – but writing, reading and literacy do need to be analysed as distinct if crucially interlinked concepts. All can be understood and exercised in ways well beyond the traditionally defined territory of the written word.

3 Ciaran O'Neill, 'Literacy and Education', in Eugenio F. Biagini and Mary E. Daly (eds), *The Cambridge History of Modern Ireland* (Cambridge: Cambridge University Press, 2017), pp. 244–60, p. 245.

4 Nicholas Wolf, *An Irish Speaking Island: State, Religion, Community, and the Linguistic Landscape in Ireland, 1770–1870* (London: University of Wisconsin Press, 2014). p. 10.

5 'Census of Ireland 1901/1911 and Census Fragments and Substitutes, 1821–51', *National Archives of Ireland*, www.census.nationalarchives.ie.

But literacy's traditional emphasis on the primacy of the textual raises distinctive political and moral problems for Ireland: 'a country', as Walter Ong observes, 'in which every region preserves massive residual orality'.[6] If the narrative of 'literacy-as-loss' is one of the most discomforting and contested elements of Ireland's language acquisition and change in the nineteenth century (and beyond), it must also be balanced by an expanded sense of what constitutes textual materials.[7] An explosion of manuscript sources in Irish matches the paucity of nineteenth-century printed books in the language.[8] Thus, what once seemed a clear story of cultural transition through literacy is increasingly being seen instead as a series of contested and complex histories.

This volume explores discourses surrounding literacy in nineteenth-century Ireland, the exercise and activation of literacy in various modes of print culture, and the implications a more nuanced grasp of reading experiences might have for our historical understandings of the relationship between education, identity, status, and the much-contested capacity to bestow a common meaning upon signs. Thus, these essays push beyond the established discourses on education and literacy to include analyses of the 'new literacies' of the period. These encompass alternative modes of communication, reading and interpretation engendered by the new technologies of the time: the visual symbolism of the *Dublin Penny Journal*; the imperial cartography honed in Ireland and deployed by the British Empire in India; the palmistry craze of the late-nineteenth century.[9] These alternative forms of interpreting sign systems are intimately connected with the practice of literacy, expansion of media, and the ways in which the world of print and writing was negotiated in Ireland. Questions about language, gender, print culture, orality and region raised in the opening essay by Ó Ciosáin resonate throughout the volume. The essays here consider literacies in both English and Irish, as well as placing both languages within wider transnational frameworks of classical and Continental language learning, and contextualised by Irish and European politics.

6 Walter Ong, *Orality and Literacy: The Technologizing of the Word* (London: Routledge, 1995), p. 69.

7 For a précis of this debate see O'Neill, 'Literacy and Education', pp. 249–51.

8 See Brian Ó Cuív, 'Irish Language and Literature, 1691–1845', in T.W. Moody and W.E. Vaughan (eds), *A New History of Ireland, vol. 4, Eighteenth-century Ireland, 1691–1800* (Oxford: Clarendon Press, 1876), pp. 374–423, p. 391.

9 For a similar approach to 'reading' the body, see Ciara Breathnach, '"Indelible Characters": Tattoos, Power and the Late Nineteenth-Century Irish Convict', *Cultural and Social History* 12.2 (2015): 235–54.

Ireland, Britain and Literacy as Loss

The history of literacy in Ireland is, of course, a history of languages and politics. The preponderance of monolingual histories of nineteenth-century Ireland means that the concept of literacy is assumed as literacy *in English*. As Helen O'Connell has noted, Irish in the period was described in terms of 'orality and illiteracy *in order to assert* the rationality of the English-language literary discourse'.[10] If the Irish language was indeed increasingly sidelined by the British administration during the nineteenth century, with literacy in English tied to employability, financial status and immigrant mobility, we must be wary of unproblematically accepting state educational and bureaucratic definitions of literacy and be sensitive to the multiple forms of competencies found in local communities and religious organisations.[11] Irish language material persists in the nineteenth century, with antiquarian and revivalist interests promoting the textualisation of many Irish works. Indeed, it may be that the monolingualism of many contemporary historians circumscribes a fuller sense of the linguistic and literate terrains of the period. As Vincent Morley has recently observed, 'the inability of so many historians of Ireland to read primary sources in the indigenous language of the country is the most striking example of the profession's failure to adapt its techniques to meet the challenges posed by the raw materials of Irish history'.[12]

The once-dominant narrative of language loss, in which English literacy displaces Irish orality, is complicated by Ó Ciosáin's interpretation of Irish print culture in this volume. As Ó Ciosáin wonders: 'What does it mean to say someone is able to read?' Re-examining works printed in Irish, in phonetical 'anglicised' forms rather than traditional orthography, he suggests that literacy in English activated and enabled, rather than closed down, literacy in Irish. Using a comparative framework, the chapter explores the ways in which denominational, gender and regional differences are expressed in the varieties of literacies in Ireland. Ó Ciosáin's conception of the nineteenth century as a period of considerable bilingual literacy, in which print actively textualised and promoted the *reading* of Irish, amplifies Wolf's description of an island composed of multiple speech communities and adaptive bilingualism.[13]

10 Helen O'Connell, *Ireland and the Fiction of Improvement* (Oxford: Oxford University Press, 2006), p. 160, our emphasis.

11 See also Nessa Cronin, Séan Crosson, and John Eastlake, 'Introduction: "The Sea of Orality": An Introduction to Orality and Modern Irish Culture', in Nessa Cronin, Séan Crosson and John Eastlake (eds), *Anáil an Bhéil Bheo: Orality and Modern Irish Culture* (Newcastle upon Tyne: Cambridge Scholars Publishing, 2009), pp. 3–12.

12 Vincent Morley, *The Popular Mind in Eighteenth-Century Ireland* (Cork: Cork University Press, 2017), p. 1.

13 Wolf, *An Irish Speaking Island.*

The interconnection of multiple languages and literacies can be traced in the case study of Douglas Hyde that follows. Máire Nic an Bhaird and Liam Mac Mathúna examine the diaristic and linguistic development of Douglas Hyde through an examination of his early journals. As the founding President of the Gaelic League, first Professor of Modern Irish in University College Dublin and first President of an independent Irish state, Hyde's linguistic ideas were integral to his literary and cultural nationalism. His inner thoughts and ideas, his linguistic development, and his coming of age in Co. Roscommon are articulated through 13 diaries housed in the National Library of Ireland. Personal, affective encounters with the Irish language are shown to be an integral part of his personal and political self-development, as Irish language becomes the written mode of both self-expression and self-creation. Hyde's diaries use phonetic, anglicised transcriptions to chart his early encounters with Irish and experiments in writing in the language. Intriguingly, Hyde's early writing in Irish utilises diacritical marks from French: suggesting how available textual models affect literacy acquisition when there is little access to works written in the language under study.

If the largely rural economy of nineteenth-century Ireland offered an impediment to literacy, given the lower scale of industrialisation compared to Britain, the growth in education in the century suggests a country invested in the politics of literacy. Indeed, during the political ferment of the 1790s and the subsequent Act of Union, the opposing forces of independence and unionism converged on the significance of literacy. As Michael Brown has noted, the 'radical revision of reading practices' undertaken by the United Irishmen 'was more than a political programme of reform or renewal. It also contained a novel cultural order, which in turn required a new kind of man'.[14] This masculine political citizen was to be forged through the interactions of 'public opinion and wider cultural production': spaces permeated by print, reading and debates over the meaning of words.[15] James Quinn's essay in this volume on the *Nation* newspaper showcases nationalist belief in the value of education – particularly education in history – in forging a self-governing citizenry. Quinn argues that many nationalists – in particular the Young Ireland movement of the 1840s – saw it as their patriotic duty to give the Irish people the 'national' education that the British government was deliberately preventing them from receiving. The core subject of this education was history, which they believed would help to create the 'imagined community' of the nation by nourishing collective memory and reinforcing national allegiances and obligations, so that the Irish would see themselves as a distinct people

14 Michael Brown, *The Irish Enlightenment* (Harvard: Harvard University Press, 2015), p. 430.
15 Ibid.

rooted in the struggles and sacrifices of the past. This they attempted to do by propagating a heroic and celebratory narrative of Ireland's struggle for independence through cheap and accessible ballad collections, historical works presented in the 'Library of Ireland', and in newspapers such as the *Nation*. Hand in hand with the provision of reading materials, Young Ireland also sought to promote literacy through the establishment of reading rooms stocked with nationalist literature to supplement or supplant official educational initiatives. Literacy was envisaged as catalysing an informed citizenry who would insist that they should govern their own destiny.

Irish associational culture and politics throughout the nineteenth century was thus animated by the power of reading, even if not all participants possessed the ability to write fluently. Even limited literacy enabled participation in the print culture and politics of the time. As an English commentator observed, repeal pamphlets were

> read to such of them as are themselves unable to read. In many of the southern towns there are repeal reading rooms, where the most zealous repeal papers are regularly read aloud to listening groups, unable to read for themselves. In those rural districts where the population is too thinly scattered to admit of establishing repeal reading rooms, the practice is for the peasantry, in each parish, to assemble every Sunday afternoon in the most convenient place in the parish, to hear the repeal weekly journals read.[16]

Such testimonies suggest the inadequacy of the term 'illiterate' to properly describe what Grant calls 'the [Irish] peasantry'.

While Quinn emphasises the political utility of literacy and history, Elizabeth Tilley's examination of the *Dublin Penny Journal* shows how antiquarian history was also being reshaped along nationalist lines by the penny magazines. Often seen as ragbags of general information, assemblages of peculiar or exotic facts, or purveyors of moral tales, these ephemeral publications are unexpected and under-examined repositories of cultural identity and indigenous knowledge. The format of such magazines was altered in the 1830s in Ireland, reflecting a sense of urgency about the gathering and preservation of evidence of the country's heritage. Tilley examines the *Dublin Penny Journal* as a case in point, as part of its mandate was to popularise and explain to a general audience the ancient chronicles of Ireland. One of the magazine's early editors was George Petrie, Head of the Memoir Section of the government's Ordnance Survey in Ireland and prominent member of the

16 James Grant, *Impressions of Ireland and the Irish, 1844*, 2 vols (London: Cunningham, 1844), II, pp. 199–200.

Royal Irish Academy. Petrie had procured for the Academy the *Annals of the Four Masters*, a record of Irish history from the deluge (dated as 2,242 years after creation) to AD 1616, and it was extracts from the *Annals* that Petrie used as a way of reuniting his audience with their own past. The *Annals* retold the story of Ireland's birth and death, a story filled both with glory and with ignominious defeat at the hands of the English. Though ostensibly listing the achievements of the Gaelic nobility, in Petrie's hands the *Annals* also suggested that the Irish peasantry might, revenant-like, reclaim their own history, and the penny journal format — cheap, conversational, nationalist – made manifest this reconstruction of reality.

If eighteenth-century Irish radical politics celebrated the progressive powers of literacy, the nineteenth-century British state likewise equated the role of education as a means to social control with literacy functioning as 'a means of teaching the lower classes their true interests'.[17] Nessa Cronin's chapter in this volume, which highlights the visual literacy of national territory and colonial space, makes clear the links between cartographic and scientific modes of reading colonial landscapes and the interpretation and containment of colonial peoples. The monetary value of English literacy within the British economy was doubtless an inducement to learn for many Irish. The 1841 census proudly noted that it was 'gratifying to see that, compared with the mass of the population, the army is by no means uneducated', with a supposed 66% of the Irish soldiers and officers in the British Army, able to 'read and write'.[18] While this number ought to be viewed sceptically as an advertisement for the colonial doctrine of moral and educational improvement, the economic advantages bestowed by reading and writing proficiency in English undoubtedly increased its popularity. Literacy in English equipped the Irish to work and move throughout the British Empire, as well as allowing many to access the means for transatlantic immigration.[19] Cronin's chapter argues that the history of the making of empire is also inextricably bound to the histories of science and cartography in the nineteenth century. Looking at the visual literacy of national territory and colonial space through the national surveys of Ireland and India undertaken in the period, she shows that the discourse and practice

17 Alan Richardson, 'Literacy', in Laura Dabundo (ed.), *Encyclopedia of Romanticism: Culture in Britain, 1780s–1830s* ([1992] London: Routledge, 2010), p. 337. This is in relation to educational aims of the Anglo-Irish writer Maria Edgeworth. See also Patrick Brantlinger, *The Reading Lesson: The Threat of Mass Literacy in Nineteenth-Century British Fiction* (Bloomington: Indiana University Press, 1998) and David Vincent, *The Rise of Mass Literacy: Reading and Writing in Modern Europe* (Cambridge: Polity, 2000).

18 1841 census report, quoted in Thomas E. Jordan, 'Queen Victoria's Irish Soldiers: Quality of Life and Social Origins of the Thin "Green" Line', *Social Indicators Research* 57.1 (2002): 73–88.

19 Graff, *Legacies of Literacy*, p. 338.

of map-making was shaped by the introduction of instruments known as 'Colby's Compensation Bars', used to accurately measure baselines under challenging climatic conditions. The language and techniques of science were translated from Dublin's Ordnance Survey to Dehra Dun, where George Everest would use them in his baseline survey of India in the 1830s. As Cronin states, 'the soldier-surveyors and civilians, local landowners and native informants, played an integral role in the material construction of empire, in the drawing and the marking out of the *graphos* of the map'.[20]

Gender, Literary Cultures and (Trans)National Communities

As already discussed, the acquisition and understanding of literacy was affected by class, gender, and region. In Britain, there was profound unease surrounding nineteenth-century discussions of women's literacy.[21] Advocates for female education posited the importance of maternal reading, while opponents invoked sexualised discourses of moral corruption and distraction from crucial domestic duties. These debates were responses to the reality of increasing female readership throughout the nineteenth century. While David Vincent notes that for nineteenth-century Britain, the rise of women's literacy levels took place more uniformly across classes than those of men, Ó Ciosáin's chapter in this volume argues that the picture in Ireland appears to be complicated by religious affiliation and region.[22] But differences in literacy are not solely tied to confessional culture. Stephanie Rains's chapter on graphology and the interactions between readers and editors in the new periodical press opens up new understandings of modes of reading and of channels of expression for female readers. Rains examines an alternative mode of reading signs: that of the graphology craze of the nineteenth century. As literacy increased exponentially during the late nineteenth century in Ireland, a central feature of the 'new journalism' style of the popular press was that readers wrote back, whether in the form of letters to the editor or entries to the numerous competitions. This Irish alternative to the Habermassian public sphere involved significant female participation. Such contests were an opportunity for readers to enjoy and display their literacy. But perhaps most

20 Nessa Cronin, 'From Dublin to Dehra Dun: Language, Translation and Mapping Ireland and India', this volume, chapter 9, pp. 159–75, p. 175.

21 Kate Flint, *The Woman Reader 1837–1914* (Oxford: Oxford University Press, 1993); James Raven, Helen Small and Naomi Tadmor (eds), *The Practice and Representation of Reading in England* (Cambridge: Cambridge University Press, 1996).

22 David Vincent, *Literacy and Popular Culture: England 1750–1914* (Cambridge: Cambridge University Press, 1993), pp. 101–03; Niall Ó Ciosáin, 'Varieties of Literacy in Nineteenth-century Ireland: Gender, Religion and Language', this volume, chapter 1.

revealing indication of the importance of writing in the popular imagination was the rise of 'graphology', which claimed to read a person's 'character' from their handwriting. Rains examines these acts of writing and what they signified for ordinary readers, many of who would have been the first in their families to write with confidence. While the economic benefits of literacy are well-charted, many of the writers Rains discovers in the archive view their handwriting as a meaningful personal characteristic: a concretisation and projection of the self enabled by the rapidly-expanding print culture of late nineteenth-century Ireland.

The relationship of literacy to gender is also present in the way in which literate culture was imbricated in notions of civility and masculinity. The emphatically textual quality of radical and progressive politics was one means of adopting the literate practices of France and Britain. Moreover, as David Lloyd has noted:

> the reconstitution of Irish masculinity and the regulation of proper gendered spaces that was undertaken by Irish nationalism generated a set of prohibitions and exhortations that focus on the unruly mouth. The oral thus stands as the most resonant metonym for Irish bodily culture and for the distinctive matrix of habits and practices that marks Ireland's colonial difference.[23]

Stephanie Newell, investigating literary culture in colonial Ghana, describes as 'paracolonial' the 'attitudes, aspiration and activities of non-elite readers who were neither the direct products of British colonialism nor the products of purely pre-colonial formations'. These readers, she argues, 'actively constituted their own literacy, seeking power from their readings and embedding English literature in local discourses about gender, education, self-help and morality'.[24] The long-standing close entanglement between Ireland, Irish educational institutions and literary marketplaces, and the British imperial order make the positioning of non-elite Irish readers within this framework particular contestable, but it is a useful reminder that the adaptation and integration of literacy practices rooted in the reading and writing of English did not necessarily mean that these could not be adapted to more localised concerns and agendas.

As Nicola Morris's chapter, for instance, shows, literacy in English could be utilised by the Methodist community in Ireland to create a countervailing

23 David Lloyd, *Irish Culture and Colonial Modernity 1800–2000: The Transformation of Oral Space* (Cambridge: Cambridge University Press, 2011), pp. 85–115, p. 3.

24 Stephanie Newell, *Literary Culture in Colonial Ghana: 'How to Play the Game of Life'* (Manchester: Manchester University Press, 2002), pp. 3–4.

religious and political discourse to that of their English brethren, allowing them to intervene in both political and religious issues. Morris's discussion of literacy, denominational identity, and Irish Methodism provides a vivid example of the deep connections between religion and literacy outlined in Ó Ciosáin's essay. With the emergence of the 'nonconformist conscience' into British public life in the 1880s, Irish Methodists responded by developing their own denominational newspaper that articulated a peculiarly *Irish* Methodist view, distinct from that being promoted in England. The establishment of the weekly *Christian Advocate* in Belfast in 1884 marked the transfer of denominational influence from the wealth of Dublin to the popular heartlands in Ulster. Thus the establishment and distribution of an indigenous Irish Methodist journal drew together a geographically dispersed denomination and developed a distinctly Irish Methodist response to current affairs.

Discussions of reading and literacy in Ireland should not, though, be positioned wholly in relation to colonial networks or to the relationship between British and Irish cultural communities. Nineteenth-century Irish readers and writers could access transnational networks, through which they could learn to read both other languages and other cultural customs, and by experiencing this, Irishness itself could become portable: part of a transnationally legible set of behaviours, modified and altered by collision and co-existence with other languages and cultures. Several essays in the collection address literacy, translation, and transnational experiences. Translation history allows us to frame Irish reading and writing within the broader contexts advocated by Biagiani and Daly. While Irish newspapers and magazines such as the *Nation* and the *Dublin University Magazine* featured a variety of both 'original' and reprinted translations, a number of Irish printers and publishers also contributed to the dissemination of translated works. Michèle Milan's chapter illustrates the role played by translators and other actors in the process, such as printers, publishers and booksellers. Throughout the nineteenth century, Irish printers and publishers such as Richard Cross, James Duffy and M.H. Gill and Sons contributed to the dissemination of what they identified as 'good reading' – an undertaking which also involved a careful selection of 'good translations'. Translation in the nineteenth-century Irish literary marketplace was therefore inextricably interconnected with discourses of morality, education, and national virtues. Looking at reading culture beyond the geographical boundaries of Ireland, Darragh Gannon examines interpretations of contemporary and historical Ireland through the Irish College in Paris. Gannon interrogates the extensive print holdings of the Irish College Old Library, acquired since the French Revolution, to illuminate student perceptions of Ireland past, present, and future – and how the reading and education of these students takes place at the nexus of European debate between religion and secularism. This transnational context is extended by

Florry O'Driscoll, who uses the case study of Dublin-born Albert De La Hoyde as an instance of transnational language learning. De la Hoyde was not yet 18 years of age when he volunteered to fight with the Papal Battalion of St Patrick in 1860, in an ultimately futile attempt to maintain Pope Pius IX's control over the Papal States. Through his letters, one can assess the individual, but also the communal significance of both the Papal Battalion and the Papal Zouaves, and the many contacts between Ireland and Italy in the mid-nineteenth century. De La Hoyde provides a perfect example of practical literacy in action, as the correspondence of the Irish soldier reveals much about the links between writing, identity, and nation at the midpoint of the nineteenth century. Gannon's and O'Driscoll's chapters both trace the reading and writing experiences of young Catholic Irishmen in France and Italy, and the ways in which their understandings of Irish nationalism and Catholic masculinity were shaped by transnational encounters.

Ultimately, this volume offers multiple perspectives on education, writing, and reading in nineteenth-century Ireland, highlighting the relationship between literacy, book history, and the history of reading, and foregrounding visual, oral, and symbolic literacies as significant modes of societal communication. It seeks to open up fresh insights into the linguistic realms of nineteenth-century Ireland and to engage on multiple levels with the politics of literacy, foregrounding this vital concept as a provocative site of class, gender, and cultural conflict rather than a narrow set of statistics or educational measurements. To read in Ireland, to read while being Irish, was to enter into contested cultural exchanges and to take part in constructing national identity after the Act of Union – but a national identity whose boundaries, inclusions, and significance were up for perpetual debate and re-definition. As this volume demonstrates, encounters with the printed page took place across manifold physical forms and through often-conflicted intellectual contexts, and in conjunction with less established, more easily-overlooked non-print modes of communication and interpretation. A diary entry, a letter, a newspaper or a periodical, a published book, the lines on a map, or the markings on a hand – these all offer crucial sites for understanding the reading communities of nineteenth-century Ireland, and how the people of these communities encountered reading, writing, and literacy in this period of rapid cultural and educational change.

Section 1
Literacy and Bilingualism

1
Varieties of Literacy in Nineteenth-Century Ireland: Gender, Religion and Language

Niall Ó Ciosáin

The description and measurement of literacy can be approached from two directions. On the one hand, it is an individual skill, achieved and practiced by specific people. On the other hand, it is a social phenomenon, and societies or groups can be characterised as 'oral', 'literate' or perhaps in a phase of 'partial literacy' or 'restricted literacy'. The two are not of course entirely distinct, and by and large the social phenomenon is the sum of the individual skills. But they are not identical either: groups can be literate as a collective, and participate in written culture, even when not all members, or even a majority, are literate as individuals. This occurs most often through the practice of reading aloud, or group reading, which was at least as common as individual silent reading in the nineteenth century, particularly outside the elite.

Literacy Levels: Reading and Writing

Most discussion of literacy in the historiography of nineteenth-century Ireland concerns the social phenomenon, reflecting the interests of the historiography of literacy in general. This takes a country or region as the unit of analysis and characterises its level of literacy as low or high, increasing or decreasing, and at what rate. Long-established regional contrasts can form part of the characterisation of a country as a whole. In nineteenth-century Ireland a highly literate north-east contrasted with an illiterate west coast, while France has traditionally been divided along a line from St Malo to Geneva, with much higher levels of literacy north of the line.[1]

1 Roger Chartier, 'The Two Frances: The History of a Geographical Idea', in Chartier,

This approach owes much to the concept of 'human capital' in economics, the 'acquired and useful abilities of all the inhabitants and members of the society' in the words of Adam Smith.[2] While this is a central element in many or most explanations of economic development, it is a difficult phenomenon to measure. For periods before the twentieth century, probably the easiest way to do so is to focus on elementary education, and on the most accessible measure of that education – literacy. Literacy levels are therefore a proxy for economic development or 'modernisation', with literacy thought of as both a cause and a consequence of that development. This was already the view of the census commissioners of 1841, who measured literacy carefully for precisely this reason:

> Still we may observe, that bad house-accommodation and defective education [ie illiteracy] seem to accompany each other. But whether the one or the other be cause or effect, there can be little doubt that the removal of either would be soon followed by the amelioration of the other.[3]

This emphasis on levels of literacy can also be found among political and cultural historians, notably those with a background in economic history.[4] The idea of a threshold level of literacy, often used by development economists, was adapted in the 1960s for a long-range explanation of political organisation by Lawrence Stone:

> The three great modernising revolutions of the West, English, French and Russian, have taken place at a time when the rate of male literacy has been between one third and two thirds, not less, not more.[5]

This has found an echo in Ireland in recent work on the 1790s, which has emphasised networks of communication, printed propaganda, and the concentration of politicisation and rebellion in the most literate areas of the

Cultural History: Between Practices and Representations (Cambridge: Polity Press, 1988), pp. 172–200.

2 Adam Smith, *An Inquiry into the Nature and Causes of the Wealth of Nations* (Dublin, 1776), Vol. 2, p. 6.

3 *Report of the Commissioners Appointed to Take the Census of Ireland, for the Year 1841.* H.C. 1843, XXIV, xxxiii.

4 François Furet and Jacques Ozouf, *Reading and Writing: Literacy in France from Calvin to Jules Ferry* (Cambridge: Cambridge University Press 1982), pp. 314–15; John Markoff, 'Literacy and Revolt: Some Empirical Notes on 1789 in France', *American Journal of Sociology* 92 (1986): 323–49.

5 Lawrence Stone, 'Literacy and Education in England, 1640–1900', *Past and Present* 42 (1969): 69–139, 138.

country.[6] In contrast, Tom Garvin in 1981 pointed to the relatively low levels of literacy in southern Ireland and the difficulties this presents for sociological explanations of the emergence of the first modern mass democratic party in the 1820s, the Catholic Association.[7]

This approach to the role of literacy is concerned largely with measurement and quantification, and then with comparison over time and between different areas or social groups. Of course this is not a straightforward procedure, and the difficulties of such measurement are well known. The most frequently and easily used measure is the ability to sign one's name, most notably on standard documents such as a parish marriage register. In England and Wales, the annual reports of the Registrar General from 1839 onwards list the proportions unable to sign at marriage, and these show a decrease from 30 per cent for men and 45 per cent for women in 1850 to almost zero by the end of the century. These figures have been extended back as far as the early eighteenth century by Schofield, using a random sample of 274 parish registers.[8] In France, the standard source is the survey carried out by Louis Maggiolo in the 1870s. He asked schoolteachers all over France to calculate the proportions signing their local marriage registers for four sample periods since the late seventeenth century, and some 16,000 teachers replied. This body of data is the basis of the standard work on literacy in France, that of Furet and Ozouf, and is extensively discussed in the first chapter.[9] In Ireland, the Registration Act of 1863 created a system similar to that of England, with annual figures produced for those unable to sign. It is more difficult to project these numbers back very far, however, given the relative paucity of parish registers in many parts of Ireland, particularly before 1800.[10]

6 James S. Donnelly, 'Propagating the Cause of the United Irishmen' *Studies: an Irish Quarterly Review* 69.273 (1980): 5–23; Nancy Curtin, *The United Irishmen: Popular Politics in Ulster and Dublin 1791–1798* (Oxford: Clarendon Press, 1994), pp. 174–227; Kevin Whelan, *The Tree of Liberty: Radicalism, Catholicism and the Construction of Irish Identity 1760–1830* (Cork: Cork University Press, 1996), pp. 65–77.

7 Tom Garvin, *The Evolution of Irish Nationalist Politics* (Dublin: Gill and Macmillan, 1981), pp. 48–60.

8 Roger Schofield, 'Dimensions of Illiteracy in England, 1750–1850', in Harvey Graff (ed.), *Literacy and Social Development in the West: a Reader* (Cambridge: Cambridge University Press, 1981), pp. 201–13.

9 François Furet and Jacques Ozouf, *Reading and Writing: Literacy in France from Calvin to Jules Ferry* (Cambridge: Cambridge University Press, 1982), pp. 5–47.

10 A few nineteenth-century Church of Ireland registers are discussed by Kirkham, along with other types of signed document such as leases from the eighteenth century: Graeme Kirkham, 'Literacy in North-West Ulster 1680–1860', in Mary Daly and David Dickson (eds), *The Origins of Popular Literacy in Ireland: Language Change and Educational Development 1700–1920* (Dublin: Trinity College Dublin and University College Dublin, 1990), pp. 73–96.

Signature data from marriage registers are in some ways an ideal way of measuring literacy. They have a very wide participation, covering up to 90 per cent of the relevant age cohort, and record differences of age and gender. They measure signing ability in a situation that is uniform, or at least very similar, across time and space, allowing for aggregation and straightforward comparison between regions, countries, and periods. Finally, they measure a skill that is being practiced and witnessed, rather than a simple declaration of ability.[11]

However, the skill being measured by signature data is that of writing, whereas literacy consists of at least two different skills, reading and writing. Normal practice in contemporary elementary schools, in Ireland as elsewhere, was to teach reading and writing sequentially and to charge separately for them, and it was not unusual for children to finish school having learned to read but not to write.[12] This was reinforced by the fact that the opportunities in later life to practice reading were far more frequent (and cheaper) than for writing, and that the ability to write was much more likely to decay over time than the ability to read. Many of those who could not sign, therefore, were nevertheless well able to read.

Given that boys would generally be kept longer in school than girls, the ability to read only was, comparatively speaking, a female characteristic. This was true of Early Modern Europe in general and was often associated with church-based literacy campaigns, both Protestant and Catholic, aiming to teach the reading of the catechism and other devotional material to all church members. As noted above, most work on literacy in Britain has focused on signature data, since the most accessible records were marriage registers, and the nineteenth-century British censuses took their lead from these and measured signing ability. The result is that, according to one study of female reading in Early Modern England, the ability to read only is 'a historically invisible skill'.[13] In other countries, however, there were instances where it was measured and visible. Conscription records for nineteenth-century France divided recruits into those who could read and write, those who could read only, and those who could do neither, although this obviously applies to men only. Danish recruits in the late nineteenth century were even

11 Roger Schofield, 'The Measurement of Literacy in Pre-Industrial England', in Jack Goody (ed.), *Literacy in Traditional Societies* (Cambridge: Cambridge University Press 1969), pp. 311–25; for a discussion in an Irish context, see John Logan, 'Sufficient for Their Needs: Literacy and Elementary Schooling in the Nineteenth Century', in Daly and Dickson (eds), *The Origins of Popular Literacy in Ireland*, pp. 113–37.

12 Schofield, 'Measurement of Literacy', p. 317; J.R.R. Adams, *The Printed Word and the Common Man: Popular Culture in Ulster 1700–1900* (Belfast: Institute of Irish Studies, 1987), pp. 20–21.

13 Heidi Hackel, *Reading Material in Early Modern England: Print, Gender, and Literacy* (Cambridge: Cambridge University Press 2005), p. 61.

more finely classified, with seven categories altogether, including a distinction between the ability to read print and the ability to read handwriting.[14]

These sources reveal sizeable cohorts that could read only. In Finland in 1880, the illiteracy rate was only 2 per cent, but the proportion of those who could read only was 87 per cent.[15] The best-known case is that of Sweden, where the percentage of readers was continuously recorded since the seventeenth century, and in some southern areas had reached 90 per cent by 1700. By contrast, writing ability did not become widespread in Sweden until the middle of the nineteenth century.[16] These extraordinary reading figures are largely religious in origin. In Sweden from the 1680s onwards, there was a major church campaign to teach reading, based around an annual catechism examination. Failure would exclude a person from church services (and by extension from other possibilities such as marriage) until the following year's test. Sweden and Finland are Lutheran, but the ability to read only is also associated with the Catholic church. Furet and Ozouf found that its distribution in France corresponded to religious indicators, and concluded that 'there was undoubtedly a specifically Counter-Reformation approach to education, aimed primarily at girls and excluding writing'.[17]

In nineteenth-century Ireland, this type of data is relatively rich, certainly compared to Britain, because the Irish census was independent of the British one, and in most respects far more sophisticated, at least between 1841 and 1861. In 1841, the British census measured literacy as the ability to sign, and took the marriage registers as its source, thereby excluding the unmarried as well as those who could read only.[18] In Ireland, by contrast, the entire population over the age of five was assessed and divided into three categories, 'read and write', 'read only' and 'neither read nor write', and the figures were collected for both women and men. Moreover, these figures are available at the level of townlands and are also divided by age cohort at a county level. This format was replicated in the 1851 census, while from 1861 the figures were given at parish level only,

14 Furet and Ozouf, *Reading and Writing*, pp. 168ff.; David Vincent, *The Rise of Mass Literacy* (Cambridge: Polity Press, 2000), p. 17.

15 Jean Queniart, 'De l'oral à l'écrit: les modalités d'une mutation' *Histoire de l'Éducation* 21 (1984): 11–35, 21.

16 Egil Johanssen, 'The History of Literacy in Sweden', in Harvey J. Graff (ed.), *Literacy and Social Development in the West*, pp. 151–82, tables on pp. 176, 180; see also 'Introduction', in Harvey Graff et al. (eds), *Understanding Literacy in Its Historical Contexts: Socio-Cultural History and the Legacy of Egil Johansson* (Lund: Nordic Academic Press, 2009), intro.

17 Furet and Ozouf, *Reading and Writing*, p. 179. There is a map of those able to read but not write in 1872, in a section devoted to church education, in Hervé le Bras and Emmanuel Todd, *L'Invention de la France: Atlas Anthropologique et Politique* (Paris: Librairie Génerale Française 1981), p. 287.

18 *Occupation Abstract, Part I. England and Wales, 1841*. H.C. 1844 XXVII, 11.

but were also broken down by religious affiliation. This body of data allows for a much more nuanced analysis of literacy and its distribution.

Female Reading Ability

The census figures show that in Ireland, as elsewhere, 'read only' was predominantly a female characteristic. The 1841 census recorded 678,000 women as being able to read and write (FRW for convenience) but substantially more able to read only (FRO), amounting to 829,000. FROs outnumbered FRWs in the great majority of counties. There were eight exceptions (Cork, Dublin, Galway, Kerry, Kildare, Limerick, Waterford, and Wicklow) along with many of the cities and larger towns (Dublin, Cork, Limerick, Waterford, Kilkenny, and Galway). Elsewhere, the ratio could be 2 to 1 or greater – Co. Londonderry had 20,000 women who could read and write but 48,000 who could read only. For males, by contrast, those who could read and write outnumbered those who could read only in every single county and city, typically by a factor of 2 (overall, 1.28 million men could read and write while 580,000 could read only).

The analyses of Scandinavia and France mentioned above link female reading only ability with religiously-based literacy, whether Protestant or Catholic. At first sight, the Irish case shows a strong relationship between FRO and Protestantism. The 1841 census did not measure religious affiliation but a religious census was conducted six years before by the Commission for Public Instruction, and this allows us to explore the relationship.[19] It turns out to be a reasonably strong relationship, with a correlation coefficient of 0.6 between the ratio of FRO and the proportion of the female population that is Protestant. This holds also for the two main Protestant denominations if we analyse them separately: the correlation with Church of Ireland women is 0.4 and with Presbyterian women 0.5.

To give full weight to the female reading only population and to analyse its distribution, however, we need to take account not just of its amount relative to those who could read and write, but also relative to those women who could neither read nor write (FN), that is to say take account of the total level of literacy as well as its nature. Reading only could be associated with a relatively illiterate area as well as with a literate one. If we simply looked at the ratio between FRW and FRO, as above, we would not see any difference between a county where 5 per cent of women could read and write and 10 per cent could read only, and another county where 30 per cent could read and write and

19 I am extremely grateful to Joel Mokyr for very generously sending me the 1835 figures converted to counties. The figures collected by the Commission for Public Instruction in 1835 were organised by diocese rather than by county, and it was a considerable undertaking to make them comparable with the census.

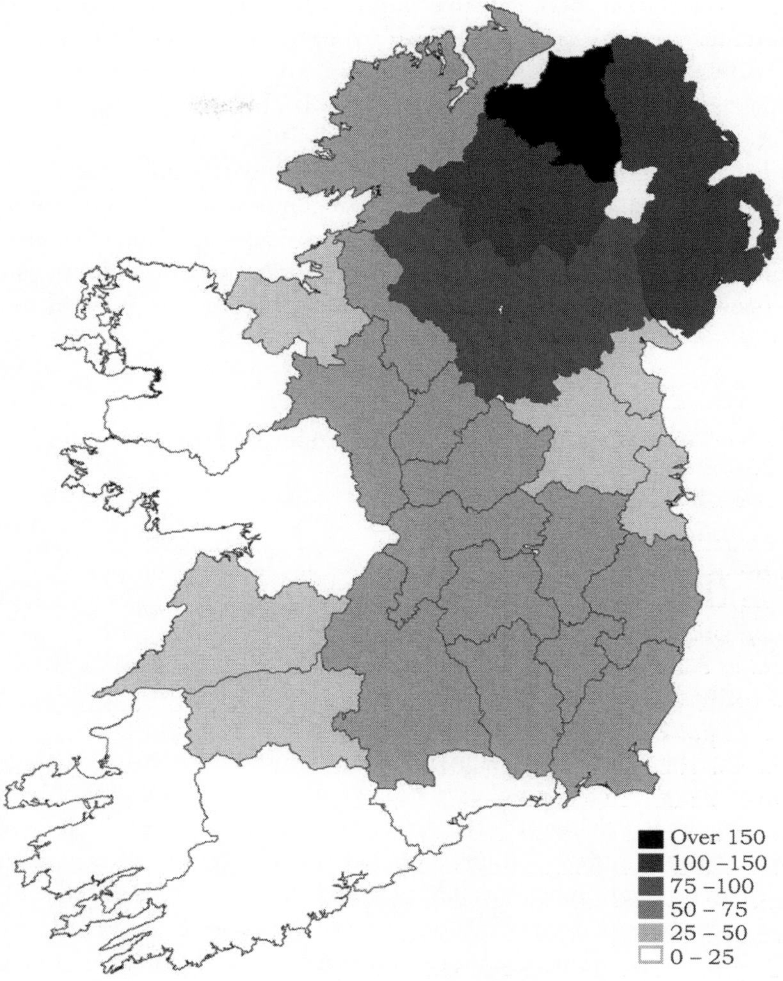

Figure 1.1: Female literacy index 1841

60 per cent could read only, although they have two hugely different levels of female literacy. A very crude way of getting around this would be to construct a measure that took account of all three categories by combining them, multiplying the ratio of 'read only' to 'read and write' by the overall literacy level:

(FRO/FRW) x (% literate females)

Figure 1.1 shows the counties in 1841 ranked on this latter index. At the top by a long way are Londonderry (156) and Antrim (135), followed by Tyrone (109) and Down (103). At the bottom are Galway (15) and Kerry (10).

The correlation between this index and the distribution of female Protestants in 1835 is a good deal stronger, with a coefficient of 0.82. The correlation with the individual denominations is also stronger, 0.76 for Presbyterians and 0.52 for Church of Ireland. This would appear to suggest that the women who can read only are mainly Protestant.

However, when we move forward to the first census that measured religious affiliation, that of 1861, and compare those numbers with the literacy figures in the same census, a different picture emerges. The proportion of women who can read only is still highest in the most Protestant province, Ulster, as is the index combining reading only and total literacy (figures in 000s in the first three columns):

Table 1.1: Female reading index by province

	RW	*FRO*	*FN*	*% Literate*	*Index*
Leinster	288	154	223	66	35
Munster	224	104	350	48	22
Ulster	300	288	287	67	64
Connaught	82	65	250	37	29

Analysing the figures by county, moreover, produces results that greatly resemble those for 1841. The correlation between the index and Protestantism is only slightly less than in 1841, 0.77. However, a closer look at the 1861 census produces a very different impression indeed. The census in fact measured literacy according to religious affiliation, and these figures reveal that FRO is predominantly associated with Catholicism. In Ulster, Catholic women who could read only outnumbered those who could read and write in a ratio of 1 to 1.45, whereas for both main Protestant denominations the reverse was true, 1 to 0.8 for the Church of Ireland and 1 to 0.72 for Presbyterians:

Table 1.2: Female reading index by religion

	FRW	*FRO*	*FN*	*% Literate*	*Index*
Church of Ireland	76	63	38	79	65
Catholic	91	132	219	50	73
Presbyterian	118	85	26	89	63

The same pattern holds throughout Ulster if we analyse it at a county level. Among Catholics in every county, FRO is greater than FRW, twice as large in the case of Tyrone (20,330 to 10,915). With one exception, FRW is larger than FRO in every county for both of the principal Protestant denominations (Church of Ireland and Presbyterian). The one exception is Church of Ireland women in Londonderry, where FRO is marginally greater than FRW (5,894 to 5,819). For Presbyterian women in the same county, however, FRW is significantly larger than FRO (14,544 to 11,943).

Overall therefore, while FRO in 1861 is spatially correlated with Protestantism, it is more of a Catholic trait; in other words, it is a characteristic of Catholic women living in more Protestant areas, albeit one shared with relatively high numbers of their Protestant neighbours as well. This suggests that FRO is not necessarily the result of elements like a more scriptural culture or of particular churches that are more mobilised and whose literacy campaigns are more effective.

The principal alternative to a religious explanation would be an economic one. It may be that women were more likely to be able to read in areas where they had more frequent participation in a cash economy. This participation would be more marked in areas of domestic industry, where women could earn money from spinning, than it would in more agricultural areas where such opportunities were fewer (eggs and dairy, mostly). The 1841 census offers some evidence to test this hypothesis in its enumeration of occupations, which was carried out at a county level. If we measure the number of spinners as a proportion of the total female population, we get figures that range from less than 1 per cent (Co. Dublin) to 29 per cent (Co. Tyrone). There is a very strong correlation between these figures and the importance of female reading only ability (i.e. the ratio of FRO to FRW), a coefficient of 0.8. However, the correlation with the literacy index (the ratio multiplied by the overall literacy rate) is a good deal less strong, 0.5. This is because there is almost no relationship between the proportion of spinners and the overall level of female literacy, which have a correlation factor of -0.03. (By contrast, there is a relatively strong correlation between female literacy in 1841 and Protestantism in 1835, 0.67.)

Reading Ability and Language

The nature of female literacy in nineteenth-century Ireland, therefore, is apparently strongly influenced by religious affiliation, but the precise nature of that influence remains very unclear. One thing that is clear, however, is the salience of a division of literacy into the separate skills of reading and writing. Even taking this into account, however, we are still left with the same problem that was presented by its measurement as a single skill. Instead of being a single binary variable, with people being either literate or illiterate, we now have two binary variables, with people being either able to read or not, and to write or not. The limitations of this approach have again been well rehearsed in the historiography of literacy over recent decades. What does it mean to say someone is 'able to read'? Reading covers a very wide spectrum of abilities and practices, from slowly and laboriously deciphering simple texts to easily scanning complex ones; from reading print to reading handwriting, as noted above in the case of the Danish conscripts; from the repeated reading of one text, possibly memorising it, to the one-off scanning of a wide range of texts, including periodicals and newspapers, what is called 'intensive' versus 'extensive' reading in the well-known typology of Engelsing.[20]

In Ireland, and elsewhere, including the other Celtic language areas, there is the added complication that the acquisition of literacy often coincided with the acquisition of a new language, to such an extent that the two processes are often conflated. In the words of Louis Cullen, language shift in Ireland was 'related to the prestige of written above oral culture, and the explosive growth in the demand for literacy'. Therefore, according to Comerford, 'as the Irish population acquired literacy it did so in English'. This was partly because, as Graff puts it, 'the new national educational system taught literacy in English, not Irish', and this was also largely true of the elementary schools that preceded it.[21]

The achievement of literacy in English is therefore often linked with absence of literacy in Irish, as if there were an inverse relationship between them. 'All of this resulted in a dramatic rise in popular literacy in English, as in the early nineteenth century the Irish language entered upon its sharp decline', writes Eagleton, while 'the increase in English speakers and readership was accompanied by a decrease in Irish-language readership', according to Rolf and Magda Loeber.[22]

This very binary formulation misunderstands the nature of literacy, however, and underestimates the complexity of the relationship between literacy and language. In fact, Irish speakers who learned to read in English thereby became more literate in Irish as a result, rather than less literate.

20 R.A. Houston, *Literacy in Early Modern Europe*. 2nd ed. (London: Pearson, 2002), pp. 211–18.

21 L.M. Cullen, *The Emergence of Modern Ireland* (London: Batsford, 1981), p. 132; R.V. Comerford, *Ireland* (London: Hodder Arnold, 2003), p. 131; Harvey Graff, *The Legacies of Literacy: Continuities and Contradictions in Western Culture* (Bloomington: Indiana University Press, 1987), p. 339.

22 Terry Eagleton, *Heathcliff and the Great Hunger: Studies in Irish Culture* (London: Verso, 1995), p. 146; Rolf and Magda Loeber, 'Popular Reading Practice', in *The Oxford History of the Irish Book Vol.IV: The Irish Book in English 1800–1891* (Oxford: Oxford University Press, 2011), pp. 211–39, p. 215.

By learning to read English they acquired the ability to read Irish as well, provided the texts that they read in Irish shared the characteristics of the texts that they read in English. The popular printed Irish-language texts of nineteenth-century Ireland were produced with just such a readership in mind. They did not imitate the elaborate orthography or the appearance of the Irish-language manuscripts that were still being written and copied up until the Famine. They used roman letters instead of Gaelic ones, and various styles of orthography that were simpler, or at least closer to English-language orthography, than that of the manuscripts. These styles can be illustrated by one of the most frequently printed Irish-language books of the late eighteenth and early nineteenth centuries. This was a small catechism and prayer book, titled *An Teagask Creestye* ['The Christian Teaching', i.e. 'The Catechism']. The conventional Irish-language spelling of this would be something like 'An Teagasc Críostaidhe', but the printed book uses English-language phonetic formations such as 'ee' instead of 'ío', thereby also avoiding accents over vowels, and also uses letters such as 'y' and 'k' that don't exist in conventional Irish orthography. This book has therefore been produced for a readership that had learned to read English, and a skill acquired in English could therefore easily be transferred into Irish, all the more easily when Irish was the reader's first language. These forms of typography and orthography also suited a print trade that functioned overwhelmingly in English. A printer working at the cheaper end of the market, producing catechisms, ballads and the like, would not have been remotely able to afford the additional specialised font of letters that would have been necessary to produce texts that used elaborate or elite forms of Irish.

Both readers and printers functioned in two languages, therefore, and their skills were transferable between languages.[23] This is often misunderstood in writing about this period, and Irish speakers who were able to read English but not the elaborate Irish of the manuscript tradition are referred to as 'literate in English but illiterate in Irish'. The discussion above makes clear that this is not so. Irish speakers who could read English could by definition read the Irish of popular printed books, and it is entirely legitimate to refer to these readers as 'literate in Irish'. Typography and orthography are conventions, and there is no one single 'correct' way of representing a language in writing.

It can also be useful to distinguish here between two different types of orthography. The first is a 'shallow' orthography, a writing system that is more phonetic, with a close relationship between script and sound, so that homonyms would be spelt in the same way, for example. By contrast, 'deep'

23 See Nancy H. Hornberger, 'Continua of Biliteracy', *Review of Educational Research* 59.3 (1989): 271–96.

orthographies are those where the relationship between script and sound is more distant, but where linguistic structures are typically more visible. Homonyms are not necessarily spelt in the same way, and word structures can make the etymology of a word clear.[24] By these standards, the written Irish of the manuscripts would be 'deep' relative to the printed Irish of cheap books, which would be more 'shallow'. This would be clear in the case of mutations of consonants at the beginning of words – for example 'bord', a table, might be spelt in the same way in both types of orthography, but 'on the table' would be rendered as 'ar an mbord' in scribal writing, and as 'ar an mord', pronounced as written (the 'b' is silent), in a popular printed text.

The advantage of a 'shallow' orthography is that it makes it easier to learn to read, and is suitable for those whose reading ability is limited. 'Deep' systems, on the other hand, have advantages for more advanced readers in that they make meaning clearer visually. Readers of Irish in the eighteenth and nineteenth centuries would have attended school for a relatively short period, and would have had irregular school attendance. A shallow orthography was far more practical and accessible for such a readership.

In Irish-speaking areas, therefore, there was a potential reading public for texts in Irish that was identical to the reading public for texts in English. Whether it manifested itself as an actual reading public, buying and reading the cheap printed texts that would be characteristic of such a public, such as the catechism described above, depended partly on its being supplied with suitable texts in Irish. In the event, there was only a limited supply, largely religious and produced in the towns of Cork, Limerick, Waterford, and south Tipperary.[25]

Conclusion

Literacy in nineteenth-century Ireland, therefore, was more than a single uniform skill, to be measured and analysed in a binary way. It consisted of a range of abilities and a variety of relationships to the written word, differing according to gender, geography, language, and other elements. Taking full

24 Mark Sebba, *Spelling and Society: the Culture and Politics of Orthography Around the World* (Cambridge: Cambridge University Press 2007), 19ff.

25 Niall Ó Ciosáin, *Print and Popular Culture in Ireland 1750–1850* (Basingstoke: Macmillan, 1997a), esp. Chapter 9, 'Languages and Literacy'. There is some general discussion of these issues in two recent histories of language in Ireland: Nicholas Wolf, *An Irish-Speaking Island: State, Religion, Community and the Linguistic Landscape in Ireland, 1770–1870* (London: University of Wisconsin Press, 2014), Chapters 4 and 6; and Aidan Doyle, *A History of the Irish Language: From the Norman Conquest to Independence* (Oxford: Oxford University Press, 2015), pp. 117–20, pp. 215–22.

account of it will involve analysing the nature of readership and of styles of reading and writing, as well as its overall level. This should bring us to a much more nuanced and contextualised understanding of politicisation, language shift, and some of the other social processes in nineteenth-century Ireland that were fundamentally shaped by literacy.

2

Douglas Hyde (1860–1949): The Adolescent Behind the Diarist

Máire Nic an Bhaird and Liam Mac Mathúna

Douglas Hyde, *Dúbhglas de h-Íde,* An Craoibhín Aoibhinn, who was born on 17 January 1860 and died on 12 July 1949, was founding president of the Gaelic League (1893–1915), first professor of Modern Irish in University College Dublin (1909–32) and first president of an independent Irish state (1938–45). His inner thoughts and ideas, his linguistic development, and his coming of age in Co. Roscommon can be seen in his own words in 13 diaries which are housed in the National Library of Ireland.[1] Hyde was an adolescent of 14 years when he embarked upon his remarkable linguistic journey. This essay examines Douglas Hyde's first diary (NLI MS G 1036), which he began writing on 9 March 1874 and which ended on 31 December 1876.

Douglas Hyde's interests in these formative years are addressed within this essay. Although his psychological and moral growth is not significantly evident in his first diary, the immense importance of language to the young Hyde is clear from the start. This diary, being the first in the collection, is the budding flower in regard to his initial acquisition of Irish. Douglas Hyde consciously acquired the Irish language in his teens by mixing with the local inhabitants of Roscommon. His interests in hunting and travel, clearly evident from his entries, are examined here. Hyde's passion for languages, especially Irish, French and Greek, and his journey towards the acquisition of the Irish language are explored. The authors will review his penmanship, including his phonetic approach to the spelling of Irish, as well as the connection between oral language acquisition and the written word. This essay highlights the complex nature of the beginning of Hyde's journey on the road of linguistic, literary and cultural nationalism.

1 National Library of Ireland archives, NLI MSS G 1036–1048.

Figure 2.1: Hyde's first diary spanning the period 1874–76 (NLI MS G 1036) (Reproduced with kind permission of the National Library of Ireland)

Egodocuments

Douglas Hyde's diaries can be classified as egodocuments.[2] The strength of his diary writing in comparison to works published by Hyde, is that the reader gets, in varying degrees, an insight into the life that Douglas Hyde spent as a youth in Co. Roscommon. The reader must always be discerning when reading diaries, as they are a reflection of the writer's personality. Bias and prejudice must be accounted for in order to truly understand their message, as noted by Ó Conaire: 'Pé scéal é, níl puinn bunúis leis an tuiscint shoineanta thraid-isiúnta gurb ionann, bonn ar bhonn, turas beatha agus a thuairisc; gur gníomh simplí aithriseach atá sa dírbheathaisnéis: gur lóchrann, scáthán nó léaspairt solais atá sa téacs caol díreach isteach i saol an duine lasmuigh den téacs' (At any rate, there is little basis for the naïve traditional understanding that a life journey is the same, side by side, with an account of it; that the autobiography is a simple imitative act: that the text is a torch, mirror or sparkle of light directly into the life of the person outside the text).[3] Personality, identity and individuality can be investigated through the use of egodocuments. The daily accounts by Hyde are a great resource and they provide an enlightening insight into the actions and pastimes of Ireland's first president as a young boy.

Douglas Hyde's Early Development

In 1867, Hyde's father Arthur was appointed rector of Tibohine, and the family moved to neighbouring Frenchpark, in County Roscommon.[4] He was home schooled by his father and his aunt due to a childhood illness, an experience which was to have a crucial impact on him, as noted by Dominic Daly:

> it was during these years that he came to know and be known by the country people around his home; it was then that he became aware of

2 'Egodocument' refers to autobiographical writing, such as memoirs, diaries, letters and travel accounts. The term was coined around 1955 by the historian Jacques Presser who defined writings in which the '"I", the writer, is continuously present in the text as the writing and describing subject'. See 'Introduction' in Rudolf Dekker, *Egodocuments and History: Autobiographical Writing in its Social Context since the Middle Ages* (Hilversum: Uitgeverij, 2002), pp. 7–20, https://repub.eur.nl/pub/17065/ (accessed 23 February 2019).

3 Breandán Ó Conaire, 'An Dírbheathaisnéis: *Genre*, Coincheap nó Cíor Thuathail? Smaointe ar Nádúr na Tuairisce Beatha', in Mícheál B. Ó Mainnín (ed.), *Léann* 1 (Béal Feirste: Shanway Press, 2007), p. 10; all translations from Irish are by the authors.

4 Janet Egleson Dunleavy and Gareth W. Dunleavy, *Douglas Hyde: A Maker of Modern Ireland* (Berkeley: University of California Press, 1991), p. 2.

> the Irish language, met the last generation of native Irish speakers, and began collecting the fragments of oral tradition which he was just in time to rescue from oblivion.[5]

Hyde was a self-made scholar and the first person to collect the oral tradition from his locality. As he did not attend school, he received initial direction from his father in the Greek language and a little teaching from Cecily Hyde at Drumkilla in French and German. He continued his own study routine after this initial guidance and thus had to develop self-directed learning skills. He relied on textbooks and reading materials found in his father's library to help him in acquiring Greek, Latin, French and German which he documents throughout the diary.[6] This practice helped nurture in Hyde his curiosity and love of study and learning, which was to be a lifelong stimulus for his own collection of the oral tradition. The seeds of Hyde, the academic, were sown from a very early age, seeds which reached fruition with the publication of his *Literary History of Ireland* in 1899: 'Hyde's *Literary History of Ireland* is a landmark in Gaelic scholarship, the fruit of thousands of hours spent in the libraries of Trinity College and the Royal Irish Academy'.[7]

During his youth, he became fascinated with hearing the old people in the locality speak the Irish language. This diary is an account of Hyde's daily life with emphasis placed on his immediate surroundings. He does not make the reader aware of the politics of the time. Outside influences remain largely unseen. He is, after all, a 14-year-old boy and although advanced in his desire for language acquisition, is very much influenced by his immediate surroundings. One of the few references to the outside world is when he mentions the 1876 Serbian–Ottoman War (1876–78) on 20 October 1876. 'Fine day. Rain in the evening. nuaidheacht na gcogadh sa bpápéir' (News of the wars in the papers).[8]

5 Dominic Daly, *The Young Douglas Hyde* (Baile Átha Cliath: Irish University Press, 1974), p. xiv.

6 For instance, he started on the *Aeneid* on 2 February 1877. 'Do thosach mé an Aeneid Bhurgeil a nuigh. Do rinne me roimhe so é ach ta se ceithre bliadhna o rinne me é agus is beag nac dhearmuighim e'. (I started Virgil's *Aeneid* today. I did it before but it is four years since I did it and I have nearly forgotten it.) NLI MS G 1037. This second volume of the diary does not contain page numbering.

7 Daly, *The Young Hyde*, pp. xvi–xvii.

8 Douglas Hyde diary, NLI MS G 1036, p. [108].

Introduction to Hyde's First Diary, NLI MS G 1036 (1874–1876)

Hyde's first diary appears to have been an accounts book owned by Bessie Hyde, his mother, and given to the young Douglas in 1874. Bessie's name is inside the front cover, however she never used the accounts book and thus Hyde acquired it from her for his diary writing.

The beginning of Hyde's first diary is predominantly written in English in a cursive script. However the second sentence is in Irish: 'Fuair Dimher bas August 1876' (Diver died August 1876).[9] This has been entered into the diary, however, at a later stage and shows the reader that Hyde had a strong bond with his dog, Diver, and that the Irish language was also close to his heart: he went to the trouble of mentioning Diver and writing about him at a later stage on this first page of his diary. His dog is mentioned throughout the diary until the dog's death. For example, in January 1875 he writes:

> Fine day, pa and Emily went to Ballagh and bought a lamp at 11/6. I waited at the swamp and killed a duck at over 50 yards with a no 4 cartridge. and afterwards went down late by moonlight to the turlough and made a nice shot at a splendid mallard rising near the swallow holes at close upon 50 yards with a cartridge of no 4, also. he was well shot. Diver fetched me out the 1st duck.[10]

He records also how, after Diver died, they got a new dog on 23 November 1876, and he compares the new dog named Shot to Diver. 'Fuair sinn madadh úr a n'ainim Shot o Narie air iasacht. Bhi sé dubh cosuil le Dimher' (We got a new dog called Shot on loan from Narie. It was black like Diver).[11]

Hyde often switches between Irish and English, that is to say he code-mixes, in the first volume of the diary. Code-mixing denotes when vocabulary and grammar aspects from different languages are used in the one discourse, or even in the one sentence, and implies complex linkages: 'Tuigfear a thábhachtaí atá sé idir théacs agus chomhthéacs a choimeád san áireamh, agus a chastacht a bhíonn an teagmháil agus a caidreamh idir dhá theanga agus dhá chultúr' (It will be appreciated how important it is to consider both text and context, and how complex the contact and relationship between two languages and two cultures are).[12] The English-Irish code-mixing highlights the learning process adopted by Hyde in his acquisition of the Irish language, although it becomes

9 Ibid., p. [1].
10 Ibid., p. 54.
11 Ibid., p. 111.
12 Liam Mac Mathúna, *Béarla sa Ghaeilge. Cabhair Choigríche: An Códmheascadh Gaeilge/Béarla i Litríocht na Gaeilge 1600–1900* (Baile Átha Cliath: An Clóchomhar, 2007), p. xv.

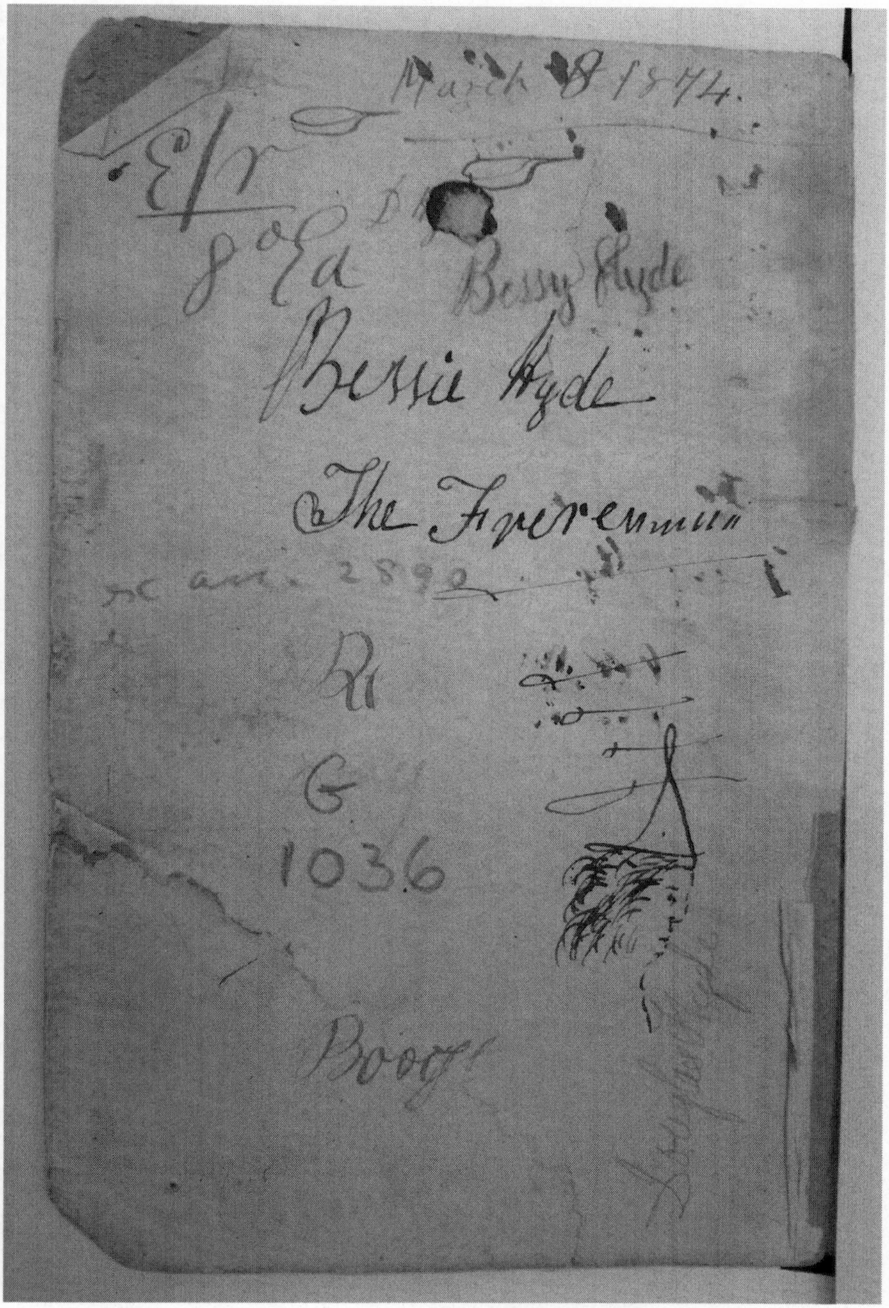

Figure 2.2: Bessie Hyde's name inside front cover of Hyde's first diary (NLI MS G 1036) (Reproduced with kind permission of the National Library of Ireland)

less frequent as he acquires more of the Irish language: 'Mórán leath mar leath atá an Ghaeilge agus an Béarla sa dara himleabhar. As sin amach i nGaeilge ar fad a scríobh sé, ionann 's, …' (Irish and English are roughly half and half in the second volume. From then on he wrote it all in Irish, almost, …).[13]

On the very first pages of the diary, the pattern of his written word is evident. Although brief in his description of events, Hyde allows the reader to create images of the life he led in Roscommon as a boy of 14 years old. His keen interest in nature and hunting can be seen from the start in his daily entries:

> Had two new lambs. (2 March 1874, p. [1])
>
> Pretty fine day. Made some cartridges. (15 April 1874, p. 8).
>
> Pa shot a jackdaw (10 March 1874, p. [1]).
>
> Since the 12th of last month we have shot 2 hares, 1 cock grouse, 47 snipe, 29 green plovers, 8 golden plovers, 4 water hens, I wild goose and 4 partridge. = Total 96 things. During the same time last year we killed only 32 things. and during the year before 80 things. (12 January 1877: G 1037, without page number)

Hyde regularly uses A and O to refer to his older brothers Arthur and Oldfield. 'A and O went to Hart's. each shot a snipe, … very hot day, went to Frenchpark' (21 August 1874, p. 33). He also refers often to his sister Annette, who was five years younger than him and to whom he was particularly close. Throughout the diary, Hyde refers to his family and to the local inhabitants.[14] His brothers, Arthur and Oldfield, are mentioned on the second page of his diary: 'Arthur came home from Dublin. Wet day. O went to London on the 21' (21 March 1874, p. 2). His sister Annette is first mentioned on page 5: 'Pa and Annette went to Frenchpark' (3 April 1874, p. 5).

Hyde was an early participant in data collection. He understood the importance of documenting important occasions and statistics – be it to do with weather, financials costs, hunting – and of maintaining social documents for future generations. He refers to the weather frequently throughout the diary.

> Snow on March 9. (1874, p. [1])
>
> Heavy [snow] on March 10 (1874, p. [1])

13 Risteárd Ó Glaisne, *Dúbhglas de h-Íde (1860–1949) ceannródaí cultúrtha 1860–1910* (Baile Átha Cliath: Conradh na Gaeilge, 1991), p. 11.

14 For a succinct comparison of Hyde's personality with that of his siblings, see Dunleavy and Dunleavy, *Maker of Modern Ireland*, p. 35.

Sunday, fine day. 15 March 1874 (p. [1])

Wet day. 16 March 1874 (p. [1])

Fine day. 17 March 1874 (p. [1])

There are also frequent references to church, e.g. 'Sunday, wet day. got extremely wet coming home from Church' (29 March 1874, p. 4). This is unsurprising since his father was rector of Tibohine parish and religion would have been important in his household. This young boy never ceases to surprise the reader as he shares his interests and pastimes. In one account he makes reference to thatching a house: 'Finished thaching [*sic*] the cowhouse' (18 March 1874, p. [1]).

Hyde's Acquisition of the Irish Language

The first entry written in Irish is on 27 March 1874: Hyde writes 'Thoine moisther war shane a l'oure ulk de Arthure oge'. (p. 3). Dominic Daly explains, 'The first two words are clear enough: Thoine moisther (Tá an máistir)' = The master is; 'war' may possibly stand for 'i bhfeirg' = angry; 'a l'oure ulk de Arthure óg' (a labhair olc de Arthur óg) means 'who spoke badly of young Arthur'.[15] It is noteworthy that *Pa* and *Ma* of the English entries are replaced by *moisther* and *moisthuress*, the equivalents of *máistir* 'master' and *máistreás* 'mistress' when Hyde writes in Irish. Thus, he adopts the perspective of the Irish-speaking community when referring to his own parents, a stance which is of considerable significance from a psychological point of view. We can see therefore that Hyde belonged to two worlds: he had his English persona, the son of Reverend Hyde, and his Irish persona, the young man who mixes with the local labourers and identifies with the local customs and language. The latter hidden persona grows in strength as Hyde develops and matures into a young adult. It is this developing second persona that gives him the strength and courage later in life to pursue a career in the Irish language instead of succumbing to his father's desires and becoming a clergyman. Hyde also takes on the local Irish language tradition of using 'óg' after names to distinguish between father and son. In English he refers to Arthur as 'Arthur'; however, in Irish he refers to him as 'Arthur Óg'. In these entries in which we have evidence of the beginning of Hyde's acquisition of the Irish language, one can see that he is using a personal, phonetic spelling with regard to the language. In this early diary, the influence of the French

15 Daly, *The Young Hyde*, p. 6.

language can also be seen in Hyde's entries, as on 1 April 1874 when he writes:

> April day Dockry's son came up for some powder and caps, gave it to him. Leau beins. A little turlough rose. great rain in the evening. Connolly went to Castlerea and got a barrel of porter, agus kan gallane d'isquu ba uch, agus trêkin ling. Arthure oge a gum budiêle d'isque ba uch agus thoine moisthuress êduc beau. (p. 4)

For example, if one looks at the spelling of *buidéal* [bottle], one sees that Hyde writes it as 'budiêle'. The circumflex accent affects the pronunciation of the 'e'. It is one of the five diacritics used in the French language.[16] The main use of this diacritical mark here is to place emphasis on the long 'e' in the word 'budiêle'. Hyde's knowledge of French at this time far surpassed his knowledge of the Irish language. It is clear from his French entries that he was comfortable reading and writing in French. The word 'budiêle' indicates to the reader that Hyde hadn't seen much Irish, if any, written down yet. If he had, he would have adopted the use of the *síneadh fada* or length mark instead of the French accent. There is also a full diary entry in French again on 4 May 1874 about hunting and shooting a rabbit. 'Je m'assuêrai [?] de tirer un coup de fusil a un des lapins mais le fusil me se trompait car le poudre êtait humide mais à la quatriême fois Je le tuai. Le pauvre lapin avait tant de peur q'il ne pouvait pas mouirir' [?] (p. 14). (I decided to shoot a rabbit but my gun failed me because the powder was wet. But I killed it on my fourth attempt. The rabbit was so scared it couldn't die.) On 19 April 1874, a mixture of languages is evident. Hyde begins his sentence in English, progresses to Greek, then to Irish and finishes in English: 'Sunday, went to Church. Ma not able to go. ******* . Edidaskon tous paidas, "mae hêne". Fine day' (p. 9). Brief as this entry is, it is a linguistic tour-de-force, with Hyde revelling in his ability to code-switch across three languages.

At first, Hyde had no experience of books or manuscripts written in Irish, as is shown by his irregular, phonetic spelling. Until he mastered Irish spelling Hyde invented a system for himself to write down on paper the sounds and words his ear heard. The following is a clear example of this: 'Kanna-mae kan budyêle iskabauck. Worra-mae sêkin faelikon' (21 August 1874, p. 33) (I bought one bottle of whiskey. I killed six butterflies.) This phonetic spelling can be seen again in the following sentence: 'La brau. Ne ve O gummuch hurabee. Paid a visit to Stillorgan' (17 April 1875, p. 162) (Fine day. O was not well at all). Thus, Hyde devised his own spelling system for the Irish language, using a personal spelling system which indicates that he was not used to reading the Irish language in his early years. Risteárd Ó Glaisne observes: 'Bhí a litriú

16 Douglas Walker, *French Sound System* (Calgary: University of Calgary Press, 2001), p. 47.

féin aige ar na fuaimeanna agus na focail a bhí á bhfoghlaim aige' (He had his own spelling for the sounds and words he was learning).[17] Based as it was on his familiarity with English spelling practices, and using the regular roman font rather than Gaelic-style letters, Hyde's idiosyncratic orthography actually paralleled the English-language phonetic systems applied to Irish in many nineteenth-century publications, as discussed in Niall Ó Ciosáin's article in this book.[18] Although he had access to a New Testament in English letters, i.e. in Roman font, which Rev. Hyde's predecessor, Mr Frenan, had left behind in the Glebe house, traditional Irish spelling does not become common in his entries until the summer of 1875, when he also begins to adopt the Gaelic script. Looking back on his progress at the end of 1878, he himself says that he didn't really know the language well until about a year and a half earlier, which would be about the middle of 1877.[19]

In August 1875, there is a clear change in Hyde's spelling which might indicate that he had started to read in Irish. For example, 'Bhi Shamus in so' (11 August, p. 72) (Séamus was here); 'Ni Bhi Moisther go maith' (11 August, p. 72) (The master wasn't well); 'La breág. … Bhí Shamus ann so' (17 August, p. 73) (Fine day. … Séamus was here). Although the spelling may not be consistent, he shows an increased awareness with regard to the sounds of the Irish language and how to transcribe them. Hyde's access to Irish language reading material helped improve his spelling significantly, cf. 'Lá bréagh' (Fine day) 24 May 1876, p. [96]. It is obvious that he is reading Irish and studying the written word: see also 'La breagh eile. Dimthig mid ag tigh Lamhin' (Another fine day. We went to Lavins's), 6 July 1876, p. 97).

Hyde's progression and development as an Irish language speaker can also be seen when studying his notes at the back of his diary. These notes show his desire to acquire not only the Irish language but Greek also. The notes begin towards the end of the notebook and continue for 39 pages. The first collection of vocabulary in his notes is dated July 1874 and is a collection of Greek words. There is then a list written by Hyde of his hunting success.

The following are some examples, which indicate the approach to spelling that Hyde adopted at the beginning of the acquisition process and his phonetic approach to spelling (NLI MS G 1036). The standard Irish forms are provided in brackets by the authors; this section has no page numbers.

Sideyour = soldier [saighdiúir]
Smalluch [=] thrush [smólach]

17 Ó Glaisne, *Dúbhglas de h-Íde (1860–1949)*, p. 11.

18 Niall Ó Ciosáin, 'Varieties of Literacy in Nineteenth-Century Ireland: Gender, Religion and Language', this book, pp. 15–27.

19 NLI G 1038, 31 December 1878, pp. 58–59. See also, Daly, *The Young Hyde*, p. 3.

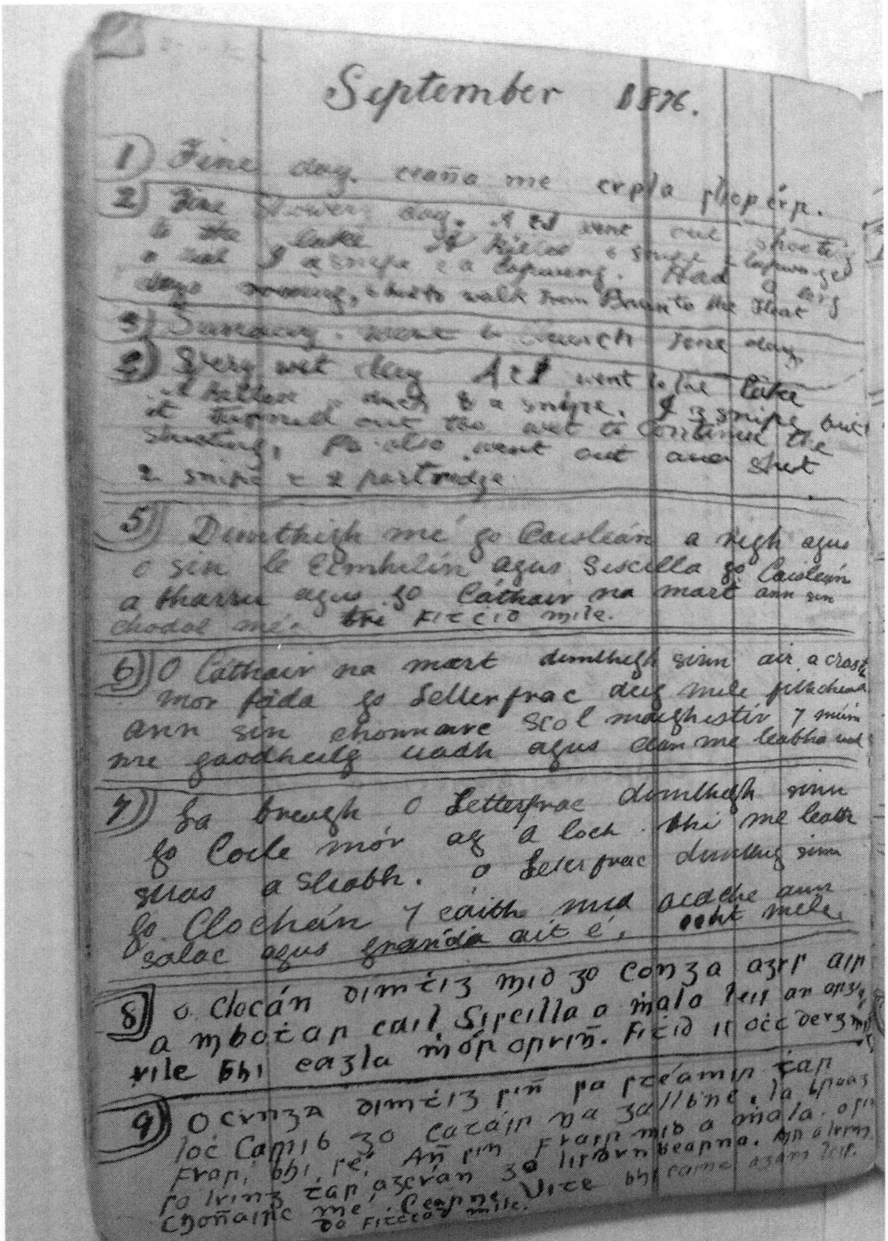

Figure 2.3: Diary entries from 1876 showing the improvement in Hyde's Irish language written skills (NLI MS G 1036)
(Reproduced with kind permission of the National Library of Ireland)

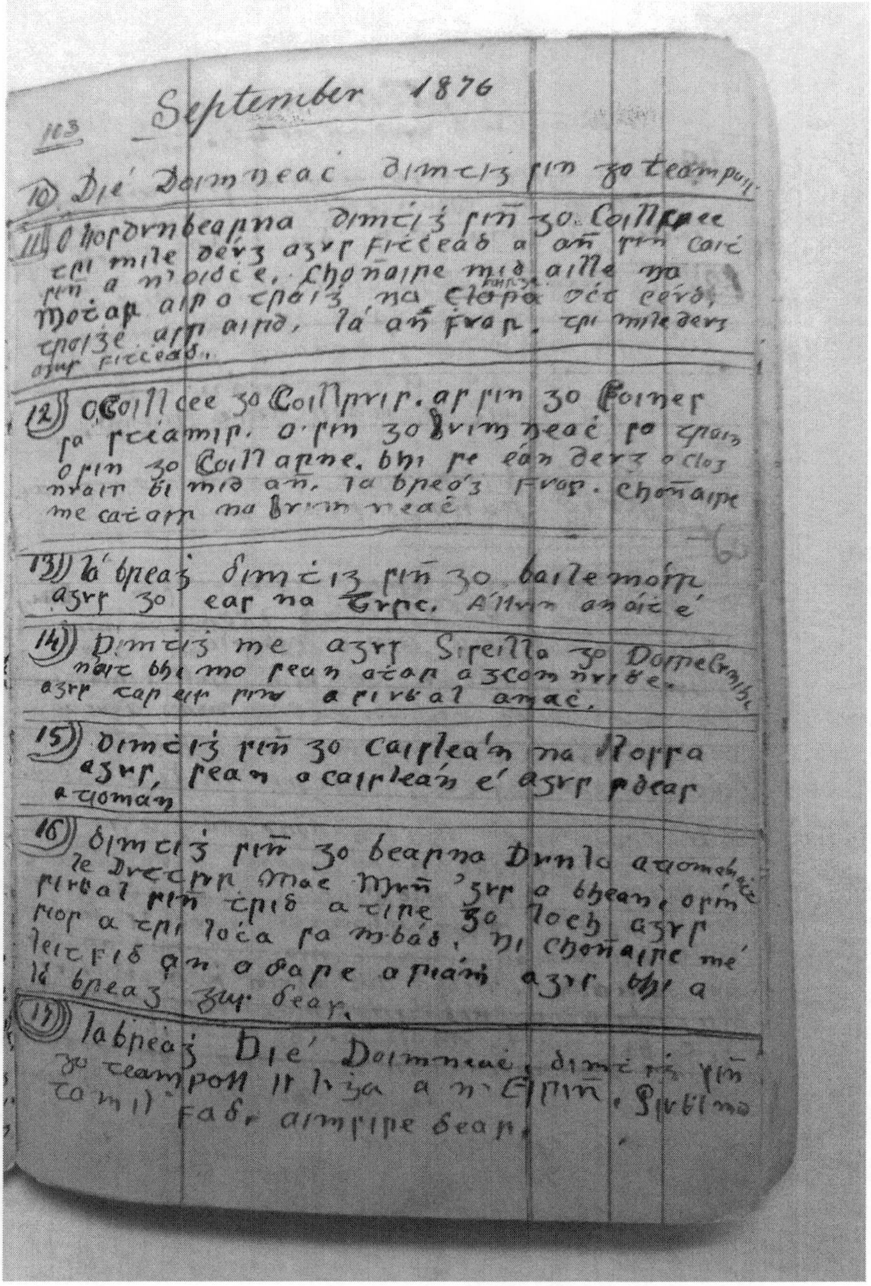
September 1876

Bolla more = town [baile mór]
Downin = deep [domhain]
Spidyoge = a robin [spideog]
Glona = a glass [gloine]
Feona = wine [fíona]
Gauryee = laughing [gáirí]
Gunweal = soon [gan mhoill]
Ochil = key [eochair]
Lig go = let it alone [lig de]
Thun = wave [tonn]
Cwehne = cry [caoineadh]

It is clear from these examples that Hyde is learning from the spoken word. If we take the example of 'Glona = a glass' and 'Feona = wine', this shows that he heard 'gloine fíona' and assumed that the nominative case of wine is 'fiona' (i.e. the genitive) instead of 'fíon' (i.e. the nominative). Other people no doubt also learned Irish in this way, particularly in earlier times, but Hyde is unusual, perhaps even unique, in leaving us evidence of the process. His Irish language competence improves and develops as the note-taking progresses. He has numerous Irish language sentences written down phonetically and then he explains them in English:

> Niel mae abultha shasue sues thau mae thirsuch = I'm so tired I am not able to stand.
>
> Shin kanella = Theres [*sic*] another.
>
> Imearth = play.

Hyde progresses in this manner and by page 30 of the notes it is clear that his Irish is quite advanced and that he has acquired a good knowledge of the language within three years. It is also obvious, as we read through the notes and see his spelling develop and become more advanced, that he has also seen the language written down.

Arthur Hyde's Diary (1876)

By 1876 Douglas Hyde was 16 years old and his penmanship had developed significantly. However, as the writing is often small and cramped, it is at times difficult to make it out, a common occurrence also in the diary of his brother Arthur, which is also housed in the National Library in Dublin

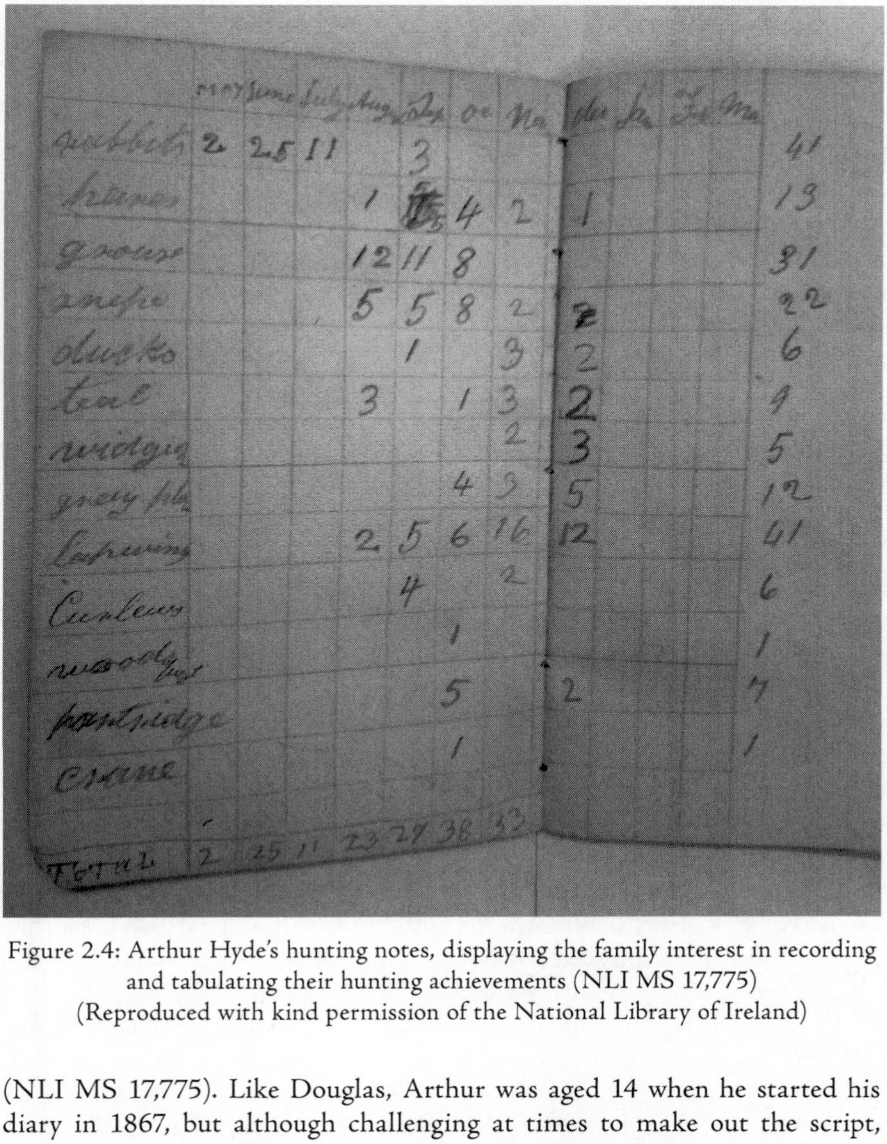

Figure 2.4: Arthur Hyde's hunting notes, displaying the family interest in recording and tabulating their hunting achievements (NLI MS 17,775) (Reproduced with kind permission of the National Library of Ireland)

(NLI MS 17,775). Like Douglas, Arthur was aged 14 when he started his diary in 1867, but although challenging at times to make out the script, it is not quite as difficult to read as Douglas's diary. There are similarities between Arthur's and Douglas's diaries. Each reveals a keen interest in hunting, in listing and in recording, both documenting their success rate. Arthur writes: 'Shot 2 rooks, did about 25 lines of Virgil' (19 March 1867, NLI MS 17,775).

The weather is also mentioned. However, Arthur wasn't as meticulous as Hyde with days and even whole months left blank without diary entries. There is a stark contrast evident between Hyde and Arthur in relation to the

Irish language. Arthur shows little interest in Irish although he learns both Latin and Greek. There is nothing written in Irish except for a drawing of Douglas Hyde with the words 'Dúbhglas de hÍde nuair bhí sé óg agus slán' (Douglas Hyde when he was young and well) (NLI MS 17,775). Did Arthur sketch this picture of his brother Douglas? We can't be sure; however, it looks as if Douglas subsequently signed his signature underneath the sketch and also wrote 'nuair bhí sé óg agus slán'. What is interesting to note, is that Douglas signed his name in Irish and described the sketch in Irish too. The captioning of the picture by Hyde is an act of self-description, indeed it is the creation of a self. Hyde who nurtured a dual persona during his adolescence, is stating which side of his persona belongs to his heart. This self-description is a strong statement from Douglas Hyde, and shows the psychological impact of Irish culture on this maker of modern Ireland, and Ireland's first president's strong allegiance to the Irish language.

Both brothers drew sketches in their diaries, however. Sketches of guns, boats and people are to be found in Arthur's diary.

Reverend Hyde wanted the sons to be fluent in Greek and Latin and insisted they spoke Latin, especially in front of the servants. Douglas and Arthur Hyde therefore adopted the use of Latin when discussing their servants in their diaries. One can presume that they did not want their servants to read their entries in relation to them and that they were following the practice of the time. The use of language is deeply inflected by class and the use of code-switching here is an expression of rank identity. Douglas and Arthur were well-educated, young gentleman and were establishing their own identity through the use of their language. 'Nova Ancilla venit' (The new servant girl comes/came) (10 April 1874, NLI MS G 1036, p. 7). Arthur Hyde, as stated, adopted this method in his diary, and wrote in Latin whenever he was mentioning the servants. In one passage he explains that a servant girl did a misdeed and was then dismissed from the job. 'Ancilla expulsa est' (The servant girl was expelled) (NLI MS 17,775).

Douglas Hyde was a chameleon of sorts and adopted language to suit different social situations. He was a man of the people and this approach to language started as a teenager and is seen in his diaries. English was his preferred language to discuss hunting, whereas Irish, which was the 'language of the people', was adopted as his first love. He was aware of social rank and class in society and adapted accordingly, which helped prepare him for his later life as a statesman.

Figure 2.5: Sketch of Douglas Hyde in Arthur Hyde's diary, subsequently signed in Irish, Dúbhglas de hÍde (NLI MS 17,775)
(Reproduced with kind permission of the National Library of Ireland)

Figure 2.6: Arthur Hyde's sketches of guns and boats in his diary (NLI MS 17,775) (Reproduced with kind permission of the National Library of Ireland)

James Hart and Hyde's Acquisition of the Irish Language

James Hart/Séamus Ó hAirt/Seamus Hart, a local worker and keeper of the bogs for Lord de Freyne, was the most influential character in relation to Hyde's Irish language acquisition. Hart had opened up the world of folklore, stories and history for Hyde. As the Dunleavys state:

> Hart had introduced Douglas to Irish history, folklore, myth, and legend; had shared with him his own store of poems and stories; had passed on to him, as if he were a son, the *seanfhocail* ... that he had received from his elders ... Hart had schooled him in histories not found in books but written across the face of the land.[20]

Hart is mentioned on the very first page of the diary and references continue throughout until his death in 1875, e.g. 'Hart gave me a black-thorn' (18 March 1874, NLI MS G 1036, p. [1]). 'Lent Hart the spade, learn'd some Irish from him' ([22] April 1874, p. 10). Many entries in Hyde's diary are brief and just make reference to Hart. For example, all that is written on 13 October 1875, p. 78, 'Fine day. Bhi Sémuis annso' (Séamus was here) which highlights the impact of their relationship upon the adolescent Hyde. Hart's influence upon Hyde in regard to the Irish language is extremely important. From May 1875 onwards Hyde uses Irish much more frequently in his diary entries. The phrase 'Ve Shamus in sho' (Séamus was here) (27 and 28 May 1875, p. 65) is frequently seen.

The diary, as already mentioned, is more an account of Hyde's daily life than an insight into his innermost thoughts and emotions. However, when James Hart dies the reader does gain considerable understanding of Hyde's emotional state of mind. On page 86, 28 December 1874, Hyde refers to the death of James Hart. The detail of his death at 8 p.m. is very emotive and we get a glimpse into the grief Hyde felt at this time. This was indeed a significant moment in the young man's life. He had lost a man who was a father figure to him and this is expressed by the lonely statement that Hyde thinks he will never find someone whom he will be as fond of in the future. This is a powerful declaration for a young boy of 14 years. We learn 'Hempul ochd clug foor Sémuis bás' (Around eight o'clock Séamus died). The day after Hart's death Douglas wrote:

> Cold stormy day. Foor sé Sémuis bás naé. Fear oc a ganool sin oc a firineach sin oc a munturach sin ní chonairc mé riamh. Bhí sé tin hempul a teachtgin agus neii sin foor se éag. Sémuis bucth rina mé

20 Dunleavy and Dunleavy, *Maker of Modern Ireland*, p. 49.

> foghlamin gaodoilig uet. Fear lé Gaelic oc a maith sin ni bhi s'a teis so. Ni higlum daoine a be dhecall feasda atá béidh dool agam oc a maith lé hu. Shocth seravid leat agus go mae do ainim banni ar neamh anis'. (29 December 1875, p. 87)
>
> (… He, Séamus, died yesterday. A man so affectionate, so truthful, so friendly I never saw. He was sick about a week and after that he died. Poor Séamus, I learned Irish from you. There will be no man with such good Irish after you. I cannot see anyone from now of whom I will be as fond of as you. Godspeed you, and may your blessed soul be in Heaven now.)

Hyde's sorrow is expressed in a simple, direct and moving passage written partly in phonetic Irish and partly in conventional Irish script on 29 December 1875, showing his respect and praise for Hart. It is clear that Hart helped nurture Hyde's own desire to acquire the Irish language. When Hart was sick, Hyde actually wrote more in English. Hart's death deeply affected Hyde and he doesn't even mention his own birthday in January the next year. Connolly, Dockry or Lavin, the other neighbours with whom he was friendly, are not mentioned for a month after Hart dying, something which would also indicate that Hyde was grieving the death of a man who had been a father figure to him. From 15 February 1876, p. 91, we hear an echo of the common entry before Hart's death of 'Ve Shamus insho' (Séamus was here); now we read 'Bhi Shán in so' (Johnny [Lavin] was here). Without Hart, one could question whether Hyde would have shown such a keen interest in the Irish language and thus grown to be such an influential character in this respect.

William Connolly who managed the Glebe estate,[21] Dockry, who was also employed by Reverend Hyde in the Glebe, and Johnny Lavin, a local labourer, were Irish language speakers and had Fenian sympathies, both factors which were to influence Hyde and mould his ideas and thoughts in the future.[22] Thus the diary shows how Hyde was mixing with local inhabitants, native speakers of Irish, from a young age, who were connected with the Fenian movement. Hyde's strong, nationalistic ideals started to develop from this time and his thoughts about politics develop as he matures. The Fenian sympathies which he felt as a teenager decreased and he gradually came to adopt a non-partisan

21 The Glebe estate was where Douglas grew up with his parents and siblings. He moved from there to Ratra House as a married man. Ratra House was *c*.200 metres from the Glebe in Tibohine, Co. Roscommon.

22 'Dockry was a Frenchpark Irish speaker with strong Fenian sympathies'; 'Johnny Lavin with his fluent Irish and Fenian sympathies' (Dunleavy and Dunleavy, *Maker of Modern Ireland*, pp. 55, 54).

approach in future years.[23] Hyde begins to focus his efforts on cultural independence as seen in his famous lecture 'The Necessity for De-Anglicising Ireland', which he gave on 25 November 1892 to the National Literary Society in Dublin. There he stated, 'we must strive to cultivate everything that is most racial, most smacking of the soil, most Gaelic, most Irish'.[24] This statement in itself echoes Hyde's childhood and the impact his relationships with Hart, Dockry, Lavin and Connolly had upon his self-identity. Hyde's exposure to Irish language and culture was intrinsically linked with the land. This was construed as the elemental racial ingredients of Gaelic identity. This image of 'smacking of the soil' is further heightened decades later in the cultural literary revival of the Irish language publishing house, An Gúm, where the central literary ideal was placed in the care of rural Gaeltacht areas where the honest Gaelic hand was working hard upon the land like in Tomás Ó Criomhthain's famous autobiography *An t-Oileánach*, published in 1929 by An Gúm.

Travel

There are references to different places throughout the diary, for example, Frenchpark, Bellanagare, Boyle, Ratra, Sligo, Ballagh, Stillorgan, Carrick, e.g. 'Went to Ratra got nothing' (15 April 1874, p. 8); 'Pretty fine day. Went to Frenchpark with Annette. Got a pair of slippers and some caps. Took a ride' (16 April 1874, p. 8). One amusing entry on 15 April 1875, p. 62, describes when Douglas and his brothers Oldfield and Arthur travelled to Dublin on the train. They went first class but had not paid for first-class tickets. They knew the system well and got off the train before the ticket station! 'He [Oldfield] A[rthur] and I went to Dublin. fine day. A[rthur] and I went half the way in a first class carriage and got out at the station before the one where the[y] took the tickets'. On pages 102–05 in Hyde's diary there is an account in Irish of his travels with his aunties Emily and Cecily: 'Dimthigh me go Caisleán a Righ agus o sin le Eimhilín agus Siscilla go Caislean a Bharru agus go Cáthair na Mart ann sin chodal mé. Tri fithchid mile' (5 September 1876, p. [102]) (I went to Castlerea and from there with Emily and Cecily to Castlebar and to Westport and there I slept. Sixty miles). On 6 September 1876 he described how he went on the long journey from Westport to Letterfrack, Connemara. Other place names documented in Irish in this trip

23 Cf. the occasion when 'Hyde responded at once with a publicly printed letter to Redmond reiterating the nonpartisan position in the League's constitution' (Dunleavy and Dunleavy, *Maker of Modern Ireland*, p. 310).

24 Douglas Hyde, 'The Necessity for De-Anglicising Ireland', in Breandán Ó Conaire (ed.), *Language, Lore and Lyrics: Essays and Lectures* (Dublin: Irish Academic Press, 1986), p. 169.

are Lough Corrib, Galway city, Lisdoonvarna, Cliffs of Moher, Killarney, Torc Waterfall, Glengarriff, Cork, Portarlington. He still goes to church during his travels: 'Dié Doimneach d'imtigh sin go teampuil' (10 September 1876, p. 103) (On Sunday we went to church). Hyde mentions towns in Mayo which he visited with Eileen and Siscilla. He discusses 'Clochán/Clifden' in Galway and refers to it as a dirty, awful place: 'O Leterfrac d'imthig sinn go Clochán agus chaith mid acache ann. Salac agus gránda ait é, ocht mile' (7 September 1876, p. [102]) (From Letterfrack we went to Clifden and we spent a night there. It is a dirty and ugly place, eight miles).

Even on his travels Hyde was a keen, diligent learner and refers to learning Irish and buying books. 'Ann sin chonnarc scol maighistir agus múin me Gaodheilg uadh agus cean me leabha[r] uad' (6 September 1876, p. [102]) (There I saw a schoolmaster and I learned Irish from him and I bought a book from him). 'Cean mé málín deas beag agus tri no ceithre leabhar 'sa Corcaigh agus péracht laiminibh' (22 September 1876, p. [104]) (I bought a nice little bag and three or four books in Cork and a pair of gloves). Travelling broadened Hyde's mind and took him out of the parochial neighbourhood of Frenchpark. He also used his travel experiences to enhance his Irish language learning. As Hyde grew, his travel was clearly linked to Irish language scholarship, using those experiences to explore bookshops, collect folklore, attend book auctions and engage in cultural discussions with people from various backgrounds in society. This cultural travel culminated later on in life with his American Tour of North America 1905–06, where he promoted and raised money for Irish language and culture.

Tobacco and Alcohol

In many respects, this diary could be equated with a social document, as it gives us a picture of life in Ireland in rural Roscommon in the 1870s. It seems strange nowadays that a young teenager just 14 years of age would be allowed drink alcohol and smoke tobacco, practices that highlight some of the many differences between today's society and that of Ireland in the 1870s. There are plenty of references to alcohol throughout the diary. Tobacco and whiskey were favourites of Hyde and his family, as is seen in his frequent entries related to them, e.g. 'Pretty fine day. Connolly went to Boyle. And bought a canister of powder and brought a hamper with "gallane d'isquebauch" potted ham, Worcester sauce, pickles etc. a heavy mist in the evening, went to Ratra and shot a fine rabbit with No 2 or 1 shot' (17 April 1874, p. 8). He also has sketches of drinks dispersed through this volume of the diary.

It is interesting to note that Hyde understood the importance of sketches for visual learners. He uses drawings here to illustrate how to set up a game

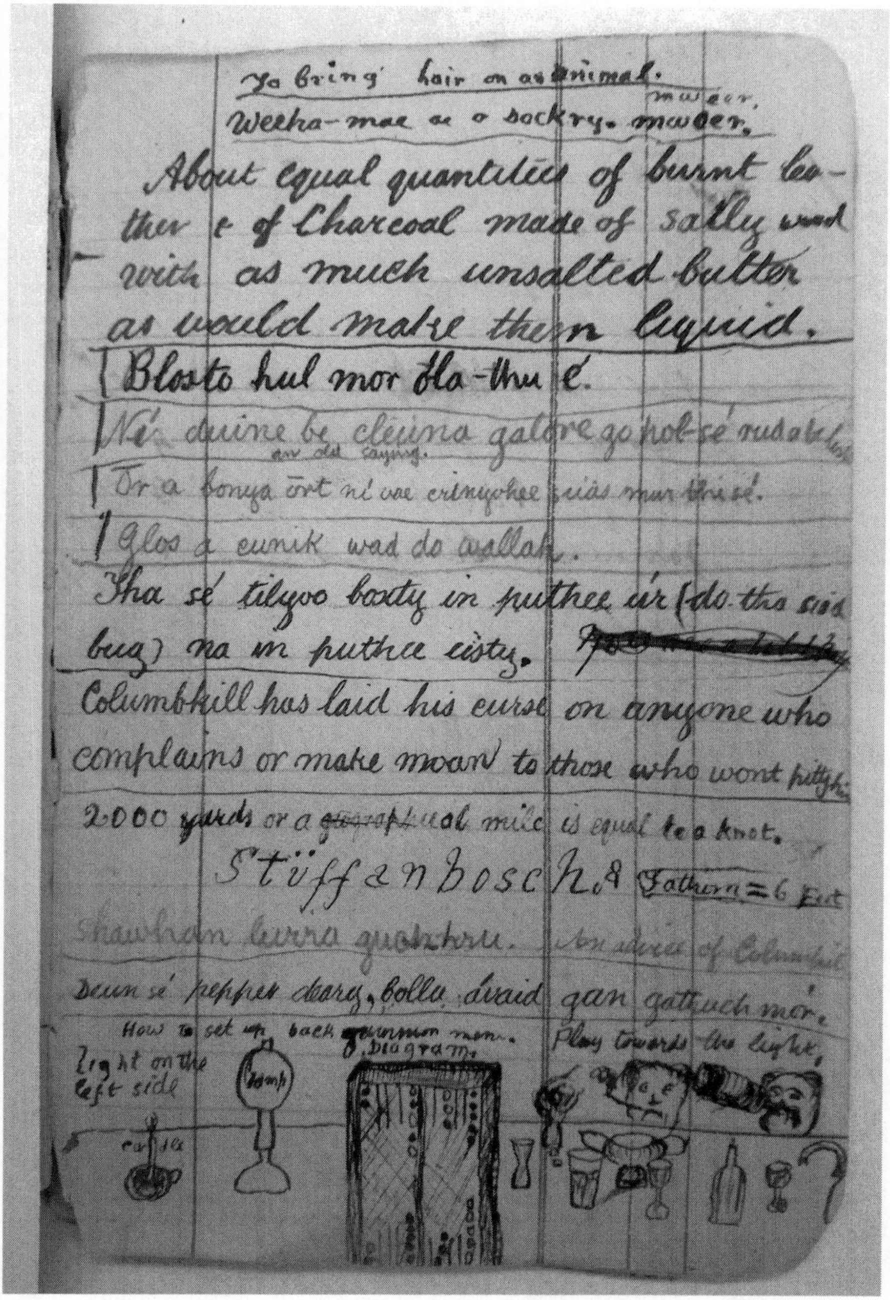

Figure 2.7: Hyde's sketches of alcohol are dispersed through this diary (NLI MS G 1036)
(Reproduced with kind permission of the National Library of Ireland)

of backgammon. There is a picture of the lamp, candle and the game itself with instructions scattered across the diagram. 'How to set up backgammon Diagram'. 'Play towards the light, light on the left side'. There are glasses on the table and two men – one smoking tobacco and the other swigging from the top of a bottle. This was associated with the English aspect of his personality. He would have seen his father play backgammon at home and clearly had a fondness for the game, thus spending time explaining how to set it up. Backgammon has often been called the aristocrat of popular games and it was considered a proper game for English gentlemen. This game thus highlights the juxtaposition of the dual persona Hyde adopted during his adolescence.

It is fitting that one of his last entries in this first volume of his diary describes presents he received at Christmas in 1876. He received an Irish language Bible, a history of the Church of Ireland and also tobacco for his pipe: 'Lá na Nodlag. … fúair me bronntanusa. Biobla Gaoideilge agus Staír na hEagluise na hEirionn agus dhá giota do'n phiobán' (25 December 1876, p. [117]) (Christmas Day. I got presents, a Bible in Irish and the History of the Church of Ireland and two pieces for the pipe). It is easy to picture the young Hyde's desire to soak up all the knowledge he could from these books. Reverend Hyde's influence and impact on the young Douglas, and Hyde's own contrasting desire to become at one with Irish language and culture is seen in the ironic present of the Bible in the Irish language.

In sum, then one can say that this diary shows us how eager, diligent and interested in local culture, the Irish language, travel and hunting the adolescent Hyde was. The importance he attached to both the written word and oral tradition is evident from the onset. Hart would have been extremely proud of Hyde when his acclaimed *Abhráin Grádh Chúige Connacht or Love Songs of Connacht*, was published in 1893, the same year he was appointed president of the newly founded Gaelic League. This diary marks the beginning of Hyde's enchantment with Irish as it was spoken by local people. Is also gives the reader an insight into the creation of Hyde, Hyde the linguist, Hyde the professor, Hyde the president. Douglas Hyde completes his first diary with this simple explanation, 'I have stopped this diary now at the end of the year and have changed to another book. Fuair me leabhar eile o Sissilla Ua Heide' (p. [119]) (… I got another book from Cecily Hyde): like any good book, this leaves the reader wanting more, which can be found in diary number two spanning the period 1 January 1877–4 September 1877 (NLI MS G 1037).

Section 2
Periodicals and Their Readers

3

The *Nation*, History, and the Making of National Citizens

James Quinn

The nationalist journalists, later known as Young Ireland, who founded the *Nation* newspaper in 1842, proclaimed their intention 'to create and foster public opinion and make it racy of the soil'.[1] This desire to forge a deeply rooted national consciousness inevitably involved looking back at Ireland's history, and drawing strength and inspiration from the achievements and sacrifices of the past. Ireland, the *Nation* insisted, had a noble record of cultural distinction and courageous resistance that should be a matter of pride to all its people, regardless of their political allegiances. It bemoaned popular ignorance of Irish history, arguing that it undermined Ireland's claims to nationhood: ignorance was the mark of the slave, while the freeman knew of the heroes and patriots who had gone before him and strove to live up to their ideals and sacrifices. The *Nation* maintained that a sustained campaign of national education was needed to overcome such ignorance, and warned that 'if the people do not persevere with a dogged and daily labour for knowledge and independence they will be slaves for generations'.[2]

The leading role in all of this was taken by Thomas Davis, one of the founders of the *Nation*, and its driving force until his death in 1845. Davis believed that overturning centuries of neglect and falsification in the writing of Irish history was an essential first step in creating a true sense of nationhood, and maintained that the primary objective of Irish literary effort should be 'to furnish Irishmen the true history of their country' and to inspire them with 'a new and informed patriotism'.[3] He was determined to refute the misrepresentations of hostile historians who he claimed had

1 *Nation*, 15 Oct. 1842. The *Nation* consulted for this article is the bound hard copy which belonged to Thomas Davis and is held in the library of the Royal Irish Academy.
2 'Irish Policy', *Nation*, 15 June 1844.
3 'National Literature', *Nation*, 20 September 1845.

made the Irish look on their past with shame by writing a version of history that falsely contrasted England's grandeur with the chaotic squabbling of the Irish: 'Our bravery they have called turbulence, our resistance rebellion, our virtue barbarity ... This must be undone before we can be a nation'.[4] Davis and his *Nation* colleagues were intent therefore on countering such dismissive imperialist polemic with a coherent narrative of the Irish past that showed it had as much pattern and purpose as that of any other country. This in turn would, they hoped, encourage its people to see themselves as the inheritors of a proud and glorious past, and inspire them to pursue their political independence in the present.[5]

The *Nation*'s educational crusade was preceded by the government's decision in 1831 to establish a national system of primary education to replace the existing patchwork of hedge and parish schools. This saw a steady increase in the state provision of primary education: from 789 national schools in 1833 to 4,321 schools with almost half a million pupils in 1849.[6] The *Nation* found much to criticise in the new system, arguing that the term 'national school' was a misnomer and that the education provided was in fact 'anti-national': state-funded schools ignored Irish literature, history and geography; the Irish language was not taught at all, and even actively discouraged.[7] Nationalists were unhappy with the assimilative and imperial character of the textbooks provided and denounced them as 'lying compendiums' which ensured that 'a boy leaves school filled with Greek, Roman and English facts, and most of them false facts, and profoundly ignorant of what it behoves him to know – the constitutional and general history of his own country'.[8]

However despite such reservations, the Young Irelanders welcomed the work of the new schools in increasing levels of popular literacy, appreciating that the *Nation*'s slogan of 'Educate that you may be free' resonated all the more when addressed to a literate population.[9] Literacy was seen as one of the essential foundations in creating an informed and discerning citizenry deserving of self-governing, and history was a crucial component in their civic education, providing the inspiring examples and cautionary warnings necessary to achieve and sustain national independence.[10]

4 'Misrepresentations of History', *Nation*, 9 December 1843.
5 M.J. Barry, 'Ireland as she was, as she is, and as she shall be', in *Essays on the Repeal of the Union* (Dublin: James Duffy, 1845), p. 12.
6 Donald H. Akenson, *The Irish Education Experiment: the National System of Education in the Nineteenth Century* (London: Routledge, 1970), p. 140.
7 'Education', *Nation*, 18 February 1843.
8 'Education', *Nation*, 14 June 1845.
9 'Growth of an Irish Nation', *Nation*, 12 July 1845; 'Popular Education', *Nation*, 27 July 1844; 'Report of the Commissioners of National Education: 1846, Part 2', *Nation*, 3 October 1846.
10 *Nation*, 8 February 1845, 3 April 1847.

As part of their campaign to bring about this independence, most of the leading Young Irelanders joined Daniel O'Connell's Repeal Association in the early 1840s. O'Connell welcomed them, believing that the accession of these well-educated young men, both Catholic and Protestant, would enhance the prestige and non-sectarian credentials of the association. From the start they were anxious to make their mark and intent on imbuing the association with a greater sense of cultural and historical awareness. Davis maintained that it was the duty of every patriot to inform himself about his country's past and that 'the Repealer who does not know Irish history is ignorant of the rudiments of his political creed'.[11] The *Nation* also argued that the study of history could also enlighten those who opposed the repeal of the Act of Union, appealing to the Presbyterians of Ulster to remember the historic role they had played in asserting Ireland's rights with the Volunteers and the United Irishmen. The paper encouraged Orangemen to emulate the Repeal Association and add reading rooms to their lodges, where they too could acquaint themselves with their country's history and learn just how ill-served they had been by England's policy of divide and rule.[12]

Repeal reading rooms had existed before the Young Irelanders joined the association, but they were few and poorly funded. O'Connell allotted only a small portion of the repeal rent to them, and saw no need for their encouragement or regulation, valuing them more for organisational and fundraising purposes than for education. In contrast, the *Nation* saw them as crucial cornerstones in constructing a national civil society. It envisaged a well-funded national network providing venues for careful reading and sober discussion and giving their members the genuinely national education denied them in state-sponsored national schools.[13] In an implicit rebuke to O'Connell's stated policy of achieving repeal through peace and perseverance, the *Nation* claimed that without an educated people, '[p]eace is cowardice and Perseverance idiocy'.[14] Davis, in particular, was sceptical of the effect of the Repeal Association's concentration on political agitation, dismissing much of it as empty speechifying and impotent posturing. Education, he maintained, was 'the only moral force in which I have any faith'.[15]

11 'Propagandism', *Nation*, 16 September 1843.

12 'Twelfth of August', *Nation*, 9 August 1845.

13 Paul A. Townend, '"Academies of Nationality": The Reading Room and Irish National Movements, 1838–1905', in McBride (ed.), *Reading Irish Histories*, pp. 19–39, p. 21. On the importance of reading rooms, see Roisín Higgins, 'The *Nation* Reading Rooms', in James H. Murphy (ed.), *The Oxford History of the Irish Book, Vol. IV: The Irish Book in English 1800–1891* (Oxford: Oxford University Press, 2011), pp. 262–73; and Marie-Louise Legg, 'Libraries' in Murphy (ed.), *Oxford History of the Irish Book*, pp. 250–54.

14 'Knowledge and Conciliation', *Nation*, 24 August 1844.

15 Thomas Davis to William Smith O'Brien [1844?], in C.G. Duffy, *Young Ireland: a Fragment of Irish History* (London: Cassell, Petter, Galpin and Co., 1880), pp. 673–74.

Anxious to counter the Anglicising tendencies of the national schools, Davis argued that the denial of suitable educational instruction was a deliberate policy adopted by the government to keep the Irish poor and ignorant. The *Nation* had begun to change this, and he hoped its efforts would be reinforced by the Repeal Association acting as the 'schoolmaster of the people of Ireland'.[16] Its reading rooms should, he advised, be immediately stocked with works of history that had some sympathy towards national aspirations, such as James MacGeoghegan's *History of Ireland* (1758–63), Francis Plowden's *An Historical Review of the State of Ireland* (1803) and Denis Taaffe's *An Impartial History of Ireland* (1809–11).[17] In an effort to reach those whose reading skills could not cope with such works, he also recommended that private reading be supplemented by reading aloud regular lectures, noting that if 'one strong-minded and earnest man' learned the outlines of Irish history, he could then pass on his knowledge to his fellow members, who could then take up more detailed studies of particular periods and build up a network of amateur scholars whose efforts could inform, encourage and sustain each other.[18]

Although they saw the Repeal Association as an important vehicle for their educational programme, the Young Irelanders were sometimes uneasy members, harbouring doubts about O'Connell's political strategy and his commitment to national independence. Given the overwhelmingly Catholic membership of the body, they were also concerned at the sectarian tendencies of some O'Connellites, and his own readiness to follow the lead of the Catholic hierarchy in matters such as third-level education.[19] They particularly disliked the unquestioning obedience of O'Connell's followers, viewing many of them as sycophants and place seekers, and believed that the absence of any real debate in the association had strengthened its leader's autocratic tendencies and was poor preparation for an independent Irish legislature. Duffy concluded that O'Connell's long enjoyment of supreme authority had made him complacent and used to getting his own way, and that the absence of any meaningful dissent over many years meant that he preferred to be surrounded by 'courtiers and lackeys [than by] counsellors and peers'.[20]

The Young Irelanders believed therefore that it fell to them to educate the obedient masses who thronged to repeal monster meetings to become discerning citizens capable of holding their rulers to account. They saw little

16 'Educate That You May Be Free', *Nation*, 5 October 1844; 'No Redress – No Inquiry', *Nation*, 15 July 1843.

17 'Repeal Reading Rooms', *Nation*, 17 August 1844, 14 December 1844.

18 'Freedom's Way', *Nation*, 30 August 1845.

19 Randall Clarke, 'The Relations Between O'Connell and the Young Irelanders', *Irish Historical Studies* III.9 (1942): 23–26.

20 Duffy, *Young Ireland*, pp. 22–23.

point in achieving legislative independence if a Dublin parliament was not a vigorous and responsible body, representing diverse interests, and elected by a population with the knowledge and judgement to make informed decisions. Education was the key, not only to attaining national liberty, but to ensuring that it was put to good use and could not be subverted by powerful individuals or institutions. The *Nation*'s programme was, in the broadest sense of the term, a republican one. 'Republican', though, was not a term that could be used lightly in the Ireland of the 1840s: most contemporaries, whether nationalist or unionist, associated it with the Puritan king-killers of the 1640s, or with French-inspired social and political levellers of the 1790s. While the Young Irelanders often praised the virtuous character and idealism of the United Irishmen, they tended to downplay their republican sympathies and ideology.[21] The *Nation* generally avoided using overt republican terminology, for fear of offending O'Connell and moderate Repealers, but its programme nonetheless drew heavily on the ideals of civic republicanism and its emphasis on political education and engagement.[22]

In all of this 'citizen-making', rising levels of literacy clearly offered an opportunity for spreading the nationalist message, but they also posed a danger in that they opened the door to the 'wrong' kind of reading matter, particularly that which portrayed Ireland's history as a series of hopeless defeats or the random violence of bloodthirsty savages. It was therefore vitally important that popular literacy be nourished with the right food and that schools, reading rooms and homes be supplied with suitably patriotic and uplifting reading matter. There was, however, a desperate shortage of such material, with most existing history books being prohibitively expensive for working people. The *Nation* did its best, devoting much of the paper to substantial articles on important people and events in Irish history, and reviewing historical works at length, but even this did not make up for the shortage of suitable books. In 1845, therefore, Davis and his *Nation* colleagues took the initiative by launching the 'Library of Ireland', a series of cheaply produced works of history, fiction and poetry that sold for the modest sum of a shilling and were intended to provide Ireland with its own national literature.

Typical history volumes were Thomas MacNevin's *History of the Volunteers of 1782* (1845) and *Confiscation of Ulster* (1846), John Mitchel's *Life and Times of Aodh O'Neill, Prince of Ulster* (1845), and Fr C.P. Meehan *History of the*

21 *Nation*, 8 July 1843 and 25 July 1845. See especially Sean Ryder, 'Speaking of '98: Young Ireland and Republican Memory', *Éire-Ireland* xxxiv.2 (1999): 51–69; and idem, 'Young Ireland and the 1798 Rebellion', in L.M. Geary (ed.), *Rebellion and Remembrance in Modern Ireland* (Dublin: Four Courts Press, 2001), pp. 135–47.

22 David Dwan, *The Great Community: Culture and Nationalism in Ireland* (Dublin: Field Day, 2008), pp. 31–39, pp. 58–61.

Confederation of Kilkenny (1846). (Other volumes assigned to various writers but never published included 'The Military History of 1798', by M.J. Barry; 'A Life of Wolfe Tone' by Thomas Davis (stalled by Davis's death); 'History of "the Great Popish Rebellion" of 1641' by Charles Gavan Duffy; 'The Williamite Wars' and 'Orators of the Irish Parliament' by Thomas Francis Meagher; 'The Life of Owen Roe O'Neill' by John Mitchel; 'and 'The Penal Days' and 'Biographies of the United Irishmen', by Thomas Devin Reilly.)[23] Although the topics chosen were diverse, this was very much a collective endeavour which portrayed events such as the Nine Years' War, the Confederation of Kilkenny and the rise of the Volunteer movement as important episodes in a continuous and heroic struggle against foreign domination that offered valuable lessons for the present.[24]

Significantly, MacNevin's *History of the Volunteers of 1782* was the first publication in the series. Young Ireland idealised the Volunteers as the virtuous citizen-soldiers of the Irish nation, portraying them as civic republicans *par excellence*, who elected their officers, debated their proposals in democratic conventions, and were determined to assert Ireland's constitutional and economic rights. Like the citizens of classical republics, they were not only politically engaged, but trained in the use of arms, and intent on holding their political leaders to account. The agitation of this citizen militia had helped to achieve Ireland's own 'Glorious Revolution' in 1782, and wrung from the British government the right of Irishmen to legislate for themselves. In lauding the Volunteers and their achievements there was the implicit criticism of O'Connell's reliance on moral force alone: concessions would be won from the British government not by mass meetings, nor by wanton violence, but by an armed and disciplined national movement that would not shirk from using force if its demands were ignored.

Given the prominent role that the classics had played in their own education, the employment of classical models came readily to the writers of the *Nation*. In his best-known ballad, 'A nation once again', Davis invoked the 'ancient freemen' of Greece and Rome and hoped to imbue his countrymen with something of their spirit and courage. In his disillusionment with modern society, John Mitchel, who became assistant editor of the *Nation* after Davis's death, regularly portrayed the classical world as an era of greater honesty and virtue, and during his trial on charges of treason felony in 1848 self-consciously adopted the role of the virtuous Roman patriot, refusing to

23 Duffy, *Young Ireland*, p. 679; C.G. Duffy, *Four Years of Irish History* (London: Cassell, Petter, Galpin and Co., 1883, p. 59; 'Listing of the Library of Ireland', *Nation*, 5 July 1845.

24 For a more detailed discussion of the Library of Ireland, see James Quinn, *Young Ireland and the Writing of Irish History* (Dublin: UCD Press, 2015), pp. 53–59.

yield to the persecution of the tyrant.[25] His most famous work, *Jail Journal* (1854), can be read as a tract of classical stoicism in its author's determination to make the best of his incarceration and his refusal to allow his spirit to be crushed by his jailors. Mitchel's suspicion of progress, idealisation of the independent yeoman farmer and determination to deny the benefits of citizenship to criminals, slaves or corrupt aristocrats, all hark back to an austere interpretation of classical republicanism.[26]

In the classical republican tradition, liberty was granted only to those who were prepared to fight for it and defend it with their lives. The works of the *Nation*'s Library of Ireland therefore paid particular attention to military history, intent on proving, in an age that placed a particular value on physical courage and martial prowess as an indicator of moral worth, that the Irish were as brave as any other nation. The Young Irelanders tried to avoid dwelling too much on historical grievances, realising that such a strategy risked creating a nation of sullen victims rather than self-respecting citizens. Instead they sought to write history in such a way as to make clear that Ireland 'has ceased to wail ... she begins to study the past – not to acquire a beggar's eloquence in petition, but a hero's wrath in strife'.[27] Influenced by Carlylean notions of hero worship, they argued that a true knowledge of Ireland's past deeds was incompatible with national subservience and sought to popularise the reputations of charismatic warrior heroes such as Hugh O'Neill, Owen Roe O'Neill and Patrick Sarsfield as Ireland's heroes and martyrs, as the Scots had done with Bruce and Wallace and the Poles with Kosciusko.[28]

When domestic history was not suitably heroic, notably during the years of Protestant oppression and Catholic quiescence that characterised the first three-quarters of the eighteenth century, the Young Irelanders shifted the focus abroad, to the valiant deeds of the Wild Geese. French victories in which Irish Brigades were prominent such as Fontenoy and Cremona were lauded as victories for Ireland achieved by Irish soldiers who remained loyal

25 *Irish Felon*, 24 June 1848.

26 See Patrick Maume, 'Young Ireland, Arthur Griffith, and Republican Ideology: the Question of Continuity', *Eire-Ireland* xxxiv.2 (1999): 155–74, 161; and James Quinn, 'John Mitchel and the Rejection of the Nineteenth Century', *Éire-Ireland* xxxviii.3–4 (2003): 90–108.

27 'The History of Ireland', *Nation*, 11 November 1843.

28 Duffy, *Young Ireland*, pp. 67–68. For the influence of Carlyle on Young Ireland, see Roger Swift, 'Carlyle and Ireland', in D. George Boyce and Roger Swift (eds), *Problems and Perspectives in Irish History since 1800: Essays in Honour of Patrick Buckland* (Dublin: Four Courts Press, 2004), p. 135; Owen Dudley Edwards, '"True Thomas": Carlyle, Young Ireland and the Legacy of Millennialism', in David Sorensen and Rodger L. Tarr (eds), *The Carlyles at Home and Abroad* (Aldershot: Ashgate, 2006), pp. 61–76; and John Morrow, 'Thomas Carlyle, "Young Ireland" and the "Condition of Ireland Question"', *The Historical Journal* LI.3 (2008): 643–67.

to their homeland and fought her battles on foreign soil. A sharp contrast was drawn between the high ideals and noble virtues of the past and the timidity and apathy of the present. In his biography of the medieval warrior chief Art MacMurrough, Thomas D'Arcy McGee praised the heroic spirit that had persisted throughout the ages in Ireland's struggles for liberty, and pointedly asked where 'the manhood, the chivalry, the love of native land' that characterised past struggles were to be found today.[29]

The Young Irelanders soon discovered that their dramatic and celebratory interpretation of Irish history lent itself well to song and verse. The *Nation* published much historical verse, which found its way into collections such as *The Spirit of the Nation* (first published in 1843) and other verse anthologies compiled by Charles Gavan Duffy (1845), Michael Joseph Barry (1845), and Denis Florence McCarthy (1846). National ballads were a particularly effective means of historical education: they could be learned quickly and their repeated performance in family and social settings confirmed and reinforced nationalist sentiments. Their reach extended to those who were unable (or not inclined) to read history, and formed a crucial link with an earlier oral tradition. Reprinted in edition after edition, songs such as 'A nation once again', 'The memory of the dead', and 'O'Donnell abú' became central to the way in which Irish people interpreted their past and proved to be Young Ireland's most enduring literary achievement.[30]

In classical republics, civic virtue was cultivated primarily by participation in the political life of the state and by bearing arms in its defence. The scope for the latter was extremely limited in the early 1840s. The rebellions of 1798 and 1803 had discredited the use of physical force in the eyes of most nationalists, and O'Connell's campaigns for Catholic emancipation and repeal of the Act of Union had been predicated on the insistence that 'moral force' alone was the path to follow. Arming or drilling in the pursuit of political goals was not a realistic option for the Young Irelanders, but they were by no means prepared to repudiate this tradition. They were, for example, enthusiastic members of the uniformed and quasi-military '82 Club founded in July 1844 to commemorate and honour the winning of legislative independence by Irish Patriots and Volunteers in 1782.[31] Their speeches, ballads and histories regularly praised Ireland's proud record of resistance in arms and honoured its heroes and martyrs. Their bellicose rhetoric put them on a collision course with O'Connell, who in July 1846 tried to bring matters to a head by compelling all members of

29 Thomas D'Arcy McGee, *A Memoir of the Life and Conquests of Art Mac Murrogh* [*sic*] (Dublin: J. Duffy, 1847), p. 133.

30 Charles Gavan Duffy, *Thomas Davis: The Memoirs of an Irish Patriot, 1840–1846* (London: Paul, Trench, Trübner & Co., 1890), p. 95.

31 Charlotte Kelly, 'The '82 Club', *Studies: an Irish Quarterly Review* xxxiii (1944): 257–62.

the Repeal Association to subscribe to a series of 'peace resolutions' condemning violence as a means of achieving political change.

At the time the question was very much an abstract one, and the Young Irelanders had neither the intention nor the capacity to take up arms. As nobody was advocating physical force in the present, the debate centred on whether it had ever been justifiable in the past. Thomas Francis Meagher claimed that history furnished many examples of when it had and famously refused to 'stigmatise the sword' that had freed nations such as the Americans and Belgians from foreign domination. John Mitchel too was not prepared to condemn the Volunteers of 1782, the founding fathers of America, or the United Irishmen of 1798, all of whom had had shown that a recourse to arms was sometimes necessary and indeed honourable. In retrospect this debate has sometimes been viewed as an insignificant squabble at a time when Ireland was about to experience the full horrors of famine, but it brought to a head two distinct conceptions of Irish nationalism. For O'Connell, it was an attempt to reaffirm his lifelong commitment solely to peaceful and constitutional politics, while the Young Irelanders regarded the resolutions as a repudiation of a noble tradition of armed resistance. For four years the *Nation* had celebrated past efforts to win Ireland's freedom by the sword. For it now to accept meekly O'Connell's resolutions would, it believed, be a base disavowal of the very kind of independent and self-reliant citizenship it sought to foster. Charles Gavan Duffy argued that accepting the resolutions meant 'presenting ourselves to our old, relentless, hereditary enemy, bound hand and foot, by a renunciation for ever, under all circumstances, of the last resource of oppressed nations'. Believing they could not repudiate Ireland's tradition of armed resistance without sacrificing their integrity, the *Nation* group seceded from the Repeal Association.[32]

In the aftermath of the split, the Young Irelanders founded their own Irish Confederation in early 1847, and the *Nation* continued to focus its efforts on political and cultural education. Its ambitious plans were, however, interrupted by the immense social upheaval caused by the Great Famine and the political disruption that followed it. The market for cheap books virtually collapsed and after stuttering on for a couple of years the publications of the Library of Ireland came to an end in 1848. The *Nation* was forced to alter its editorial line and devote increasing amounts of space to agrarian and economic matters, publishing, for example, the radical agrarian proposals of James Fintan Lalor in 1847–48. Duffy noted that as economic conditions deteriorated, the pride and self-reliance that were to form the basis of the nation's civic virtue were being eroded by fear and destitution.[33]

32 *Nation*, 18, 25 July, 1 August 1846.
33 Duffy, *Four Years of Irish History*, p. 256.

It was partly to arrest this slide into moral degradation that the Young Irelanders decided to take up arms in July 1848. As the government began to pass repressive legislation and arrest activists, they believed that they had to strike to keep faith with the tradition of gallant resistance they had championed in the *Nation* for the previous six years. In making its call to arms, the paper's editor noted that '[w]e fight, because the honour, the interest, the necessity, the very existence of this ancient nation depends upon our valour and devotion at this hour'.[34] A sense of historical duty, however, proved to be an insufficient basis for an insurrection. The leaders of the Irish Confederation had no military experience and few arms, and their attempt to mobilise a rural population demoralised by three years of hunger and disease fizzled out in days, with relatively little disturbance and few casualties. The Confederation was shattered by imprisonment and exile, and its newspapers and publications prohibited.

The events of July 1848 showed that the *Nation* had clearly not succeeded in transforming the Irish masses into the active and disciplined citizens of their dreams, but time was to show that it had not entirely failed either: the importance of education in national renewal and the duty of every nationalist to inform himself or herself about their nation's past were powerful legacies. In using newspapers and cheap mass-produced books to inspire a greater sense of national awareness, Young Ireland can be seen as a classic example of Benedict Anderson's argument of nineteenth-century nationalism's use of print-capitalism to create the mass solidarity that formed the basis of a new nationally based 'imagined community'. This was a community that stretched back into the past and forward into the future, bound together by a knowledge of the glories and sacrifices of previous generations. The sense of belonging to such a community provided sustenance through difficult times and helped Irish nationalists endure their setbacks and continue to work towards achieving national independence.[35]

Young Ireland was crucial in helping to establish print culture as an integral part of nationalist movements, and almost all the significant organisations that followed placed great reliance on having their own newspaper and reading rooms. Prominent Fenians such as John Devoy, Thomas Clarke Luby, William O'Brien and John Denvir attached great importance to their youthful reading in nationalist reading rooms and acknowledged the part that the works of Young Ireland had played in moulding their nationalist outlook. Some such as Luby wrote heroic, celebratory history in the Young Ireland tradition; Liverpool-based John Denvir was inspired by the Library of Ireland to produce

34 C.G. Duffy, 'The Toscin of Ireland', *Nation*, 29 July 1848.

35 Benedict Anderson, *Imagined Communities: Reflections on the Origins and Spread of Nationalism*. Revised ed. ([1983] London: Verso, 2006), pp. 6 and 36.

an illustrated series of cheap books that circulated among Irish communities in Britain.[36] The *Nation* itself did not disappear, but was revived in 1849, and continued for almost another fifty years, mostly under the editorship of the brothers A.M. and T.D. Sullivan. The Sullivans saw themselves as guardians of the Young Ireland tradition (although their editorial policy was rather more conservative and Catholic than that of the early *Nation*) and, under their guidance, the *Nation* still sought to educate its readership through a combination of fiery journalism, historical essays and stirring songs.

By the early 1880s the term 'Young Ireland' enjoyed a new vogue, being adopted by several newly formed nationalist literary societies.[37] This development was greatly assisted by the writings of surviving Young Irelanders, notably Charles Gavan Duffy, who in a series of influential works popularised an account of the Young Irelanders as idealistic, non-sectarian and incorruptible patriots, disdainful of any form of personal gain and motivated solely by the desire to bring about their country's political and cultural regeneration.[38] Such a myth held a great appeal to the young enthusiasts of the new literary societies who were anxious to remind people that there was more to Irish nationalism than the parliamentary and agrarian agitations of the 1880s, and often contrasted the idealism and cultural vitality of Davis and his colleagues with what they saw as the soulless materialism of contemporary constitutional politics. As had the Young Irelanders, they sought to sow the seeds of national pride by teaching history to the younger generation, and encouraged them with incentives such as prizes for the best essays in Irish history in the hope that 'knowledge of our country's history, our country's song, will help to buoy every Irishman in their march for political independence'.[39] In June 1885 third place in the Young Ireland society's historical essay competition went to 14-year-old Arthur Griffith, whose prize consisted of Mitchel's *History of Ireland* and *Jail Journal* and Duffy's *Ballad Poetry of Young Ireland*.[40]

During the 1880s many of these nationalist and literary societies were affiliated to the Parnellite Irish National Land League, and were described as 'the true heirs-at-law of Thomas Davis's reading rooms of forty years ago'.[41]

36 John O'Leary, *Recollections of Fenians and Fenianism* (2 vols, London: Downey & Co., 1896), pp. i, 2–3, 50; T.C. Luby, *Illustrious Irishmen* (New York: Kelly, 1878), pp. iii–iv; John Devoy, *Recollections of an Irish Rebel* (New York: Chase D. Young, 1929), pp. 39, 290, 378; William O'Brien, *Recollections* (London: Macmillan, 1905), p. 56; John Denvir, *The Life Story of an Old Rebel* (Dublin: Sealy, Bryers & Walker, 1910), pp. 37, 137.

37 On the Young Ireland societies of the 1880s, see M.J. Kelly, *The Fenian Ideal and Irish Nationalism 1882–1916* (Woodbridge: Boydell and Brewer, 2006), pp. 16–31.

38 Duffy, *Young Ireland*; idem., *Four Years of Irish History*; idem., *Thomas Davis*.

39 *Dublin Evening Telegraph*, 7 January 1884.

40 Brian Maye, *Arthur Griffith* (Dublin: Griffith College Publications, 1997), p. 13.

41 J. Pope-Hennessy, 'What do the Irish Read?', *Nineteenth Century* XV (1884): 925–26.

By this time the national schools had done their work, and the receptivity to national literature was greatly aided by the fact that literacy rates had advanced significantly from the 1840s, from less than 50 per cent to over 80 per cent.[42] Even the reading rooms of non-political bodies such as mechanic's institutes, temperance clubs and religious societies usually included nationalist newspapers, history books and collections of patriotic verse. In 1883 a priest in charge of a Catholic Young Men's Society noted that its members read almost exclusively Irish history, poetry and biography, most of which was written by the Young Irelanders and their followers.[43]

The making of Irish citizens perhaps took somewhat longer than the Young Irelanders had originally envisaged in the 1840s, but it was a process that once started proved difficult to stop, and exerted a profound influence on the development of Irish nationalism. Through the influence of bodies such as the Young Ireland societies and the Irish Literary Society, and the writings of figures such as A.M. Sullivan and Arthur Griffith, the ideals of Young Ireland became a central part of Irish nationalist cultural discourse from the late nineteenth century onwards. Their use of literature and history for propagandist purposes resonated strongly with the zealous generation that emerged out of the cultural revival. The civic ideals of Young Ireland did much to influence a new conception of Irish nationalism, priding itself on its rectitude and virtue, and imposing duties of political education and self-improvement on its adherents. Chief among these was the learning and propagation of Irish history. A thorough knowledge of Ireland's past struggles was seen as an affirmation of patriotism in advanced nationalist circles, and the reading, teaching and discussion of Irish history were central activities in militant nationalist organisations such as the Dungannon Clubs, Inghinidhe na hÉireann and Fianna Éireann. Many of the generation who carried through the revolution of 1916–21 saw themselves as acting in a long tradition of struggle and resistance and claimed that it was primarily their understanding of Irish history that motivated them to seek their country's independence. This history was often derived from the songs and books of Davis, Mitchel and their followers.[44]

42 Mary Daly and David Dickson (eds), *The Origins of Popular Literacy in Ireland: Language Change and Educational Development 1700–1920* (Dublin: Trinity College Dublin and University College Dublin, 1990), pp. 114–17; Marie-Louise Legg, *Newspapers and Nationalism: The Irish Provincial Press 1850–1892* (Dublin: Four Courts Press, 1999), pp. 44–46.

43 Pope-Hennessy, 'What do the Irish Read?, p. 930.

44 Cahir Davitt, Bureau of Military History (BMH), WS 993, p. 1; Kevin O'Shiel, BMH, WS 1770, p. 67; Sean O'Neill, BMH, WS 1219, p. 1, p. 33; Eamon Broy, BMH, WS 1280, p. 9; Sean Ó Ceallaigh, BMH, WS 1476, p. 1; Michael McCormick, BMH, WS 1503, p. 1; Thomas Reidy, BMH, WS 1555, p. 1; Patrick Lyons, BMH, WS 1645, p. 1; Thomas Hevey, BMH, WS 1668, p. 4.

The Gaelic Leaguer and IRB-man, P.S. O'Hegarty, for example, a nationalist historian of some importance himself, argued that despite the failure of Young Ireland's insurrectionary efforts in 1848, 'in the long run, they won. The written word remained. The principles of nationality expounded in the *Nation* were never again wholly obscured. They became an integral part of the Irish consciousness'.[45] Young Ireland's writings had a profound effect on those who saw the past as heroic and noble in contrast to a corrupt and debased present. If Ireland's future was to match its past, then this nobility and heroism would have to be regained, and many believed that this could only be done by Ireland's citizen-soldiers taking up arms and proving the existence of Irish courage and virtue once again.

45 P.S. O'Hegarty, *A History of Ireland under the Union 1801–1922* (London: Methuen, 1952), pp. 628, 378.

4

Watchmen to the House of Israel? Irish Methodism and the Religious Press

Nicola Morris

The nineteenth century saw the peak in periodical culture in Ireland and Great Britain with nearly 20,000 different titles published.[1] Their average longevity was 28 years and approximately 40 per cent of these journals were religious, most commonly published on a monthly or weekly basis. Patrick Scott has thus suggested that 'subscription to a periodical, almost irrespective of its content matter, served Victorians as a kind of religious self-identification', a means of feeling part of a broader, more dynamic, movement than that provided by the local chapel.[2] Methodism contributed to this trend: its first monthly magazine, the *Arminian Magazine*, launched in 1778 and was published continuously (under various titles) until 1969.[3] Over the course of its run, *Arminian Magazine* was joined by a multiplicity of complementary and competitive journals, amongst which were: the *Watchman* (1832–84); the *Methodist Recorder* (1861–present); the *Methodist Times* (1885–1937); and the first dedicated Irish journals, the *Irish Evangelist* (1859–84) and the *Irish Christian Advocate* (1883–1971).[4] Each

1 Patrick Scott, 'Victorian Religious Periodicals: Fragments That Remain', in Derek Baker (ed.), *Sources, Methods and Material of Ecclesiastical History: Papers Read at the Twelfth Summer Meeting and the Thirteenth Winter Meeting of the Ecclesiastical History Society*. Studies in Church History, 11 (Blackwell: Oxford, 1975), p. 325.

2 Ibid.

3 This magazine was known as the *Arminian Magazine*, 1778–97; the *Methodist Magazine*, 1798–1821; the *Wesleyan-Methodist Magazine*, 1822–1912; the *Magazine* (of the Wesleyan Methodist Church), 1913–31; and again the *Methodist Magazine*, 1932–69. At the time of its closure in 1968 it claimed to be the 'oldest magazine in the world'. Frank Cumbers, 'The Methodist Magazine, 1778–1969' *Proceedings of the Weseyan Historical Society*, 37:3 (1969): 72–76.

4 The *Christian Advocate* only closed because on 20 October 1971 an IRA bomb destroyed their Belfast headquarters. Robin Roddie, 'Reporting and Recording', *Methodist Newsletter* (January 1998), p. 15.

of these journals originally represented an ascendant wing of the church, and reflected the contemporary theological and political debates. Thus, the theological and political shifts within Methodism can be charted through the pages of these journals. The emergence and decline of each of these newspapers also suggests that subscription was a method of identifying with particular ideas and thus of defining identity through a reading community.

It is notable therefore, that the first significant Irish publication, the *Irish Evangelist,* did not appear until 1859, during the Ulster Revival. Until then, Irish Methodists were dependent on receiving denominational content and news from periodicals published in England. Overall, Methodists were a highly literate section of the Irish population. In 1861, the census recorded that 73.1 per cent of Methodists over the age of five could read and write, with the figure rising to 91.5 per cent in 1901.[5] Ulster Methodists had the lowest levels of literacy at only 66.7 per cent in 1861, rising to 95.7 per cent in 1901, lower than the other three provinces who all recorded figures in 1901 over 99 per cent.[6] This lower figure for Ulster can be explained by the fact that it was the only region in which there was a significant number of working-class Methodists residing in the larger conurbations, especially Belfast. Nevertheless, the Methodist literacy figures are significantly above the Irish national average for the century, which stood at 41.3 per cent in 1861, and which had only risen to 79.4 per cent in 1901.[7] Given these high rates of literacy among Irish Methodists it is unclear why little distinctive Irish content was produced in the early nineteenth century. It would appear that the size of the denomination may have been the key determining factor, with the total number of full members fluctuating between 20,000 to 28,000 over the course of the century.[8] In 1861, the census 45,399 people identified themselves as Methodists, constituting just under 1 per cent of the total Irish population, significantly above the denomination's own enumeration for that year of only 23,551 committed members (37,758 if Primitive Wesleyans are included).[9] The relatively small membership thus made it less economical to publish a specifically Irish journal, but it also suggests that many may have relished the

5 *Census Ireland, 1861 and 1901.*

6 Ibid.

7 Ibid.

8 *Irish Conference Minutes,* 1800–1900. Membership was 19,292 in 1800; 23,800 in 1820; 27,047 in 1840; 22,860 in 1860; 24, 463 in 1880 and 27,745 in 1900. This compared to British Methodist membership which grew from 88,334 in 1800 to 410,384 in 1900. The Irish and British Conferences were the ruling bodies of Methodism and the printed minutes of the Conferences can be accessed at the Methodist Church Archives, John Rylands University Library, Manchester and the Methodist Historical Society of Ireland Archive, Edgehill Theological College, Belfast.

9 *Census Ireland, 1861.*

opportunity to feel part of a larger whole through reading about successes elsewhere. As a small evangelical and evangelistic religious community in Ireland, Methodists closely allied themselves with a global mission, intimately associating with the struggles of other Methodist communities abroad who also had to content with an 'inhospitable society and environment'.[10] The Ulster revival however, gave Irish Methodists evangelistic success of their own to boast about, and a nexus around which they could develop and strengthen the distinctly Irish aspects of their denominational identity.

All of the Methodist periodicals aimed to support and encourage devotion among the faithful, largely adopting the pattern set by their founder John Wesley in his first journal, the monthly *Arminian Magazine* (see note 3 for other iterations). John Wesley commenced preparation for the *Magazine* in August 1777, by publishing a series of *Proposals for, by Subscription, the Arminian Magazine; consisting of Extracts, and Original Treatises on Universal Redemption*.[11] As the first editor, Wesley proposed that the journal should contain 'no news, no politics, no personal invectives' and 'nothing offensive either to religion, decency, good nature, or good manners'.[12] It thus published only material that Wesley and the later editors' determined revealed God's work in the world, namely: sermons, biographies, missionary notices, histories, book reviews, obituaries, religious poetry and conversion narratives.[13] It was polemical and attempted to edify the readership, educate Methodists in the distinctive features of their brand of evangelicalism, and provide inspiration for their daily lives. It was published in a small format, with the page size eight inches by five inches, with the frontispiece consisting of an engraving of a notable minister or evangelist. Throughout its existence the *Magazine* remained under Conference control, which appointed a minister as editor, and required quarterly reports on its business. It was published by the official publishers to the denomination (initially J. Paramore at the Foundery, Moorfields) and distributed through the connexional book rooms at City Road in London and Whitefriar Street in Dublin.[14]

The magazine was designed to promote the official connexional brand of theology and praxis and provide practical examples of piety to the readership.

10 N.W. Taggart, *The Irish in World Methodism, 1760–1900* (London: Epworth Press, 1986) p. x.

11 John Wesley, *The Journal of John Wesley in Four Volumes*, Vol. 4 (London: Wesleyan Conference Office, 1904), p. 102 and Luke Tyerman, *The Life and Times of the Rev. John Wesley, MA*, Vol. 3, 3rd ed. (London: Hodder and Stoughton, 1876), p. 281.

12 Tyerman, *Life and Times of John Wesley*, p. 281.

13 A.O. Winkles, '"Excuse What Difficiencies You Will Find": Methodist Women and Public Space in John Wesley's Arminian Magazine', *Eighteenth-Century Studies* 46:3 (2013): 416–17.

14 *Arminian Magazine*, 1779.

Thus, the four different titles under which the *Magazine* published marked the changing identity of the denomination over the 191-year period. Initially launched as the *Arminian Magazine*, the name was chosen to emphasise the theological position advocating that the individual must exercise of freewill to choose the way of salvation.[15] This was in opposition to the Calvinist doctrine espoused in other periodicals, such as the *Gospel Magazine*, that a person's salvation (or damnation) was predestined and immutable.[16] The name changes from 1798 onward reflected the developing denominational identity, firstly as distinct from Church of England, then later as specifically Wesleyan as various groups split from main body, before reverting to the *Methodist Magazine* after Methodist re-union in 1932. These changes followed divisions within England and were largely irrelevant to the *Magazine's* Irish audience. Irish Methodists were sincerely attached to theological Arminianism, particularly where they were in competition with Ulster Presbyterians and all were determined to permanently associate themselves with the Wesley's theology. However, Irish Methodism did not suffer from the fissiparousness of their English brethren and, after the only split in the denomination in 1818, both factions retained 'Wesleyan' in their official title.[17] Nevertheless, Irish readers remained comfortable with the identity being promulgated by the *Magazine*, and reading it gave a sense of connection to a larger whole; reassuring them that despite the relative weakness of Methodism in Ireland, they were part of a successful international movement.

There was a relatively short-lived Irish edition of the *Magazine* that ran from 1802–22, which was typeset and published by Robert Napper of Capel Street, Dublin, for the Methodist book room located at 13 Whitefriar Street.[18] It was slightly shorter than the English edition, lacked an annual index and sold for 6½d a month, rising to 10d in 1812.[19] Generally speaking, the articles included in the Irish edition were taken from the English edition, although occasionally articles of specifically Irish interest were substituted. Similarly, controversial articles might be omitted from the Irish edition, for example in 1804 a 'horrifying' account of the 1798 rebellion in Wexford was excluded.[20]

15 Tyerman, *Life and Times of John Wesley*, p. 281.

16 Ibid., pp. 87–94.

17 The larger portion of Irish Methodists only split entirely from the Church of Ireland in 1818, using the label 'Wesleyan Methodist'. The smaller faction decided to maintain its connection with the Church of Ireland and became known as the 'Primitive Wesleyan Methodists'.

18 D.B. Bradshaw, 'The Irish Edition of the "Methodist Magazine"', *Proceedings of the Wesleyan Historical Society* 13:3 (1921): 56–60, 57.

19 *Wesleyan-Methodist Magazine* (Irish edition), November 1811, cover.

20 A. Wallington, 'The Arminian and Methodist Magazine: British and Irish Editions', *Proceedings of the Wesleyan Historical Society* 13:1 (1921): 11–12; David Hempton,

Rather curiously, the section 'Irish Missionary notices' did not appear in the Irish edition; presumably Irish readers were expected to already have this information through their minister. The most interesting addition to the Irish edition was substituting the frontispiece engraving with a series of portraits of Irish preachers, introduced in 1806.[21] These rooted the Irish edition in the country, and visually reinforced the distinct evangelical and Methodist tradition within the country. This was key for maintaining Irish Methodist identity, and although the Irish edition only lasted 20 years, the pattern of identifying and revering ministers and evangelists who worked in the country continued throughout the century, for example in C.H. Crookshank's *History of Methodism in Ireland* published in 1885.

The launch of the weekly broadsheet newspaper, the *Watchman*, in 1835 was a new departure in Methodist publishing: this was an explicitly political journal and published in broadsheet newspaper format. The early years of the nineteenth century had seen significant political upheaval culminating in Catholic emancipation in 1829, and the Great Reform Act of 1832. Many Methodists had been enfranchised in 1832 and political radicalism was growing in popularity, especially in the Methodist circuits of the north of England. Soon, the journal had a weekly circulation print-run of around 3,700, and as the mouthpiece of the Rev. Jabez Bunting, considerably more influence than any Irish organ could hope to achieve. Bunting, a leading English minister and noted Conservative, determined that the time was ripe for a 'religious monitor on political subjects' that would have the effect of 'moderating the effervescence of party feeling following the political chaos emanating from the general election in January 1935'.[22] The *Watchman* was clearly targeted at the urban, respectable and financially comfortable Methodists that had seen most benefit from the Reform Act, not the lower-class radicals, and the price of 7d for the first issue reflected that.[23]

Whereas the editor of the *Magazine* was appointed by Conference, the *Watchman* was technically independent of connexional control and was owned and operated by the Wesleyan Methodist Newspaper Company controlled by a board of wealthy laymen and ministers.[24] Despite this

Methodism and Politics in British Society, 1750–1850 (Stanford, CA: Stanford University Press, 1984), p. 119.

21 Wallington, 'The Arminian and Methodist Magazine', p. 57.

22 *Watchman*, 7 January 1835; David Hempton, '"*The Watchman*" and "Religious Politics" in the 1830s', *Proceedings of the Wesleyan Historical Society* 42:1 (1979): 2–13, p. 3.

23 This price reduced to 5d until 1860 then 3d until it ceased business in 1884: J.L. Altholz, *The Religious Press in Britain, 1760–1900* (New York: Greenwood Press, 1989), p. 89.

24 Louis Billington, 'The Religious Periodical and Newspaper Press, 1770–1870', in Michael Harris and A.J. Lee (eds), *The Press in English Society from the Seventeenth to Nineteenth Centuries* (London, 1986), pp. 89–108, p. 106.

independence, Bunting's profile and status within the denomination ensured that it was viewed as an official organ designed to 'represent the opinions and protect the interests of the Wesleyan Methodists'.[25] The title of the new journal revealed its mission: taking an image from Ezekiel, the journal conceived of itself as a sentinel sent to warn the people of approaching disaster that would become inevitable unless an alternative course was charted. Bunting had stated in 1827 that 'Methodist was as much opposed to democracy as to sin', and he believed that public affairs needed to be directed by men of property.[26] He feared that the widening of the franchise would lead to the election of radical politicians opposed to his conservative views but that this could be stemmed among Methodists by the educated analysis and opinion from the editorial staff, who would steer politically engaged Methodists towards conservative and Tory views. For Bunting and the *Watchman*, conservative principles meant the defence of the Protestant constitution of the United Kingdom. In practice, therefore, the newspaper supported the Established Church as a protector of the constitution and as a bulwark against Catholicism. Similarly, they opposed the system of National Schools as it legitimised Catholic religious instruction even to Protestant children.[27] Catholicism in all its forms was considered to be inimical to 'true' religion and a danger to the British state.[28] Given that the majority of its population were Catholic, Ireland was naturally seen as being at the frontline of the defence of the constitution, where 'the battle, both religiously and politically, [was] to be fought'.[29]

This conservative political stance was appealing to Irish Methodists as the *Watchman* was vocally opposed to O'Connell, condemning his 'system of Popish agitation' and strongly siding with the Tories regarding the contentious elections to the Dublin City seat.[30] In 1837, the journal praised unnamed Methodist ministers in the city for having 'broken through their habitual reserve' to campaign against O'Connell, conveniently overlooking the denominational ruling that clergy should not comment on political matters in an official capacity.[31] The *Watchman* was in fact regularly to demonstrate that the 'no politics' rule instituted by Wesley was not immutable; you just needed influence and respectability to break it. Given that most Methodists agreed

25 *The Times*, 8 January 1835.

26 Robert Currie, *Methodism Divided: a Study of the Sociology of Ecumenalism* (London: Faber, 1969), p. 165.

27 *Watchman*, 1 March 1838.

28 See Linda Colley, *Britons: Forging the Nation 1707–1837*. Rev. ed. (London: Pimlico, 1992), pp. 330–32.

29 *Watchman*, 13 January 1836.

30 Ibid., 23 December 1835.

31 Ibid., 19 July 1837.

with the *Watchman* that 'Protestantism is the only agency of regenerating Ireland', finding 'theological' reasons for opposing Irish legislation was straightforward.[32] All the perceived problems and deficiencies of Ireland were laid at the door of religion, and thus could not be alleviated by liberal policies that ceded ground to Catholics.[33] Thus, the journal opposed reform of the Irish municipal corporations, on the grounds that it would 'strengthen the cause of Popery, and increase its influence in the legislature of the Empire' on the basis that what was 'theologically wrong could never be morally right'.[34] All of these positions had the enthusiastic support of Irish Methodists and while Irish affairs were central to the political debate in the United Kingdom there was no need for a distinctly Irish journal, when supporting the English newspaper was likely to have more political impact.

However, while Ireland was the battleground chosen for battles over Catholic encroachment and education, Irish affairs were not considered by the *Watchman*'s editors as inherently interesting to their readers. Consequently, the journal only gave comprehensive coverage to Ireland when an English issue was at stake, such as education. This was particularly notable in the absence of any coverage of the Famine, or indeed the Ulster Revival of 1859. While the Famine was clearly a humanitarian disaster, the *Watchman* typically only gave extended coverage to matters of high politics, not charity, tragedy or the social condition. Methodism was not a church of the social elites, particularly in Ulster, and a significant proportion of its congregations were affected by the famine. This resulted in the connexion losing one-third of its members between 1846 and 1856, largely to emigration, and forcing the Methodists to withdraw from a number of districts.[35] It was not that British Methodists were unsympathetic to the plight of the Irish, indeed the Wesleyan Methodist Relief Fund distributed over £20,000 between 1845 and 1851, money which was distributed 'without any regard to denominational distinction'.[36] However, the lack of acknowledgement of the impact of the disaster by the denomination's leading journal must have rankled and it is thus not surprising that for Irish Methodists relying on English publications became much less satisfactory. The only major Irish issue that the *Watchman* discussed at length during these years was the Young Ireland

32 Ibid., 1 February 1838.

33 Ibid.

34 Ibid., and Hempton, '"*The Watchman*" and "Religious Politics"', p. 8.

35 *Irish Conference Minutes*, 1846–56. The Irish Conference Minutes for 1847 complain especially vociferously about the numbers driven to emigration because of the 'distracted state of Ireland', but do not mention the famine specifically.

36 T.P. O'Neill, 'The Charities and Famine in Mid-Nineteenth Century Ireland', in Jacqueline Hill and Colm Lennon (eds), *Luxury and Austerity* (Dublin: UCD Press, 1999), p. 163, and *Irish Conference Minutes*, 1847.

rising of 1848, which was roundly condemned, and William Smith O'Brien mocked for taking 'refuge in a cabbage garden'.[37] But even with regard to this incontrovertibly political issue, the journal limited its coverage, claiming they 'had an article of some length in type, on Irish affairs, but the pressure on our space, compels us, at the last moment, to lay it aside', clearly demonstrating that they believed that Irish matters were of little interest to their general readership.[38]

For Irish Methodists, the revival of 1859 thus marked some good news after a prolonged period of struggle, yet this was not reflected in the English press. The refusal to discuss the revival in the *Watchman* was consistent with their conservative values and opposition to radicalism. Wesleyan experiences with revivals in the north of England in the early nineteenth century was that it led it political radicalism and was 'not only divisive, but silly and degrading'.[39] However, the milieu of Irish Methodism had an entirely different conception of revivalism which, particularly in Ulster, had come to be considered as desirable, and as a preferably regular occurrence necessary for the 'ongoing reform and renewal of the church'.[40] The revival was thus rapidly characterised within Wesleyanism as of a peculiarly Irish character not to be encouraged in England. Irish Methodists, however, were not content to sit on the sidelines during the 'year of grace' and to let the other denominations claim the credit, rather they wished to be clearly associated with evangelistic success. As a result of apparent English disinterest in Irish affairs and the development of an identifiably Irish form of evangelical revivalism, a new distinct Irish Methodist identity began to emerge, and this required its own journal to celebrate and disseminate Irish Methodist success.

It was the Ulster Revival and the increased awareness of the unique Irish milieu that encouraged the launch of the first Irish Methodist periodical, the *Irish Evangelist*. This monthly newspaper was first published in October 1859 under the management of a Dublin solicitor Theodore Cronhelm. Expectations were high for the new journal as it was anticipated that the widely dispersed but literate membership would relish the opportunity to be more informed about events in other Irish circuits. The *Irish Evangelist* was edited by the Rev. Dr William Crook, a notable essayist within the denomination who had published a number of books and articles on the global spread of evangelical

37 *Watchman*, 3 August 1848.

38 Ibid.

39 Hempton, *Methodism and Politics in British Society*, p. 96.

40 Andrew Holmes, 'The Experience and Understanding of Religious Revival in Ulster Presbyterianism, c.1800–1930', *Irish Historical Studies* 34:136 (2005): 361–85, 385; D.W. Miller, 'Did Ulster Presbyterians Have a Devotional Revolution?', in J.H. Murphy (ed.), *Evangelicals and Catholics in Nineteenth Century Ireland* (Dublin: Four Courts Press, 2005), pp. 38–54, p. 43.

religion.[41] His principal interest was to chart the successes of Irish Methodists in mission, both at home and abroad, and the *Irish Evangelist* reflected these interests. It aimed to promote and chart the successes of Methodist mission in Ireland, effectively becoming the newspaper of record for the denomination circulating news about revival around the various Methodist circuits.[42] It was subtitled 'a journal of the present, and herald of the future' suggesting that the revival was going to institute a new era of evangelical commitment across the country.[43] Methodists claimed credit for the evangelical revival within the other Protestant denominations, and were consequently newly confident in their work of saving Ireland from 'Romish influence and superstition'.[44] Given its self-appointed role as a herald, the *Irish Evangelist* broadly conformed to the model of the *Methodist Magazine* in focusing on edifying the readership and largely avoiding comment on overtly political issues. However, it did interpret its remit as commenting on moral and ethical issues, so did enter the political debate on questions such as disestablishment and education, where it took a broadly conservative stance supporting the Established Church and opposing concessions to Catholics.[45] This editorial policy led the paper to reasonable circulation, but it was held back by a lack of capital investment which prevented it from increasing the frequency of its publication.[46]

Although the *Irish Evangelist* chose to largely eschew discussions of overtly political affairs, the 1860s also marked the beginning of a political divergence between Irish and British Methodism. After Bunting's death in 1858, political liberalism was in the ascendancy in the English church, as demonstrated by the falling circulation of the *Watchman*, and the launch of the *Methodist Recorder* in 1861.[47] Like the *Watchman*, the *Methodist Recorder* was published in broadsheet format, but at only 1d was a cheaper alternative.[48] The new weekly was more supportive of Liberal political views, but despite being an ostensible rival to the *Watchman*, the two newspapers were rapidly consolidated under the control of a single board of management.[49] In contrast to the more conservative *Watchman*, the *Recorder* supported the extension of the franchise to all householders and came out in its first year as favouring the

41 See for example, William Crook, *Ireland and the Centenary of American Methodism* (London: Hamilton, Adams and Co., 1866).
42 C.H. Crookshank, *A History of Methodism in Ireland* (London, T. Woolmer, 1888), v.3 p. 524.
43 *Irish Evangelist*, October 1859.
44 Crookshank, *A History of Methodism in Ireland*, v.3, p. 525.
45 See for example, *Irish Evangelist*, March 1868, March 1869 and March 1870.
46 Roddie, 'Reporting and Recording'.
47 According to Altholz, the *Watchman*'s circulation fell from around 3,200 in 1855 to 2,000 in 1865: Altholz, *The Religious Press in Britain*, p. 89.
48 Ibid.
49 Ibid.

disestablishment of the Irish Church. These were the positions of William Arthur, an Irish-born missionary who became President of Conference in 1868, and who believed that liberty of association and liberalism in politics provided the best terrain for Protestant evangelism.[50] This was strongly opposed by the majority of Irish Methodists, who held to the conservative position that an attack on the Established Church was an intolerable concession to Catholicism that would turn the island irrevocably from the principles of the Reformation that had established the population of the United Kingdom as a 'free and enlightened people'.[51] Somewhat ironically, the most significant impact of the disestablishment on Irish Methodism was precipitating the re-union between Wesleyans and Primitive Wesleyans in 1878, after which membership grew steadily for the remainder of the century.[52]

The 1867 Reform Act enfranchised a significant number of British nonconformists for the first time, and the general election the following year appeared to propel Gladstone to power on the back of these votes.[53] Wesleyan Methodists were conscious that they were the second largest denomination in England, after the Established Church, and they had a prime minister who was apparently eager to listen to their views. Indeed, during the period between 1870–1914, the religious press was recognised as the ideal medium through which to organise nonconformist opinion, and had the effect of both educating the electorate and exerting pressure on politicians.[54] The *Methodist Recorder* clearly saw itself taking on this role for liberal Methodism, taking over the mantle from the *Watchman*, whose conservative principles seemed outmoded. However, this swing towards political liberalism was not matched among Irish Methodists, who rather than respecting Gladstone's religious values, were deeply suspicious of his apparent willingness to offer concessions to Nationalists. Moreover, they could not accept that there was anything principled in the grand old man's *volte-face* regarding the Irish church: rather they saw it as a gross betrayal.

This trend of political divergence between the Irish and British churches continued and by 1883 Irish Methodism was finding the lack of a homegrown weekly journal containing news and discussion of current affairs to be a

50 William Arthur, *Ought Not the Two Methodist Bodies in Ireland to Become One?* (Dublin, 1869) and idem, *The Householder's Parliament: A Word to the Electors of 1885* (London, 1885).

51 *Irish Conference Minutes* 1868 and *Wesleyan-Methodism Magazine*, 1867, p. 711.

52 *Irish Conference Minutes*, 1878.

53 D.W. Bebbington, *The Nonconformist Conscience: Chapel and Politics, 1870–1918* (London: George Allen & Unwin, 1982), pp. 1–17.

54 R.J. Helmstadter, The Nonconformist Conscience', in Gerald Parsons (ed.), *Religion in Victorian Britain, Vol. 4, Interpretations* (Manchester: Manchester University Press, 1988), pp. 62–63.

problem. The major issues of concern to Irish Methodists were less frequently in accord with those of their British brethren. British nonconformity was now solidly Liberal in politics, a situation that was illustrated by the cessation of the *Watchman* in 1884 and the corresponding launch of a more radical broadsheet, the *Methodist Times* in 1885, identically priced with the *Recorder* at 1d. The *Methodist Times* was edited by the prominent minister Hugh Price Hughes, patterned on the *Pall Mall Gazette* in both visual style and tone, and operated through a stock company under the presidency of William Alexander McArthur, a scion of an upwardly mobile Irish Methodist family.[55] The *Methodist Times* represented advanced Liberal opinions and essentially operated as the polemical organ of Hughes to promote his social and political principles. Hughes subtitled it 'A Journal of Religious and Social Movement', and it advocated significant social reform.[56] Hughes was disposed to applaud Gladstone's efforts to bring 'justice to Ireland' and support his policy of land reform. By contrast, most Irish Methodists did not share this confidence in Gladstone and while they were open to some form of land reform, they were adamant that this should not be, or perceived to be, giving in to threats by criminals engaged in the Land War.[57] They believed that those English Liberals who were prepared to deal with the 'enemies of Union', leader of the Irish Party, Charles Stuart Parnell and the Land League, were in fact 'gullible'.[58] Now that both major journals of British Methodism were staunchly Liberal, the time was judged opportune for an Irish weekly covering political affairs.

Given the increasing political divergence between British and Irish Methodism, discussions thus commenced as to whether the *Irish Evangelist* could become a weekly publication despite its lack of capital investment. However, before these conversations reached their conclusion, a group in Belfast, led by I.S. Allen (a printer by trade) and the Rev. Dr John Donald, seized the initiative and launched a new title, the *Irish Christian Advocate* in November 1883. This new broadsheet was competitively priced at 1d and rapidly overtook the *Irish Evangelist* and the two titles merged the following

55 William Alexander McArthur was born in Sydney in 1857 son of Alexander McArthur. He was a merchant and banker and was elected as the Liberal MP for St Austell in 1887. Alexander McArthur was born in Derry, went into partnership as Colonial Merchant with his brother William and was elected to New South Wales Legislature and as Liberal MP for Leicester. Sir William McArthur was born in Malin, moved to London in 1857, and was an alderman and later Lord Mayor of the city. He also was a Liberal MP for Lambeth.

56 Christopher Oldstone-Moore, *Hugh Price Hughes: Founder of a New Methodism, Conscience of a New Nonconformity* (Cardiff: University of Wales Press, 1999), pp. 121–23; *Methodist Times*, 7 January 1886.

57 Arthur, *The Householder's Parliament*, p. 13; *Christian Advocate*, 18 December 1885.

58 Arthur, *The Householder's Parliament*, p. 13.

year.[59] That the *Advocate* was launched in Belfast is indicative of the change in the balance of power within Irish Methodism that occurred over the course of the second part of the nineteenth century; away from the long-established affluent community in Dublin (and to a lesser extent Cork) and towards the densely populated industrial region of Ulster.[60] The *Advocate* conceived of itself as the mouthpiece of this community, now in the ascendant within Irish Methodism through weight of numbers.

For the first 18 months of the *Advocate's* life, it was edited by Rev. Dr John Donald, before Rev. Dr Henry Evans was given permission by the Conference to give up his circuit work and become the full-time editor of the journal.[61] Evans was eager to engage with contemporary political issues, and adopted a dynamic approach for the *Advocate's* articles and editorials. Characteristic of this style was the dominance of the editorial column, frequently polemical in style, exhorting the readership to consider specific aspects of the social or political condition. This was complemented by commissioned articles from high-profile Methodists in support of the chosen cause, and the publication of extensive correspondence to the editor, engaging the readers in lively debate on current affairs. Evans was very clear about the issues he believed were facing contemporary Methodism, and was not afraid to tackle them head on, even when this brought the journal into conflict with Methodists in other parts of the British Isles.

This first became evident in the coverage given to the 1885 general election campaign, during which Evans's political bias became quite clear. The campaign began unexceptionally, with Evans encouraged his readers to consider the candidates' 'attitude to moral questions', and to eschew voting on purely party grounds.[62] He focused the election coverage on candidates' attitudes to education, control of drink traffic and repeal of the Contagious Diseases Acts, which were expected to be key issues during the next parliament. Education had remained at the top of the Methodist political agenda since the Act of 1870: this was further emphasised in 1885 when the system of National Schools appeared to be under attack both from the English radicals and the Catholic hierarchy.[63] Irish Methodists were urged strongly to resist this plank

59 Roddie, 'Reporting and Recording'.

60 Methodism was seeing its most significant growth in this area, especially Belfast, whose Methodist population had leapt up between the 1861–81 from 4,929 to 9,141 and had grown again by 1901 to 21,506. *Census Ireland* 1861, 1881, 1901; See also, N.K. Morris, 'Predicting a "Bright and Prosperous Future": Irish Methodist Membership, 1855–1914', *Wesley and Methodist Studies* 2 (2010): 91–114.

61 Roddie, 'Reporting and Recording'.

62 *Christian Advocate*, 27 November 1885.

63 *Wesleyan-Methodist Magazine*, p. 701; Alan O'Day, *Parnell and the First Home Rule Episode, 1884–7* (Dublin: Gill and Macmillan, 1986), pp. 104–06.

of the radical programme and defend the rights of parents to direct their children's education.[64] The issues highlighted were ones on which Liberal candidates tended to perform well, however, the *Advocate* maintained that they were acting in a non-political manner.

Some Liberal sympathies were, however, reflected in the coverage that the *Advocate* gave to the three Methodist parliamentary candidates standing in the 1885 general election. An electoral advertisement placed by Thomas Shillington, the radical Liberal candidate in North Armagh, was given prominent place in the journal, and commended by Evans to the readership.[65] Key to Shillington's campaign was advocacy of land reform and support for female suffrage, and the *Advocate* considered him to be 'a safe pair of hands' on questions of social morality, education, temperance and repeal of the Contagious Diseases Acts. Shillington was the only Methodist candidate identified by the journal in November 1885 as standing in Ireland and they decried the fact that the denomination was so anonymous.[66] Despite the *Advocate*'s support, Shillington's campaign was doomed to failure, due to opposition from local weavers, and the popularity of his Orange and Conservative opponent, Major Edward Saunderson.[67]

However, Evans failed to give any coverage to the two other Methodist candidates that stood in the election. He was unable, or more likely, unwilling, to recognise either Jeremiah Jordan of the Irish Parliamentary Party standing for West Clare, or E.S.W. de Cobain standing as an Independent Conservative in East Belfast, as members of the denomination. Jordan was a prominent member of his local Methodist church in Fermanagh, a notable temperance campaigner, Sunday school teacher and former local preacher. One personal correspondent of Jeremiah Jordan, Alexander Duncan of Co. Kildare, claimed that a letter he had written to the newspaper had been declined solely because it advocated support for the Irish Parliamentary Party.[68] It was only after the results of the election had been announced that the *Advocate* deigned to recognise Jordan, denouncing him for associating 'with a band of men who ignore the moral law and trample underfoot the laws of the land', suggesting that he had forfeited the right to call himself a Methodist.[69]

64 Arthur, *The Householder's Parliament*, p. 14.
65 *Christian Advocate*, 27 November 1885.
66 Ibid.
67 Major Edward Saunderson, (later Colonel), first leader of the Irish Unionist parliamentary party. The Liberal MP for Co. Caven 1865–74, the Land War pushed him towards an aggressive Orangeism (he joined the Order in 1882), and he was returned for North Armagh as a Conservative in 1885, a seat that he held until his death in 1906.
68 Alexander Duncan to Jeremiah Jordan, 16 December 1885 (PRONI, D2073/2/1).
69 *Christian Advocate*, 18 December 1885.

This anti-nationalist attitude does not, however, explain the failure of the *Christian Advocate* to identify as Methodist the Independent Conservative candidate for East Belfast E.S.W. de Cobain, who identified himself as a 'the candidate of the working classes'.[70] Despite *The Times* publishing an article summarising the biographies of parliamentary candidates, identifying de Cobain's father as a Wesleyan minister, the *Advocate* contained no coverage of his campaign.[71] De Cobain was a controversial candidate for the Belfast constituency, standing as an independent in opposition to the official Conservative candidate, specifically appealing to the working man. Moreover, de Cobain had previously been Grand Master of the Grand Orange Lodge of Belfast for five years, and was, at the time of the election, a Deputy Grand Master of Ireland.[72] While the working-class areas of Belfast were where Methodism was experiencing the most growth, Cobain's provocative and rowdy campaign did not fit well with the self-conscious respectability of the Methodist leadership, or Evans's literary aspirations for the *Advocate*. In this sense the *Advocate*'s political stance was very similar to that of the *Watchman* earlier in the century: conservative, middle class and suspicious of the masses' involvement in politics.

The revelation of the 'Hawarden Kite', indicating Gladstone's support for Home Rule legislation, caused the *Christian Advocate* to react with immediate horror. In its next issue, the editor wrote an extensive rebuttal of the proposals, asking 'on what grounds is a separate legislature needed for Ireland?'[73] The arguments were advanced using religious terms: Nationalism was described as the 'spawn of an alien creed' and Home Rule was a 'war on the Crown rights of Christ'. Moreover, it claimed that the loyal Protestants of Ireland were being abandoned by those who should defend them, to the rule of the disloyal Catholic majority.[74] The *Advocate* was derisive about the suggestion that Gladstone was 'fully aware' of the situation of the Protestant minority in the country, and would ensure adequate safeguards were instituted for their protection. Thus, the *Christian Advocate* was convinced that 'the only hope for a United Ireland is as an integral part of the United Empire …Ulster will never acquiesce'.[75]

Apart from specific objections to Home Rule, the *Christian Advocate* also sought to cast doubt on whether Gladstone could continue to be considered an 'imperial statesman' or 'responsible politician' if he could 'countenance the cry for Home Rule' without due regard to Protestant and Imperial

70 *Belfast Evening Telegraph*, 12 November 1885.
71 *The Times*, 27 November 1885.
72 Ibid.
73 *Christian Advocate*, 24 December 1885.
74 Ibid., 24 December 1885 and 8 January 1886.
75 Ibid., 24 December 1885.

interests.[76] Gladstone's apparent perfidy was exacerbated by the reaction of the English Methodist press to the situation, specifically the support given by the *Methodist Times* to the proposal. The emergence of Home Rule, however, as the key political issue in British politics, focused Hughes's attention on the Irish situation and he rapidly elevated it to the 'highest priority of Christian politics' through the medium of his newspaper.[77] Although it adopted similar religious imagery to the *Christian Advocate*, in dramatic contrast to the Irish newspaper, the *Methodist Times* aligned itself with the policy for Home Rule, declaring that: 'Nothing is so important as that evangelical Christians should realise that "believing in Christ" means a great deal more than believing in Him as a personal Saviour. It means ... Christ's way of treating Ireland'.[78] For Hughes, this meant listening to and accommodating the demands of Nationalists in Ireland. Hughes was a supporter of democracy and believed that 'if the leaders of the church and society mended their ways, embraced democracy, and addressed the needs of the masses, they might establish the authority of Christ in all aspects of earthly life'.[79] Thus, for Hughes, Home Rule was a pre-requisite for the conversion of Ireland to evangelical religion.

The publication by the *Methodist Times* of 'An Irish Methodist's Reasons for Supporting Home Rule' by Jeremiah Jordan, newly-elected Nationalist MP for West Clare, only served to add fuel to the fire.[80] The suggestion that Jordan might be a representative voice of Irish Methodism appalled many Irish pew-dwellers, and sparked a flurry of correspondence to both the religious press and to the nationalist *Freeman's Journal*. The latter portrayed Jordan as representing Irish Methodism in the House of Commons, which, while accurate in the sense that he was a Wesleyan Methodist elected for an Irish constituency, obscured the reality that a majority of his co-religionists were firm supporters of the unionist cause. In a letter to the *Freeman's Journal*, a third-generation Irish Methodist, Matthew Tobias, expounded on this theme before extensively criticising the *Methodist Times*, deriding it as 'very much a Radical organ, with very few subscribers'.[81] The theme of the unrepresentative nature

76 *Christian Advocate*, 8 January 1886.
77 Oldstone-Moore, *Hugh Price Hughes*, p. 150.
78 *Methodist Times*, 14 January 1886.
79 Oldstone-Moore, *Hugh Price Hughes*, p. 131.
80 *Methodist Times*, 7 January 1886.
81 *Freeman's Journal*, 16 January 1886. The extent of the circulation of the *Methodist Times* at this point is unknown, although it was later the most widely read of the Methodist journals. By 1900, the *Methodist Times* had a readership of 150,000. (Greg Cuthbertson, 'Pricking the "Nonconformist Conscience": Religion Against the South African War', in Donal Lowry (ed.), *The South African War Reappraised* (Manchester: Manchester University Press, 2000), pp. 169–87, p. 178.)

of the *Methodist Times* was adopted by the *Christian Advocate* in its next issue, which, borrowing a phrase from Mr Tobias, ran a substantial article headed 'The *Methodist Times* (so called)', which criticised both the conduct and content of the newspaper. Stating that although the *Advocate* was 'greatly grieved to so openly reprove our contemporary', it questioned the motives of Hugh Price Hughes, accusing him of 'wanton meddling' in matters that did not concern him.[82] The article suggested that an Englishman had no business commenting on Irish affairs, which he could not possibly understand. Furthermore, the *Advocate* argued that as a Methodist, Hughes had a duty to listen to and support the opinion of his brethren who had direct experience of the matter. While this attitude, that the English had no business interfering in Irish affairs, seems to have been popular among Irish Methodists, it also appears to have been primarily an argument of convenience. When British sources promoted an anti-Home Rule agenda, the *Christian Advocate* was quick to cite them.[83] The *Advocate* had no time, and certainly no column space, for those Methodists either in England or Ireland who dissented from what it believed to be the only reasonable course: opposition to any form of Home Rule.

Evans's strident opinions, political campaigning and divisive rhetoric were not as popular as he had hoped, and circulation of the *Advocate* remained modest under his leadership. His time as editor was not financially successful and he was removed from post and returned to circuit work after only three years. The editorship was thus passed in 1888 onto Rev. C.H. Crookshank, who had recently completed his three volume history of Irish Methodism, from its origins to the Ulster Revival (published 1883–85). In many ways, under his editorship the *Advocate* returned to the traditions of the *Irish Evangelist*, focusing on Methodist activity, missions and reports of revival. Crookshank did not completely abandon the political commentary in the newspaper, though he generally pursued it with less partisan fervour than his predecessor. A clear exception to this was the citation of Parnell as co-respondent in the O'Shea divorce case, when, in the winter of 1890–1, the growing gulf between Irish and British Methodism was again revealed.

The reaction of the London *Methodist Times* to the court hearing of the 15–17 November 1890 was immediate and damning of the Irish leader. On the 20 November, the journal declared that 'Of course Mr Parnell must go', before apologising to its readers that circumstances required it to make such an obvious statement.[84] The newspaper maintained that its previous support for Home Rule and unwavering backing of Parnell over the Pigott forgeries,[85]

82 *Christian Advocate*, 22 January 1886.

83 See for example, *Christian Advocate*, 16 April 1886.

84 *Methodist Times*, 20 November 1890.

85 In 1887 *The Times* printed a series of letters purporting to demonstrate that Parnell

vindicated 'our right to speak as friends of the Irish people' and provided evidence that its criticisms of Parnell were in no way born of anti-Irish feeling.[86] The *Methodist Times* insisted that:

> if the Irish race deliberately select as their representative an adulterer of Mr Parnell's type they are as incapable of self-government as their bitterest enemies have asserted. So obscene a race as in those circumstances they would prove themselves to be would obviously be unfit for anything except a military despotism.[87]

While the London journal argued that that while it did 'not underestimate the immense and unique services' that Parnell had rendered to the Irish people, there 'ought to be two limits to their gratitude. It ought not to exceed their patriotism and it ought not to exceed their faith in God'.[88] It was inconceivable to the editor Hughes that a man who was immoral in his personal life was fit to lead a party or a nation, declaring that 'what is morally wrong can never be politically right'.[89] Moreover, Parnell's moral defectiveness was compounded by his failure to immediately resign. When the Irish Party re-elected Parnell as leader, the *Methodist Times* declared that this had 'placed Parnellism outside the pale of Christian civilisation' and expressed the hope that Jordan and all the 'respectable members' of the party would rally around Michael Davitt: the only prominent nationalist to have publicly called for Parnell's resignation.[90] While Hugh Price Hughes apparently had little to gain politically by compelling Parnell to resign, however, he had built his own career as a leading Methodist minister on successive campaigns for social purity and morality in public life.[91] Hughes's principal concern was to maintain the creditability of himself and his paper with the Methodist reading public by continuing to promote the principles of social purity. To do this, he needed to

apparently expressed regret at having to condemn the Phoenix Park murders of Lord Frederick Cavendish and Thomas Burke. After the investigation of a special commission the letters were proven to have been forgeries created by Richard Piggott.

86 Ibid., 27 November 1890.

87 Ibid., 20 November 1890.

88 Ibid.

89 Ibid.

90 Ibid.; *Freeman's Journal*, 21 November 1890; Frank Callanan, *The Parnell Split, 1890–91* (Syracuse, NY: Syracuse University Press, 1992), p. 12.

91 Hughes was a senior member of the Methodist Conference's Committee for Social Purity and had been the prime motivator of the 'Forward Movement' within British Methodism and the establishment of the London Mission (*Wesleyan Conference Minutes of Great Britain, 1891*). For further discussion see Oldstone-Moore, *Hugh Price Hughes*; and Dorothy Price Hughes, *The Life of Hugh Price Hughes* (London: Hodder and Stoughton, 1904).

make a public condemnation of Parnell, and in doing so he received significant support from other Methodists and other nonconformists in England who previously espoused Home Rule. Writing to *The Times*, 'a Wesleyan Minister' coined the phrase 'nonconformist conscience' to describe and commend the concerted effort of Hughes and his allies to remove Parnell from power.[92] This was, however, adopted as a derogatory term by the national press to imply that nonconformists were selective about the areas of morality about which they protested. One correspondent suggested that 'the inconsistency of the "conscience" is glaring', and verged on the hypocritical.[93]

The *Christian Advocate* also believed that the outrage of the *Methodist Times* concerning Parnell's actions was inconsistent with its earlier stance. While the *Advocate* claimed to be delighted by 'such a noble stand for social purity' made by the *Methodist Times*, it suggested that it should be combined with a permanent change in the political outlook of the journal. Indeed, the *Advocate* maintained that a failure to do so would indicate that Hughes was in fact 'more influenced by anxiety for the success of a political party than desire for the spread of social purity'.[94] The Belfast newspaper considered Hughes's barrage against Parnell a vindication of its opposition to the Nationalist party. Highlighting the *Methodist Times*'s intemperate condemnation of the Irish as proving themselves 'incapable of self-government', the *Advocate* likewise argued that the Irish people had for many years 'blindly' followed nationalist leaders without regard for their personal morality. Nevertheless, despite hailing the *Methodist Times*'s coverage of the crisis as a victory for its long-held principles, the *Advocate* continued to appear sceptical of the motivation for Hughes's *volte-face*, and implied that it might yet be demonstrable hypocrisy. One correspondent, Thomas Moran of Enniskillen, suggested that it was inconsistent of Hughes to condemn Parnell for breaking the seventh commandment regarding adultery, when it was common knowledge across Ireland that he had frequently incited and applauded the breaking of commandments six and eight (those forbidding murder and theft).[95] This caused much anger among Irish Methodists, who suggested that their English brethren were selective in their use of scripture and ignorant of the tactics of the Nationalist movement in Ireland.

This spat between the journals highlights the difference in politics and expectations the Methodist readership had in Ireland and England. While both newspapers claimed to espouse the same religious principles, the political applications were quite different. Irish Methodists maintained that conservative policies designed to protect the Protestant constitution and the Union were

92 *The Times*, 28 November 1890.
93 Ibid., 8 January 1891.
94 *Christian Advocate*, 28 November 1890.
95 Ibid.

better for Ireland, while their English brethren supported increasing liberalism and democracy. The *Advocate* was thus a vital component in building and maintaining this distinctly Irish identity, which might otherwise have been lost in the broader trends in Methodist thought across the islands. Periodical readership was not merely a means of maintaining denominational identity but also created a distinct Irish national variety of Methodism.

While clearly opposing the Irish Parliamentary Party and Home Rule, during the second Home Rule crisis the *Advocate* under Crookshank was not so obviously partisan or Ulster-centric as in 1886. Significant coverage was given to the Ulster Convention of 17 June 1892, with the contributions of the Methodist speakers particularly stressed.[96] The Methodist speakers given coverage in the *Advocate* were representative of the church in the province, with the Rev. Dr McCutcheon, principal of Methodist College Belfast, the Rev. Wesley Guard from the clergy, and T.F. Shillington and Frank Johnston representing the 'industrial classes' and Robert Greer, JP, the middle classes. These speeches were notable for their political moderation, stressing the apolitical stance of the denomination and declaring they had 'no sympathy with the "No Popery" cry' but sought only a 'pacific compromise'.[97] The *Advocate* was careful to place the Convention within the broader context of Irish (and not exclusively Ulster) unionism and the traditional Methodist stance of respect for duly appointed authority.[98] Similar coverage was also given to Methodist contributions at a meeting of southern unionists in Dublin.[99] This emphasised that the issue was not confined to Ulster, and that Methodists across Ireland should stand together in resisting the policy, not abandoning southern brethren to their fate. Irish Methodism was, and would continue to be, an all-Ireland church.

Coverage of the second Home Rule crisis was Crookshank's swan-song, and he retired in 1893. He was replaced by the Rev. Richard Cole, an experienced journalist and minister. Cole was a leader writer for the *Belfast Telegraph*, and Methodist correspondent for the *Northern Whig* and *Irish Times*, and was to edit the *Advocate* for the next 20 years. While a committed unionist himself, he steered the journal away from political controversy and strove to create a periodical of general Methodist interest. He increased the coverage of the annual Methodist Conference, introducing a daily edition for this event in 1895, and tended to focus on the specific experiences of individuals and circuits in a lively engaging manner. Thus in a reversal of his predecessor's policy that Nationalists could not be considered true Methodists, Cole felt it

96 *Christian Advocate*, 21 June 1892.
97 Ibid.
98 *Christian Advocate*.
99 *Christian Advocate*, 28 June 1892.

appropriate to publish a fulsome obituary of Jeremiah Jordan praising him as a 'an ardent temperance reformer, and a loyal Methodist', whose political beliefs did not compromise his faith.[100] Similarly, he would not give free coverage to the Ulster Covenant or associated religious services, insisting that the only insert would be that of a commercial advertisement for the regular fee.

Cole specifically prioritised the development of an all-Ireland Methodist community over political campaigning. He increased the coverage of the annual Methodist Conference, introducing a daily edition for this event in 1895, and expanded the reporting of items such as the prizegiving ceremonies at the two Methodist grammar schools, annually listed all Methodist graduates of Ireland's universities and encouraged informal reports of work undertaken overseas. Under Cole's leadership, the experiences of individuals and circuits formed the core material of the *Advocate*, and he successfully created the sense that every Methodist in Ireland could be known and loved by the whole church. The decision to take the journal in that direction reaped its rewards as he steered the *Advocate* through the difficult times of the First World War and partition, keeping the journal afloat when other periodicals (with much larger constituencies) such as the Presbyterian *Witness* folded.[101]

Over the course of the nineteenth century therefore the Methodist press changed significantly, with new journals appearing and failing as different factions of the church were in the ascendant. These journals tended to announce their analysis of events boldly, from the title page forwards, and developed a readership that reflected their views. The relationship of Irish Methodists to this religious press was consequently dependent upon their political and spiritual values being fairly represented. When English journals could provide appropriate coverage of denominational and political affairs, there was little incentive to start a new publication, so Irish Methodists both consumed them and used them to persuade their English brethren of their views. As the dominant politics of British nonconformity became more liberal over the course of the century, the London journals became less satisfactory as they failed to reflect Irish realities or opinions. The need for a specifically Irish Methodist press was thus identified from the mid-century, and from its inception developed and expressed a distinctly Irish sense of identity. However, when English and Irish interests diverged from the mid-century onward, a distinctive Irish newspaper was seen as desirable. Irish concerns and Irish successes were explicitly identified and expressed. While the *Irish Evangelist* confined itself to 'religious' content, its expectation and reporting of revival were different from the English experience and absent from their press. The creation of the *Christian Advocate* in 1883 marked the political

100 Ibid., 5 January 1912.
101 Roddie, 'Reporting and Recording'.

divergence between the two churches, and although the journal did not develop in the manner anticipated by its first two editors, this development was the foundation of an enduring Irish community voice within Methodism which lasted until the 1970s.

5

The *Dublin Penny Journal* and Alternative Histories

Elizabeth Tilley

As is so often the case in the study of periodicals, concrete evidence about influence and impact is hard to find, and we are repeatedly forced to rely on the statements provided by the magazines themselves: circulation figures, when advertised, are frequently inflated, boasts about a title's national importance are often puffs written by friends of editors. In Ireland, the situation is compounded by the fact that domestic periodicals were always in direct competition with those originating in England and Scotland, so that the self-reporting of inflated sales figures occasionally served purposes beyond the obvious. Further, it was recognised that the Irish domestic market for periodicals would always be partly comprised of Irish readers living abroad; consequently, declared circulation most often included the figures gathered from agents in cities such as Manchester and Liverpool. The ways in which English and Irish periodicals were intertwined make it difficult to try and claim too much about the place and cultural force of any particular Irish title. However, the argument that follows suggests processes through which a cultural re-thinking of material history was performed, at least for a short space of time, within the pages of an Irish weekly: the *Dublin Penny Journal*,[1] that did try to focus on Ireland, that assumed an intelligent and curious readership, and that provided original material of high quality.

The most difficult period for periodical production in Ireland, in terms of new titles published, as well as the quality and longevity of those titles, was the 30 years following the Act of Union in 1800. By contrast, the (roughly) 20-year period between 1830 and the famine years at the end of the 1840s saw an explosion of new titles, though the lifespan of most of them was still no more than a year. The reasons for this dramatic increase are numerous: they include greater political stability in the country, Catholic Emancipation

1 The *Dublin Penny Journal* ran from 1832–36.

in 1829, the coming of age of many of Ireland's greatest nineteenth-century literary figures (Lever, Lover, Le Fanu, Carleton, Hall, Banim, etc.) whose works appeared most often in serial form, the rise of Mechanics' Institutes and the associated drive for public education, as well as the establishment, or re-invigoration of literary and scientific societies like the Royal Irish Academy.[2] The period was also a very lucrative one for English printers and booksellers, as the adoption of the steam press made mass production of cheap periodicals economically viable. It is no accident that in form, and often in outlook, Irish periodicals copied English models; for instance, the venerable *Dublin University Magazine* (1833–77) consciously followed the format and generally conservative editorial view of *Blackwood's Magazine*. English penny weeklies, like the *Penny Magazine* (1832–45), produced by the English Society for the Diffusion of Useful Knowledge (SDUK), or *Chambers's Edinburgh Journal* (1832–1956), catered for the working class and were often heavily subsidised by religious or educational societies. Ireland also had versions of these, most notably in the *Catholic Penny Magazine* (1834–35) and its rival the *Protestant Irish Penny Magazine* (1835–36). The subject matter of these Irish penny weeklies was not exclusively Irish, and their high moral tone, as in their English models, was not always an inducement to buy.

Again, the *Dublin Penny Journal* (*DPJ*) stands out as a truly original product. 'Impact' is difficult to quantify, but it does appear that the journal exemplified a new spirit of enquiry and cooperation in Irish popular culture in the 1830s, one that saw an extraordinary sharing of discoveries and information between socio-economic groups and religious persuasions. The *DPJ* existed – against the odds – for four years, from 30 June 1832 to 25 June 1836, in a market that was already saturated with cheap literature of various kinds. In September of 1832 the editors reported circulation at 30,000 copies weekly; that figure was probably the highest number the *DPJ* ever achieved but, even after the initial enthusiasm wore off, circulation was respectable given such a poor market. The *DPJ*'s first year of production, before its editorial management changed, is generally acknowledged as its best.[3] The circumstances surrounding the first appearance of the magazine in 1832 are fairly well known; the plan for an Irish penny paper appears to have

2 See Tom Clyde, *Irish Literary Magazines: An Outline History and Descriptive Bibliography* (Dublin: Irish Academic Press, 2003), p. 20 and *passim*; Barbara Hayley, 'A Reading and Thinking Nation: Periodicals as the Voice of Nineteenth-Century Ireland', in Barbara Hayley and Enda McKay (eds), *Three Hundred Years of Irish Periodicals* (Dublin: Association of Irish Learned Journals, 1987), pp. 29–47.

3 For a full treatment of the importance of the *Dublin Penny Journal* in pre-Famine Ireland, see Francesca Benatti, *A National and Concordant Feeling: Penny Journals in Ireland, 1832–1842* (Unpublished PhD thesis, NUI Galway, 2003).

been that of Church of Ireland clergyman Caesar Otway, but it is clear that the driving force behind the project was the antiquarian George Petrie, and it is Petrie's personality and interests that take centre stage in the journal, at least during the first year. His artwork, his reporting of the results of his antiquarian research, and his speculations about the uses to which Ireland's built environment had been employed in the past are the most startling departures from the norm in the *DPJ*. These are characteristics that set it apart from English versions of the type, though it is clear that the founders were also imitating the physical format of English penny magazines through adopting the same kind of physical space – two tightly printed columns of text on every page, heavily illustrated, and cheap. Crucially, though, the *DPJ* was unique in the fact that it acknowledged no sponsor – religious or political – and as such was free from the sort of overbearing moral tone or polemic discernible in other titles from the same period. The *DPJ* was also unique in the fact that from the outset the editors restricted themselves to Irish concerns and adopted an editorial voice that assumed a literate, inquisitive and fiercely national (though not republican) audience. It was an audience with a penny a week to spare, whose time was precious, and who were amongst a new generation of readers more used to perusing newspapers than fiction or long essays. The articles offered in the *DPJ* were in the main original, not extracts from other magazines. Feedback from readers was encouraged, with letters and signed observations from correspondents around the country given prominence.

The editors were anxious to claim the benefits of both reading and circulating the paper in Ireland, and they appealed to the moral, intellectual, and commercial interests of the public in soliciting support for the enterprise:

> Sagacious people say that the present extraordinary demand for penny publications will die away; that it is a *fever* just approaching its crisis—a mania which will soon reach its grand climacteric ... So far from thinking that the demand for these publications will subside, we think it will increase, and that a change will be produced by them upon the state of public feeling as extraordinary as it will be beneficial. Setting totally aside the great *moral* influence, and the great *mental* power which they will exercise, let us just see what good they effect in the way of creating a *new trade* in the country. Say there are forty thousand penny magazines sold in all Ireland weekly; (perhaps there are more) this brings in upwards of one hundred and sixty pounds per week, and the profits resulting from this sum give employment not merely to paper makers, to printers and to booksellers, but to a great many honest poor people, who not having a trade, or unable to exercise it, through various causes, are finding a means of subsistence by hawking

> the cheap publications. Now, if every gentlemen [*sic*] in Ireland were to encourage all his friends, servants, and dependants to buy each, say *one* a week, there would soon be upwards of an hundred and fifty thousand sold of the cheap publications, treble the number of poor people would be employed in selling them, a vast mass of information would be diffused, *thought* would be awakened, the public mind would receive a prodigious impulse, and the very face of society would be changed.[4]

The emphasis here on the necessity of 'public feeling' to be engaged in order to boost sales of the *DPJ* at home suggests that, like the English penny weeklies supported by bodies such as the SDUK, the remit of the *DPJ* was never wholly commercial, though the editors did say that 'our ambition is to rival even the great London penny publications'.[5] The plan sketched out in the extract above, for social and economic inclusion through a shared sense of history and culture, places the ideology behind the creation of the *Dublin Penny Journal* far beyond English (and some Irish) penny enterprises that focused almost exclusively on either entertainment or on the perceived need for moral reform of the working-class reader.[6]

Petrie was an artist, as well as an activist for the popularisation of high culture, someone with clout in Dublin's scholarly community.[7] He was a life member of the Royal Irish Academy, partly in recompense for the services he had shown the body. Petrie had made some significant antiquarian purchases on behalf of the Academy, purchases that ultimately formed the nucleus of the collection of the National Museum of Ireland.[8] In 1831 the seventeenth-century manuscript entitled the *Annals of the Four Masters* came on the market from a private library; Petrie bought the manuscript for £53 and presented it to the Royal Irish Academy at cost price, foregoing the substantial profit he might have made had he sold it abroad.[9] As the *Annals* was in poor condition,

4 *Dublin Penny Journal*, 1.8 (1832), p. 64.

5 *Dublin Penny Journal*, 1.14, 29 September 1832.

6 See Elizabeth Tilley, 'Periodicals' (pp. 144–73), and Robin J. Kavanagh, 'Religion and Illustrated Periodicals in the 1830s' (pp. 342–57), in James H. Murphy (ed.), *The Oxford History of the Irish Book, Vol. IV: The Irish Book in English, 1800–1891* (Oxford: Oxford University Press, 2011).

7 The standard work on Petrie's life is William Stokes, *The Life and Labours in Art and Archaeology of George Petrie, LL.D., M.R.I.A.* (London: Longmans, Green, and Co., 1868). See also Peter Murray, *George Petrie (1790–1866): The Rediscovery of Ireland's Past* (Cork: Crawford Municipal Art Gallery; Kinsale, Co. Cork: Gandon Editions, 2004).

8 Petrie was instrumental in securing the Cross of Cong and the gold torques from Tara, amongst other items, for the Academy Museum of Antiquities (see Stokes, *The Life and Labours in Art*, p. 79 and *passim*).

9 Stokes notes that Petrie was offered '£100 over the purchase-money for the manuscript, and [was] subsequently pressed to name any sum that would induce him to resign it. In

Petrie was also instrumental in arranging for its physical conservation, in addition to the transcription and translation of its contents from Irish into English. It is not possible to over-emphasise the importance with which the *Annals* were (and are still) regarded.[10] The manuscript was written in Irish between 1632 and 1636 by four scholars, all of whose signatures appear on the title page. The work is a chronicle of Irish history up to 1616, and its pages detail the births and deaths of kings, accounts of battles and invasions, together with an enormous amount of data about prominent families, both their ancestry and their descendants. The information the *Annals* contained was copied from older manuscripts that have since been lost, so the historical value of the labour of the Masters is enormous. The *Annals* were seized upon in the nineteenth century as physical evidence of Ireland's prominence before the coming of the English, and so became part of a reconstruction of a Gaelic heritage crucial to the nationalist enterprise.

This is clear from the speech Petrie gave on the occasion of his presentation of the *Annals* to the Royal Irish Academy,[11] the text of which was reprinted in full in the *Dublin Penny Journal* in the 8 June 1833 issue. In it Petrie emphasised the public significance of the manuscript and the opportunities wide ownership of such a treasure offered in balancing the historical record.[12] It would not have seemed at all odd that such reportage was in the *DPJ*'s remit; the speech was part of an outline for a programme of recovery of Ireland's history, and this link between the activities of learned societies like the Royal Irish Academy and the magazine – seen as naïve on Petrie's part by some later critics – can be viewed as one of the first attempts to create common ground between classes and political groups after Catholic Emancipation in 1829.[13] In the end the *Dublin Penny Journal* published over

acknowledgement of the zeal evinced by Petrie in the service of the Academy, and the pecuniary sacrifice involved in it, he was unanimously elected a life member' (ibid., p. 78).

10 See Edel Bhreathnach and Bernadette Cunningham (eds), *Writing Irish History: The Four Masters and their World* (Dublin: WordWell, 2007).

11 The speech was delivered to the Royal Irish Academy on 5 March 1831.

12 Joep Leerssen has studied the importance of learned societies in the emergence of Ireland's public sphere after Catholic Emancipation in 1829, and compares their rise to the role the salon played in France, and the coffee house in England: see Leerssen, *Hidden Ireland, Public Sphere* (Galway: Arlen House, 2002), p. 33. The connection between this emergence and the press is a crucial part of his argument.

13 David Greene, in a retrospective essay on Petrie and the Royal Irish Academy, published in the Academy *Proceedings* in 1972 noted: 'the idea that they [the middle class] would extend their patronage to the Royal Irish Academy [and by extension the *Dublin Penny Journal*] for its work in rescuing the traditions of a people whom they feared and despised is so ridiculous that it is hard to imagine how Petrie could have put it forward'. Quoted in Elizabeth Tilley, 'The Royal Irish Academy and Antiquarianism', in James H. Murphy (ed.), *The Oxford History of the Irish Book, Vol. IV: The Irish Book in English, 1800–1891* (Oxford: Oxford University Press, 2011), p. 476.

20 articles on the *Annals*, mostly translations and commentaries produced by Irish language scholar John O'Donovan.[14] Bernadette Cunningham has traced the cultural importance of O'Donovan's later edition of the *Annals*, published between 1848 and 1851, and we know that extracts appeared in the Young Ireland newspaper *Nation* in the late 1840s, but it is important to remember that there were earlier versions of the translations, the earliest of which seems to be in the *DPJ* in 1832, shortly after Petrie acquired the manuscript. In other words, wide dissemination of the material the *Annals* contained was from the outset a prime motive behind its acquisition. These occasional articles on aspects of the *Annals*, along with Petrie's illustrated essays on Irish antiquities, became the *DPJ*'s version of a series – the points of repetition that helped establish continuity and coherence in what might otherwise be seen as a randomly ordered miscellany. It seems reasonable to assume that repetition within the cheap penny format helped develop reader tolerance towards such scholarly material, and was part of the 'effect', if not the overtly stated mission, of the *DPJ*.

Clearly Petrie and O'Donovan between them laid great emphasis on the physical evidence of the past and on the written records of Irish civilisation before the arrival of the English; the result was the creation, or perhaps the resurrection, of a symbolic map of Ireland, studded with material objects and written records as proofs of sophistication and learning. For instance, Figure 5.1 shows a portion of an article on Irish surnames, written and signed by Petrie, from the 1 September 1832 issue. The article was a translation of a portion of the *Annals*, giving English approximations of Irish words and using Roman type to display the Irish language. The passage concerned a gathering of nobles in Dublin in 1585, and it was included, as Petrie said, for its historical importance, but he was also careful to note that it illuminated 'the ancient rank' of the ancestors of present-day readers as well as the multiple connections between these historical persons and their modern descendants. Information about these modern descendants was given in the footnotes. Ultimately the footnotes took up almost as much space on the page as the text, and Petrie concluded the article with an invitation to readers to amend the record as part of an ongoing project of memory-making, to correct any errors spotted and add to the evidence given. Thus, oral, modern witness was solicited and treated with the same seriousness as the evidence of the Masters, and a mark of this seriousness was represented graphically on the page. In the process antiquarian discussion was removed from the rarefied

14 O'Donovan worked as a translator for James Hardiman in the Office of Public Records, and later for the Ordnance Survey under Thomas Larcom (to whom he taught Irish) and Petrie. See J.H. Andrews, *A Paper Landscape: The Ordnance Survey in Nineteenth-Century Ireland*, 2nd ed. (Dublin: Four Courts Press, 2002), p. 122.

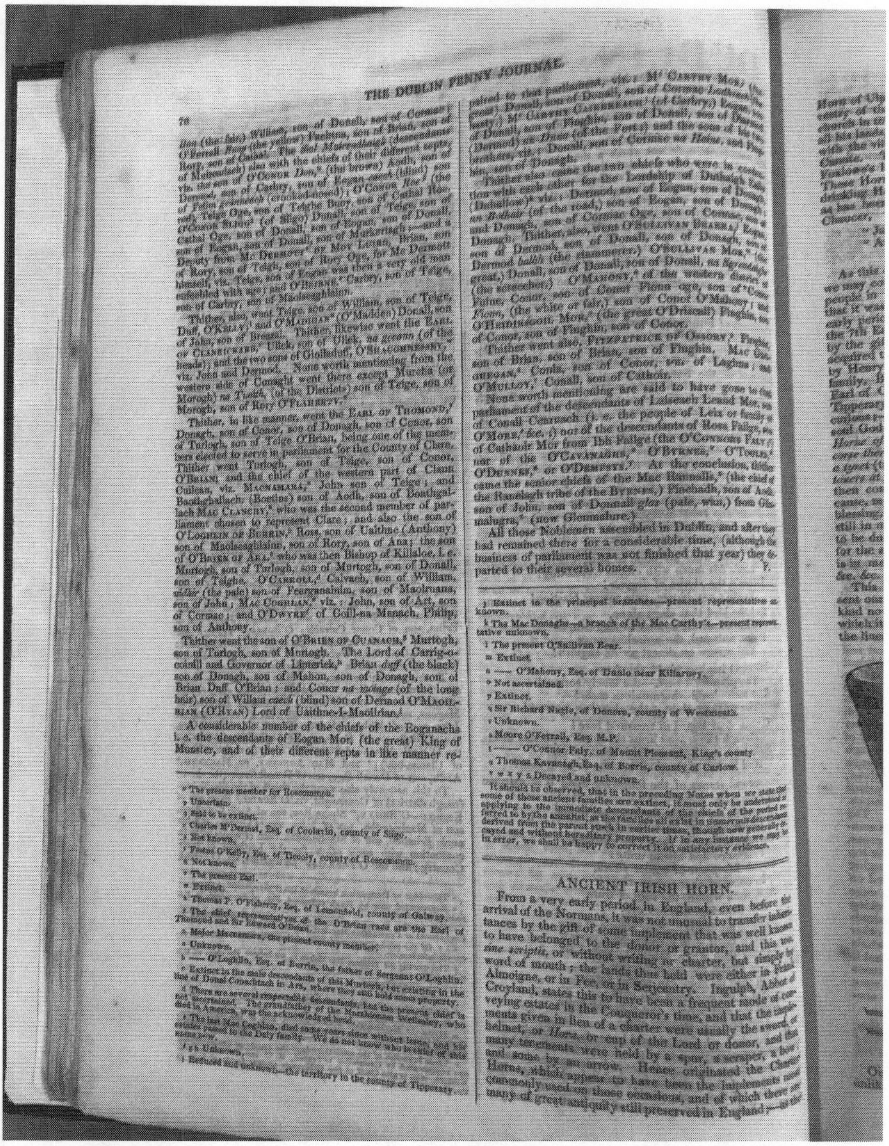

76 THE DUBLIN PENNY JOURNAL.

All those Noblemen assembled in Dublin, and after they had remained there for a considerable time, (although the business of parliament was not finished that year) they departed to their several homes. P.

ANCIENT IRISH HORN.

From a very early period in England, even before the arrival of the Normans, it was not unusual to transfer inheritances by the gift of some implement that was well known to have belonged to the donor or grantor, and this was *sine scriptis*, or without writing or charter, but simply by word of mouth; the lands thus held were either in Frank Almoigne, or in Fee, or in Serjeantry. Ingulph, Abbot of Croyland, states this to have been a frequent mode of conveying estates in the Conqueror's time, and that the implements given in lieu of a charter were usually the sword or helmet, or *Horn*, or cup of the Lord or donor, and that many tenements were held by a spur, a scraper, a bow, and some by an arrow. Hence originated the Charter Horne, which appears to have been the implements most commonly used on those occasions, and of which there are many of great antiquity still preserved in England;—

Figure 5.1: *Dublin Penny Journal* (1 September 1832), p. 76
(Courtesy James Hardiman Library, National University of Ireland, Galway)

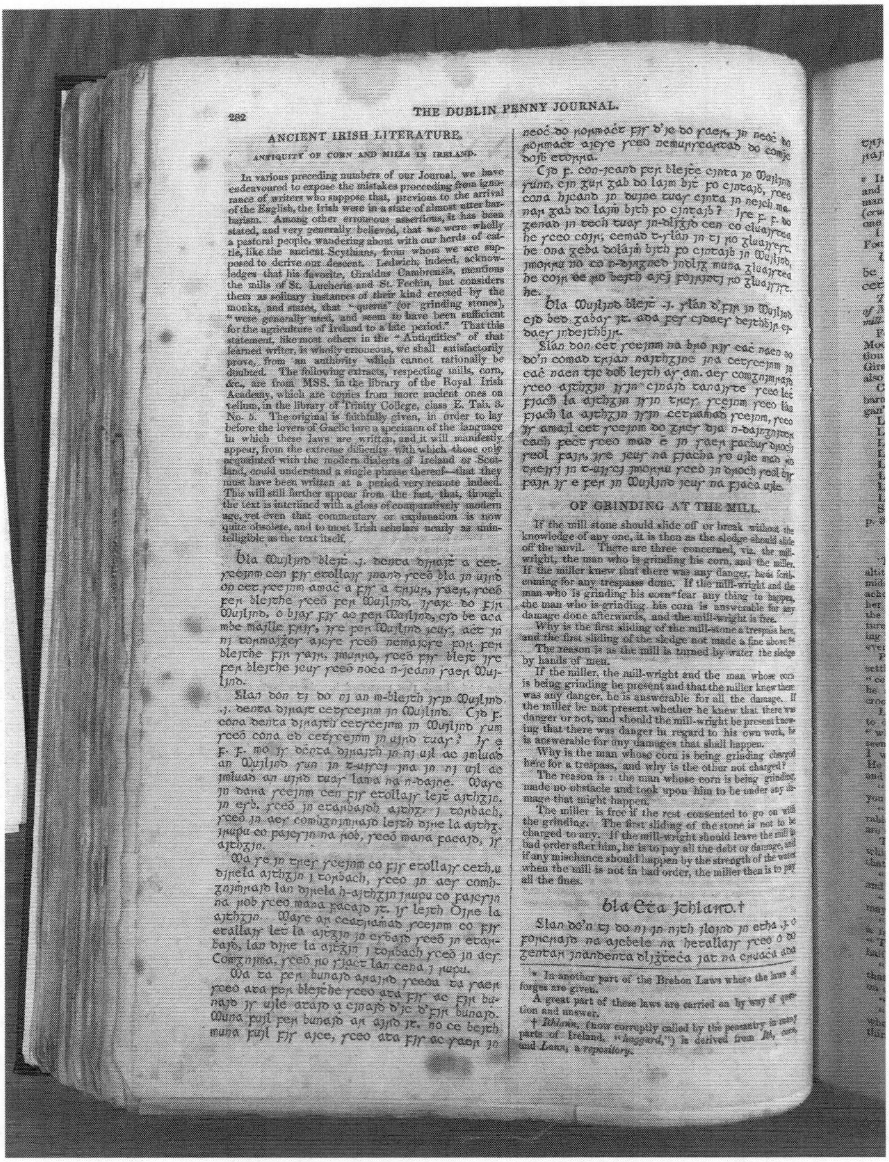

282 THE DUBLIN PENNY JOURNAL.

ANCIENT IRISH LITERATURE.

ANTIQUITY OF CORN AND MILLS IN IRELAND.

In various preceding numbers of our Journal, we have endeavoured to expose the mistakes proceeding from ignorance of writers who suppose that, previous to the arrival of the English, the Irish were in a state of almost utter barbarism. Among other erroneous assertions, it has been stated, and very generally believed, that we were wholly a pastoral people, wandering about with our herds of cattle, like the ancient Scythians, from whom we are supposed to derive our descent. Ledwich, indeed, acknowledges that his favorite, Giraldus Cambrensis, mentions the mills of St. Lucherin and St. Fechin, but considers them as solitary instances of their kind erected by the monks, and states, that "querns" (or grinding stones), "were generally used, and seem to have been sufficient for the agriculture of Ireland to a late period." That this statement, like most others in the "Antiquities" of that learned writer, is wholly erroneous, we shall satisfactorily prove, from an authority which cannot rationally be doubted. The following extracts, respecting mills, corn, &c., are from MSS. in the library of the Royal Irish Academy, which are copies from more ancient ones on vellum, in the library of Trinity College, class E. Tab. 3. No. 5. The original is faithfully given, in order to lay before the lovers of Gaelic lore a specimen of the language in which these laws are written, and it will manifestly appear, from the extreme difficulty with which those only acquainted with the modern dialects of Ireland or Scotland, could understand a single phrase thereof—that they must have been written at a period very remote indeed. This will still further appear from the fact, that, though the text is interlined with a gloss of comparatively modern age, yet even that commentary or explanation is now quite obsolete, and to most Irish scholars nearly as unintelligible as the text itself.

OF GRINDING AT THE MILL.

If the mill stone should slide off or break without the knowledge of any one, it is then as the sledge should slide off the anvil. There are three concerned, viz. the mill-wright, the man who is grinding his corn, and the miller. If the miller knew that there was any danger, he is forthcoming for any trespass done. If the mill-wright and the man who is grinding his corn* fear any thing to happen, the man who is grinding his corn is answerable for any damage done afterwards, and the mill-wright is free.

Why is the first sliding of the mill-stone a trespass here, and the first sliding of the sledge not made a fine above?[a]

The reason is as the mill is turned by water the sledge by hands of men.

If the miller, the mill-wright and the man whose corn is being grinding be present and that the miller knew there was any danger, he is answerable for all the damage. If the miller be not present whether he knew that there was danger or not, and should the mill-wright be present knowing that there was danger in regard to his own work, he is answerable for any damages that shall happen.

Why is the man whose corn is being grinding charged here for a trespass, and why is the other not charged?

The reason is : the man whose corn is being grinding, made no obstacle and took upon him to be under any damage that might happen.

The miller is free if the rest consented to go on with the grinding. The first sliding of the stone is not to be charged to any. If the mill-wright should leave the mill in bad order after him, he is to pay all the debt or damage, and if any mischance should happen by the strength of the water when the mill is not in bad order, the miller then is to pay all the fines.

* In another part of the Brehon Laws where the laws of forges are given.

A great part of these laws are carried on by way of question and answer.

† *Ithlainn*, (now corruptly called by the peasantry in many parts of Ireland, "*haggard*,") is derived from *Ith*, corn, and *Lann*, a *repository*.

Figure 5.2: *Dublin Penny Journal* (2 March 1833), p. 282
(Courtesy James Hardiman Library, National University of Ireland, Galway)

atmosphere of the learned society and recast in a new genre, newly accessible, out of private hands and into the public sphere. Again, this was recovery work, performed with the assistance of those it most nearly concerned, and possible, I would argue, in no other form than that of the *DPJ*.

Similarly, material reproduced from other Irish manuscripts that were already accessible to scholars, but not to the general public, found its way into the *DPJ*. Figure 5.2 shows a portion of an article from the 2 March 1833 issue asserting the great age of Ireland's grain mills, against the assumptions of earlier antiquarians that the country lacked any organised system of agriculture. John O'Donovan wrote the article; his copy came from a collection of Irish texts held by the library of the Royal Irish Academy and by Trinity College (and O'Donovan thoughtfully included the shelf numbers of these in case the reader wished to consult them directly). The portions of text given in Irish type are highlighted here, though O'Donovan also offered an English translation to follow the display of Irish, and he reassured readers that he didn't expect them to comprehend the Irish text, because of its age and the older form of Irish in which it was written.[15]

So why did he bother to include the Irish version at all? The appending of the original was vital as it provided a visual affirmation of authority; it was the typographical equivalent of Petrie's expressed anxiety elsewhere in the *DPJ* to preserve physical remains through artistic representation. Present and past were visually as well as semantically paired, and ownership was established through such representation. Literacy equals the ability to interpret and to employ the symbolic system of a culture, to create meaning that is both individual and universal, and it resides in the visual as well as in the textual. In O'Donovan's translations it was felt to be important that the page display its difference from English type as well as from English versions of Irish history. And it was, ultimately, irrelevant that the Irish version would have remained incomprehensible to the vast majority of readers; its meaning was visual rather than semantic, its Gaelic authority unassailable, and decoding it involved appreciating the authenticity of its appearance, something made possible through its presentation in this format in the *DPJ*. The result was the creation of what has been called an 'alternative history', part of the process of 'gaelicising the memory of the past'. When John O'Donovan's translation of the *Annals* was published in volume form, the same sort of parallel structure was used, again, as a way of 'visibly demonstrating the authenticity of texts' in yet another manifestation of an alteration in Ireland's public sphere.[16]

15 Speakers of Irish were not necessarily able to read Irish script, either in its old or in modern form.

16 Bhreathnach and Cunningham, *Writing Irish History*, p. 69; Leerssen, *Hidden Ireland, Public Sphere*, p. 13.

O'Donovan, Eugene Curry, James Clarence Mangan, and others all served under Petrie in the topographical section of the Irish Ordnance Survey, whose headquarters was Petrie's home.[17] The role of the Ordnance Survey in the interpretation of so much of this historical material has been well studied, and it is assumed that one of the great consequences of the work of the Survey was to recast aspects of Ireland's popular culture in a form acceptable to its elites. Thomas Larcom, director of the Survey, remarked that 'in writing the history of a place-name one has taken a long step towards writing the history of the place itself'.[18] The unspoken corollary was that existing histories, written from a foreign point of view and ignorant of popular culture, were error-ridden, biased, and incomplete.

The presentation of documents like the *Annals* and extracts from Ordnance Survey findings in the *DPJ* demonstrated that it was equally crucial to make this re-aligned history available to the 'lower orders'. Through the texts and representations of material remnants of Ireland's past, a link was forged between the built and the linguistic landscape and the present inhabitants, emphasising the role of their ancestors in creating it. However, the transmission of culture is never pure or exact, especially when translation is involved, and O'Donovan's work has been criticised as often overwhelming the main text, footnotes and explanatory material ultimately replacing the narrative they were intended to illuminate. In this argument, the cultural fixity that was one of the products of the process could be seen as a further distortion of a history that was again appropriated – a rebirth but also a mutation. But it seems to me that this danger is to a certain extent mitigated by the form in which O'Donovan's information was transmitted. That is, the *DPJ* was not a neutral space; its assumed readership was not the cultural elite or the scholar. As Petrie had boasted in the first issue: the journal was cheap, its articles pithy and short, and its very existence provided employment to those who would sell it on the streets. It was 'owned' by its readers, who don't seem to have been shy about writing back to the editors, and, as has been noted, were encouraged to do so. Ultimately, the extent to which this dialogue influenced the plan of cultural recovery is unknown, but it is crucial to acknowledge the fact of the dialogue in the first place.

In the 14 July 1832 issue of the *DPJ*, the woodcut presented below the masthead was a view of Dublin, taken from Phoenix Park (Figure 5.3). The outline used as the basis for the woodcut was by Petrie, though unsigned. It appears that Petrie employed as his original a drawing he himself had provided a year earlier for G.N. Wright's expensive volume aimed at tourists,

17 See Rachel Hewitt, *Map of a Nation: A Biography of the Ordnance Survey* (London: Granta, 2010), p. 272 and *passim*.

18 See Andrews, *A Paper Landscape*, p. 156.

[SECOND EDITION.]

THE

DUBLIN PENNY JOURNAL,

PUBLISHED EVERY SATURDAY.

No. 3. Vol. I. J. S. FOLDS, 56, GREAT STRAND-STREET. July 14, 1832.

Dublin, from the Phœnix Park.

DUBLIN.

A few years ago, at a public meeting in the city of Glasgow, a worthy old man who had made a sort of tour throughout Ireland, dilated in a speech upon its miserable condition, painted it in dark and gloomy colours, and concluded with a warm and earnest appeal to those present, to "take pity on that unhappy country." This roused the blood of one of the audience—and he was an Irishman! He could not sit still and hear the land of his birth caricatured, or permit any one to go away with false impressions; and so, in parliamentary phrase, he "got on his legs," and in glowing and energetic terms rebutted the charge of Ireland being a miserable and a degraded country. Dublin, he told them, was one of the finest cities of Europe, having a greater number of benevolent institutions than any one of a similar size throughout the world; while with genuine Irish eloquence he enlarged upon the politeness and hospitality of its inhabitants, the splendour of its public buildings, and the variety of its literary and scientific associations. When he concluded, a dissenting and well-known clergymen of Glasgow, an intelligent and liberal man, started to his feet, and exclaimed,

"Breathes there the man with soul so dead,
"Who never to himself hath said,
"*This is my own, my native land!*

Thunders of applause followed, and the honest and outspoken defender of his native metropolis sat down amid the approbation of a large audience.

Now look at the wood-cut, and say if, even in this indistinct view, Dublin does not deserve the appellation of "a *fine* city?" True it wants *something* which London and Edinburgh have; we are told that our metropolis wants the business and the bustle of the English, and the singular and romantic air of the Scottish metropolis. But in our miniature way, we are much more busy and bustling here than in the "great city." London is the elephant of cities, enormous but calm, and performing its mighty efforts with such habits of regular and unostentatious strength that we only become conscious of what is doing, by reflection upon what has been and must be done. It is true, that in the *great* thoroughfare from Charing Cross to Whitechapel there is a rushing sound of men and carriages and horses, travelling to and fro: but this is emphatically the great thoroughfare, and what are four or five miles of street, compared with the huge mass of London? In "the city," the calmness and utter absence of outside show, where we know there is such prodigious business, and prodigious wealth, seems very extraordinary to an Irishman. And again in Edinburgh, beautiful and romantic as it is, its old town huddled upon the hill, and guarded by the fortress which perched on high, frowns upon all around, and fills the eye from whatever point you view the place, or its new town, swelling away round the base of the rock, built of "*rale* stone," and justifyng in some degree the appellation which the modern Athenians have assumed, the "city of palaces;" even it, can it boast of such a view as one may have, standing upon Carlisle Bridge, and looking eastwards, westwards, northwards, and southwards? First, the long continued line of quays extending right through the centre of the city, from Ringsend point to the Military road, a distance of nearly three miles. In the direction of the Bay, the Custom-house (see our first number) rising at a little distance in all the beauty of truly classical architecture, and surrounded by ships and other vessels of considerable size, which approach quite close to the bridge; to the west, the bridges crowded with busy mortals passing and repassing; in the distant perspective, the Four Courts, and different churches, whose domes and spires are seen towering above the intervening buildings; while still further off, the Wellington Testimonial (occupying the fore ground in our wood-cut,) may be distinctly observed rising above the trees in the Phœnix Park. To the north, Sackville street, one of the most splendid streets in Europe, having in its centre the noble pillar erected in memory of the immortal Nelson; on the left of it, the Post Office, a specimen of elegant and chaste architecture, while southwards is Trinity College and the Bank.

What associations does that noble building, with its handsome dome—the Four Courts—create in the mind? Every man in Dublin knows what a delightful place the hall of the

Figure 5.3.1: *Dublin Penny Journal* (14 July 1832), p. 1
(Courtesy James Hardiman Library, National University of Ireland, Galway)

Figure 5.3.2: G.N. Wright, *Ireland Illustrated*
(London: H. Fisher, Son, and Jackson, 1831), p. 22
(Courtesy James Hardiman Library, National University of Ireland, Galway)

entitled *Ireland Illustrated*, published in London by Fisher. The drawing as reproduced in the *DPJ* caught the attention of the English publisher and he filed a court action against John S. Folds, proprietor of the *DPJ*, citing piracy. However, the argument was not so much about contested copyright as it was the perception that through the reproduction as a woodcut in a penny journal the worth of the original drawing had been affected. The dispute was announced in a short editorial, probably written by Folds, on the final page of the 2 February 1833 issue:

> A London publisher, conceiving that we have copied some of our illustrations from his work, has endeavoured to obtain, though without success, an injunction from the Court of Chancery, to restrain our publication. Supposing that we have done so, what injury has he sustained thereby? has he a copyright in our public buildings and ancient edifices to prohibit us from taking the same view of them which his artists have done? Certainly not, and though we might have been a slight gainer in the way of expense at the outset of our little work, by copying the outlines of some of his plates, he could be no loser … what person that has the slightest pretensions to judgment or taste in

> the fine arts, will believe that these effects of a finished steel engraving, could be transferred to such humble efforts of the wood-cutter as ours? The thing is quite ludicrous. (p. 256)

Folds was being slightly disingenuous here, as he does not mention the fact that Petrie was the artist of both works. In any case, Folds's contention was that copyright could not be held over a public view. Fisher also claimed that sales of his volume had fallen off since the publication of the *DPJ*, another charge that the editors found ridiculous, as the ostensible market they were targeting was completely separate from the upper classes who would be drawn to Fisher's publications.[19] The lawsuit failed, but largely because copyright could not be proven to extend to pictures, and in any case the judge seemed sure that the argument was really about money rather than a point of law. Folds clearly thought this worth repeating, as he quoted the judge's remarks:

> I cannot … help remarking, that I never in my life beheld the workings of the spirit of monopoly more clearly evinced than in the present instance; and I consider it proper to state, that no rational man can for a moment entertain a doubt that the sole object of the plaintiffs is to put down this Penny Journal—a meritorious publication, calculated to excite a taste amongst the poorer classes for acquiring useful knowledge.[20]

Why were the English publishers so hostile? It would be wonderful to be able to prove that such was the market saturation of the *DPJ* that the upper classes, looking for artwork for their walls, were ignoring expensive collections of engravings in favour of the humble woodcuts the *DPJ* provided. But this is probably not the case; the dispute that ended in the lawsuit really seemed to originate in a disagreement between Petrie himself, who had been under contract to produce drawings for *Ireland Illustrated*, and the publishers, who had been annoyed at the slow pace at which Petrie supplied them with his work, as his tardiness in turn held up the production of engraved plates. Whatever about the personalities in the case, from a theoretical point of view this re-appropriation of images is important. It signalled a determination to provide universal access to cheap art and a re-alignment of Ireland as subject

19 Fisher's annoyance may have originated in the amount – £20 – that he paid the engraver (Goodall) for the plate of Petrie's *Dublin from the Phoenix Park*. See Murray, *George Petrie*, p. 69. Murray also notes that 'Petrie's view of *Dublin from the Phoenix Park* is virtually identical to an engraving in the National Library of Ireland after a view by Samuel Frederick Brocas, which can be dated to this period. Petrie's rivalry with the Brocas family must have been intense'.

20 *DPJ*, 1.36, 2 March 1833, p. 288.

rather than object, as a space owned rather than as a tourist destination. In this sense the process can be seen, again, as part of the formation of a new public sphere; in effect the penny journal regained control of the representation of the Irish landscape and offered it up as part of a recontextualisation of history. A new set of memories was formed, indissoluble from visual remains, to which Petrie added textual records and interpretations of those records favourable to the originators, in a palimpsest of which the final layer was the penny journal itself.

As has been noted above, the *DPJ* managed to exist without political or religious sponsorship, but this does not mean that it wasn't after some sort of support. However, it does appear that though the intellectual community viewed it in a benevolent light, the middle classes – or perhaps it is simpler to say the book-buying classes – failed to see its worth. In the Preface to the first volume of the journal in 1833, reference was made to the 'enemies' of the magazine: booksellers reluctant to take copies of it to sell because the return they would realise was so low, and English publishers like Fisher who objected to the cheap reproduction of images and were worried about the competition it posed to the English magazines they sold in Ireland. The Preface, existing as a sort of Afterword to the entire year's issues, was in fact a direct address to an entirely different audience: the scholar and gentleman, as the writer of the Preface called him, someone who would recognise the value of the content of the journal, but who might balk at a public display of its lower-class appearance. In a clear-sighted evaluation of the influence of form on meaning, the writers of the Preface acknowledged that the penny numbers were 'suited to the pockets of the poorer classes of society'. However, the bound volume was presented as being worthy of 'the library of the scholar and the gentleman'.[21] In other words, it was acknowledged that the penny paper and the bound volume contained exactly the same information, but that material itself attracted cultural capital based simply on the form in which it was encased. And, ultimately, it was these middle or upper-class readers that the editors hoped would aid the distribution of the penny journal, in its paper-covered format for their dependants, and in its cloth-bound format for themselves. In the end it was this was class that failed them, not the working class. Education via historical rebirth was not, it seemed, universally welcomed. When the *DPJ* passed to other editorial hands in July of 1833, its shape and focus changed entirely and it resembled, ironically, a cheaper version of Wright's *Ireland Illustrated*.[22]

21 'Preface', *Dublin Penny Journal*, vol. 1 (1833).

22 For the history of this change see '*Dublin Penny Journal* (1832–1836)', in Laurel Brake and Marysa Demoor (eds), *Dictionary of Nineteenth-Century Journalism in Great Britain and Ireland* (Gent: Academia Press, 2009).

In 1840, roughly ten years following the first publication of the *DPJ*, Petrie tried the penny journal format again, this time as sole editor. His *Irish Penny Journal* was virtually indistinguishable from its earlier manifestation,[23] and though equally worthy, ceased publication after only a year. But here too can be found the materials of reclamation. In Petrie's description of his impressions of Monasterboice (see Figure 5.4), a similar re-casting of the landscape according to use and popular memory overtook the sort of static presentation of Ireland's landscape so prominent in works like that of Wright. In Petrie's commentary accompanying his drawing he said:

> In concluding these notices of a spot so long the abode of piety, art, and learning of remote times, we may add, that in its present deserted and ruined state, it is a scene of the deepest and most solemn interest; and the mind must indeed be dull and earthly in which it fails to awaken feelings of touching and permanent interest; silence and solitude the most profound are impressed on all its time-worn features; we are among the dead only; and we are forced, as it were, to converse with the men of other days.[24]

Cultural memory was being both evoked and manufactured here through print, a process that depended on familiarity with the landscape in its present form, as well as imagination enough to recreate its past forms.[25] The silence of the land was something Petrie had cause to notice again during the Famine, but here he is referring to the difficulty of making the physical and built landscape give up its historical secrets to the living. In terms of material culture, the silence is a gap that Petrie filled with the minutiae of Irish history, a cultural retrieval that both created and standardised memory. Objects, names, rituals, texts, pictures, were all used as repositories of meaning. Without the reconstruction and replication of Irish history before the English that Petrie performed in the penny press, cultural memory – already fast disappearing – would have been very difficult for Young Ireland and later groups to enact.

The *DPJ* was a communal project that failed in its attempts at the resurrection of a national history, but it was one that actively sought input

23 The *Irish Penny Journal* ran from 4 July 1840 to 26 June 1841. Format and audience repeated that of the *Dublin Penny Journal*, though some content ventured beyond Ireland and its concerns.

24 *Irish Penny Journal*, 1.7, 15 August 1840.

25 See Sydney J. Shep, 'Cultures of Print: Materiality, Memory, and the Rituals of Transmission', *Journal of New Zealand Literature* 28 (2010): 183–210. Shep's subject matter is very different from that discussed here, but her framework and comments on the manufacture of public memory are most useful to my argument.

THE IRISH PENNY JOURNAL.

NUMBER 7. SATURDAY, AUGUST 15, 1840. VOLUME I.

REMAINS AT MONASTERBOICE, COUNTY LOUTH.

To the observing and imaginative traveller, our island must present a great number of peculiarities of aspect which will not fail to excite his notice, and impress themselves indelibly upon his mind. The scantiness of wood—for its natural timber has nearly all disappeared—and the abundance of water, are two of the characteristics that will most strike him; and, next to these, the great extent of prospect usually afforded to the eye in consequence of the undulating character of its surface. Sparkling streams are visible everywhere, and shining lakes and noble rivers come into view in rapid succession; while ranges of blue mountains are rarely wanting to bound the distant horizon. The colours with which Nature has painted the surface of our island are equally peculiar. There is no variety of green, whether of depth or vivid brightness, which is not to be found covering it; they are hues which can be seen nowhere else in equal force; and even our bogs, which are so numerous, with all their mutations of colour, now purple, and anon red, or brown, or black, by their vigorous contrasts give additional beauty and life to the landscape, and assist in imparting to it a sort of national individuality. Our very clouds have to a great degree a distinctive character—the result of the humidity of our climate; they have a grandeur of form and size, and a force of light and shadow, that are but rarely seen in other countries: they are *Irish clouds*—at one moment bright and sunny, and in the next flinging their dark shadows over the landscape, and involving it in gloomy grandeur. It is in this striking force of contrast in almost every thing that we look at, that the peculiarity of our scenery chiefly consists; and it appears to have stamped the general character of our people with those contrasting lights and shades so well exhibited in our exquisite and strongly-marked national music, in which all varieties of sentiment are so deeply yet harmoniously blended as to produce on the mind effects perhaps in some degree saddening, but withal most delightfully sweet and soothing. A country marked with such peculiarities is not the legitimate abode of the refined sensualist of modern times, or the man of artificial pleasure and heartless pursuits, and all such naturally remain away from it, or visit it with reluctance; but it is the proper habitation of the poet, the painter, and, above all, the philanthropist; for nowhere else can the latter find so extensive a field for the exercise of the godlike feelings of benevolence and patriotism.

Yet the natural features of scenery and climate which we have pointed out, interesting as all must admit them to be, are not the only ones that confer upon our country the peculiar and impressive character which it possesses. The relics of past epochs of various classes; the monuments of its Pagan times, as revealed to us in its religious, military, and sepulchral remains; the ruins of its primitive Christian ages, as exemplified in its simple and generally unadorned churches, and slender round towers; the more splendid monastic edifices of later date, and the gloomy castles of still more recent times—these are everywhere present to bestow historic interest on the landscape, and bring the successive conditions and changes of society in bygone ages forcibly before the

Figure 5.4: *The Irish Penny Journal* (15 August 1840), p. 1
(Courtesy James Hardiman Library, National University of Ireland, Galway)

from readers, that understood the transmission of history as complicated and multi-faceted, and that tried to use the power of the form of the text – the penny journal format – to complement the impact of Ireland's built environment and its linguistic heritage on the landscape of time. The journal tried to manufacture memory, to unbury a true reflection of Ireland's past in a physical form calculated to appeal to those most nearly concerned, both culturally and politically, in its resurrection. The very existence of the *DPJ* and its assertion that sufficient material of interest could be found in the country to fill its pages constituted an act of cultural resistance to attempts to conceptualise Ireland in terms of a series of importations of meaning from elsewhere.

Section 3
Translation, Transmission and Transnational Literacies

6

Room with a View: Reading Ireland in the Irish College Old Library, Paris *c.*1870–1900

Darragh Gannon

This essay examines interpretations of contemporary and historical Ireland through the eyes of Irish seminary students resident at the Irish College in Paris, *c.*1870–1900. It interrogates the extensive print holdings of the Old Library, in addition to select items in the Irish College archives, to illuminate student perceptions of Ireland's past and present. This study locates the experience of 'reading' Ireland in the Irish College, Paris, at the intersection of seminal political changes in Ireland and France, the epicentre of European debate between religion and secularism and along the frontier of the nineteenth and twentieth centuries.[1]

The period 1870–1900 was denoted by compelling political, religious and social tensions in both Ireland and France. These years witnessed the emergence of mass politico-cultural mobilisation in Ireland through the Home Rule, Land League and Gaelic League movements. The Irish Catholic Church both embraced and eschewed these campaigns. These decades also marked the consolidation of the French Third Republic. France developed a constitutional democracy which emphasised republican secularism over religion, to the diminution of Catholic influence in public life. Moreover, this period also prompted rich debate over the role of the Church in the modern era. The First Vatican Council was established to situate the Catholic Church more definitively within a European society increasingly influenced by the ideas of rationalism, liberalism and materialism. Meanwhile, the period under review

1 The author would like to acknowledge the Centre Culturel Irlandais, Paris, for its generous award of the 2014 Irish College Library and Archives Fellowship. Special thanks to CCI Director Ms. Nora Hickey M'Sichili, and her staff, for their support of this study.

also offers an opportunity to weigh the impact of the Cullenite revolution, the Irish Church's instrumental, institutional conformity to Roman Catholic practices, devotions and doctrines, on an Irish religious community at the heart of an increasingly secular France. This study investigates the impact of these layered influences on interpretations of Ireland at the Irish College in Paris between its centenary and the end of century.

Scope and Content

The Old Library at the Irish College in Paris is an invaluable repository from which to elicit the nuances of Irish student perspectives of Ireland. The loss of its original collections during the French revolution necessitated the assembly and arrangement of new titles for the student population.[2] What items were acquired in this re-collection process? What thematic motifs recur in these volumes? What contemporary influences may have informed the selection of these texts? As Gerard Long has observed, the collecting patterns of certain libraries in the course of the nineteenth century could be manifestations of changing scholarly interest in Ireland or part of broader European trends towards assembling print collections.[3] The reinvestment in the Old Library collection throughout the nineteenth century may have also impacted on the reading culture of Irish College students. Niall Ó Ciosáin has noted that the initial numerical limitations of a library can lead to an individual reading single texts in an 'intensive manner'.[4] To what extent did this reading rhythm influence student perceptions of Ireland's past? In the latter half of the nineteenth century the reading of Irish history was increasingly of concern to the Catholic hierarchy. As Colin Barr has emphasised: 'history ... was a subject that not only could be safely taught by Catholics from Catholic books in a Catholic environment, but one which could only be accurately taught in such an environment'.[5] Close inspection of the Old Library's holdings in 1870 and the intensity to which volumes were acquired thereafter can offer fresh

2 *Bibliothèque patrimoniale*, Centre Culturel Irlandais, Paris, http://www.centreculturelirlandais.com/modules/movie/scenes/home/index.php?fuseAction=bibliotheque.

3 Gerard Long, 'Institutional Libraries and Private Collections', in James H. Murphy (ed.), *The Oxford History of the Irish Book: the Irish Book in English, 1800–1891* (Oxford: Oxford University Press, 2011), pp. 281–97.

4 Niall Ó Ciosáin, 'Oral Culture, Literacy and Reading, 1800–50', in James H. Murphy (ed.), *The Oxford History of the Irish Book: the Irish Book in English, 1800–1891* (Oxford: Oxford University Press, 2011), pp. 173–91, p. 176.

5 Colin Barr, 'University Education, History and the Hierarchy', in Lawrence W. McBride (ed.), *Reading Irish Histories: Texts, Contexts and Memory in Modern Ireland* (Dublin: Four Courts Press, 2003), pp. 62–79, p. 69.

perspectives as to how student communities at the Irish College developed an Irish historical memory.

How did the Irish College in Paris view the cultural, social and political changes which were taking place in Ireland in the closing decades of the nineteenth century? As Florrie O'Driscoll's essay in this volume attests, the Irish College in Rome was central to the co-ordination of Irish nationalist efforts in opposition to Italian nationalism.[6] The Irish College in Paris too, potentially, was a contested site of national development. Historians have increasingly identified the reading room as one of the key educational loci of nationalist movements in Ireland.[7] The collections of the Old Library evince an Irish student community in Paris responsive to *live* developments in Irish politics in the late nineteenth century. The presence of printed editions such as *Lettres d'Irlande* (1889) and the collation of weekly newspapers such as *The Tablet* indicate an active learning culture in current affairs. The existence of contemporary Irish ephemera, journals and photographs within the college's archives supports this view. What image(s) of Irish political change were fostered within the Irish College? The Old Library also provided a public space for dialogue on events in Ireland. As Paul Townend has written, the reading room in Irish culture 'linked a set of reading practices … with national development'.[8] While college libraries nominally espoused religious and spiritual learning, reading these collections, in practice, fostered a broad range of literacy skills such as independent reading, discourse analysis, and critical thinking. This intellectual environment also sharpened the rhetorical skills and shaped the leadership abilities of aspirant priests engaged in political debate. Patrick Boyle, then College Superior, stated of the students who returned to Ireland: 'Many of them hold the highest points of confidence in their diocese'.[9] What texts were students exploring and what discussion was stimulated by a reading of these contemporary sources? A forensic examination of the core arguments found in late nineteenth-century titles will be supported by an investigation of key collections in the college archives, including the Patrick Boyle papers and the college annual reports. It is only through this holistic approach that scholars can establish the *mentalité* of students at the Irish College towards contemporary politics.

Finally, to what extent did the religious impetuses of the Catholic Church

6 Florrie O'Driscoll, 'May God Bless You and All at Home': Mid-Nineteenth Century Irish Views on Italy through the Letters of Albert Delahoyde, 1860–1870', this book, chapter 7.

7 Paul Townend, '"Academies of Nationality": the Reading Room and Irish National Movements, 1838–1905', in McBride (ed.), *Reading Irish Histories*, p. 31.

8 Ibid., p. 19.

9 Patrick Boyle, *The Irish College in Paris from 1578 to 1901* (London: Art & Book Co., 1901), p. 108.

in the late nineteenth century and the growing secularisation of European public life, impact Irish College students? Does the Old Library collection reveal the continued lived legacy of Cardinal Cullen's ultramontanism decades after his death, and to what degree was the trend towards secularism in France during the Third Republic a cause for concern or indeed curiosity among students at the Irish College? How might these European influences have affected Catholic priests' later service in Ireland? The collections held in the Old Library offer subtle indicators as to students' reading of these competing ideological forces. Meanwhile, significant archival deposits such as the college correspondence will offer personal testimonies to the interactions of students with these contemporary ideas. This essay, ultimately, offers a unique insight into that 'curiously Franco-Irish institution', the Irish College in Paris.

The Irish College, Paris, 1870–1900: A History

The Irish College in Paris was an outstanding landmark of Irish education and emigration in late nineteenth century Europe. Irish collegiate communities had existed in France from the late sixteenth century and were formally recognised by Louis XIV who granted them a permanent home on Rue du Carmes in 1677 (in what became the 5eme arrondissement). A further property was purchased on the nearby Rue du Cheval Vert in 1769 which became the permanent home of the Irish College from 1775 onwards. Despite damage to its buildings and collections during the revolutionary period, the Irish College was recognised in 1805 as an essential centre of Irish culture by Napoleon, who officially changed its street address to Rue des Irlandais two years later. Irish ecclesiastics would continue to train for the priesthood there throughout the nineteenth century. Closing his report to the Catholic hierarchy of Ireland in June 1900, the rector of the Irish College, Patrick Boyle, reflected on that institution's experience of the nineteenth century: 'the College has continued its work amid various vicissitudes. It has passed through three revolutions, and two sieges. But like the city in which it stands, it may claim the device, *Fluctuate nec mergitur* ["tossed but not sunk"]'.[10] Boyle's rather protective summation of the college's experience was indicative not only of its exposure to the tumultuous events of the Napoleonic wars, 1848 rebellions and Franco-Prussian war, but also of its laboured administration in the aftermath of these events.

10 Quoted in Ciaran O'Neill, *Catholics of Consequence: Transnational Education, Social Mobility and the Irish Catholic Elite, 1850–1900* (Oxford: Oxford University Press, 2014), p. 202.

Although not directly damaged by the conflict in 1870–71, the Irish College at Rue des Irlandais never fully recovered from the effects of the Franco-Prussian War. Its ancillary buildings at Arcueil, part of suburban Paris, had been almost totally destroyed, first by invading Prussian soldiers and, subsequently, by a band of disaffected French troops. The repair effort, it was estimated, would cost upwards of 20,000 francs. The financial weight of the restoration process pressed hard on the staff and students of the Irish College over the next three decades. A campaign to actualise an indemnity fund offering recompense for damage inflicted on British property in France was largely unsuccessful during the 1870s, despite the public attention given to the claim by the support of the Irish Parliamentary Party leader Isaac Butt.[11] Its financial effects would percolate every aspect of life at the Irish College from the standard of living for students to the standard of entrance examination for aspiring students. As Ciaran O'Neill has commented of the institution during this period, it existed in a 'sense of suspended animation'.[12]

The Franco-Prussian War, indirectly, imposed further limitations on the development of the Irish College in the late nineteenth century. The French Third Republic, born into the conflict, applied heavy administrative control of the institution in its aftermath. In 1873 the French government established a *Bureau Gratuit* – a seven person administrative board – to manage the Irish College's structures and temporal affairs. Five were appointed by, and were responsible to, the secular government. Though such a reform was entirely within the remit of the new political regime and formed part of a wider policy of centralised government, it created tensions between French political leaders and Irish ecclesiastical leaders. The approval now required from the Minister of Public Instruction before the appointment of new college staff transgressed implicit Irish Church control of the Irish College. Important decisions affecting the educational potential of that institution could now be made elsewhere in Paris. It would be an uncomfortable end to the nineteenth century for the students and staff of the Irish College.

Environments of Education: Calendar

Students preparing for the priesthood at the Irish College Paris in the late nineteenth century committed to four years of intensive training, scholarship and reflection. Their devotion to the spiritual mission was the focus of every month spent in Paris as structured by the College authorities. The year

11 Justin Dolan Stover, 'Witness to War: Charles Ouin-la-Croix and the Irish College, Paris, 1870–71', in *Études irlandaises* xxxvi (2011): 27–28.

12 Ciaran O'Neill, *Catholics of Consequence*, p. 198.

began, however, not in Paris but in Dublin. Each September, entrance examinations to the Irish College were held at Blackrock College in Dublin.[13] Prospective candidates who had been nominated by their dioceses faced a full day's test of their religious, linguistic and logical abilities. Those applying for first philosophy, for example, were tested in Latin, Greek, algebra and geography. Candidates for second philosophy and first theology, meanwhile, took exams in Latin composition, logics, metaphysics and ethics.[14] Applicants were also rigorously screened with regard to their character. Students were expected to bring to Blackrock their bishop's letter of recommendation in addition to proof of their baptism, confirmation and state of health. A personal interview with each prospective candidate followed in the afternoon. The 'doubtful ones' were 'questioned orally'.[15] According to its entrance registers, 593 Irish students in total entered the Irish College, Paris, between 1870 and 1900.[16]

Within days of being accepted to the Irish College, students were expected to make their way to Paris, arriving on the date of the feast of St Matthew the Apostle (21 September). Classes began the following Monday. Students at the Irish College attended lectures on every day of the week. The period between September and February was particularly intensive. The college calendar notes only a few dates on which 'class as usual' did not take place such as the Days of All Saints and All Souls respectively. These holy days of obligation, however, were swiftly followed by a monthly subject examination. In late February the mid-year examinations began. These took place over a week, ending on Shrove Tuesday.[17] The second term, running from February to June, was slightly shorter but no less intensive. Holy Week, which could fall in either March or April, broke up the students' repetitive lecture schedule. Holy Tuesday was a half-day for class while Spy Wednesday was a 'free day'. Visits to churches in the fifth arrondissement and Notre Dame marked the students' experience of Holy Thursday and Good Friday respectively. On Holy Saturday and Easter Sunday religious ceremonies were held at the Irish College chapel, while Easter Monday was given over to free time. The remaining calendar notes for March and April

13 '"College calendar" (manuscrit, incomplet), année 1873' (Centre Culturel Irlandais (CCI) archive, Collège: administration, A2.b109).

14 '"Entrance exam[s] and information for freshmen": information relatives aux conditions d'entrée, 1919–24' (CCI Archive, Collège: administration, A2.b188).

15 Ibid.

16 'Registre des élèves entrés au college entre 1858 et 1938' (CCI Archive, Collège: administration (registres) A2.c4).

17 For details of examination subjects and questions see: 'Carnet manuscrit sur les examens, 1892–94' (CCI Archive, Collège: administration, A2.b144). See also: 'Register of exams, 1895–1932' (CCI Archive, Collège: administration, A2.b150).

evidence the otherwise continual cycle of lectures at the Irish College. The annual end of year examinations were held across seven days in early June.[18] Those who fell below pass standard were reported to their bishops.[19] On their completion, students were warned by the college authorities that 'it is strictly forbidden to eat or drink in hotels or restaurants in Paris'.[20]

Vacation time between June and September was slightly less exacting though no less supervised. Students typically had the option to return to Ireland or remain in Paris, spending the summer at the college's suburban retreat at Arcueil. Those who chose the former were instructed to 'bring back certificates of good conduct from their parish priest' to attest to their application of religious principles and practices in their home diocese during their time away.[21] Those who selected the latter option were expected to continue their studies privately for four days of the week, Tuesdays, Fridays and Saturdays being set aside as 'days of recreation'. Closely planned excursions to locations outside the city were organised for those staying at Arcueil, including trips to Versailles, St Germain, St Denis and Vincennes. Visits to sites in the city itself, meanwhile, were carefully monitored. The Palais des Beaux Arts, Galerie du Luxembourg and Musée du Luxembourg were cited as inappropriate places to visit on account of potential exposure to indecent pictures. Individual students, meanwhile, were not allowed to purchase books from shops while walking through Paris.[22] Concern over the students' exposure to Parisian life was particularly acute in the early 1870s during which time the villa at Arcueil was inaccessible. This was patent in the annual reports prepared for the bishops of Ireland by the college rector, Thomas McNamara, who consistently warned of the students being open to 'serious injury to their health' for their remaining in Paris.[23]

18 '"Collège calendar" (manuscrit, incomplet), année 1873' (CCI Archive, Collège: administration, A2.b109).

19 'Reports of the Irish College, 1890–1917' (CCI Archive, Collège: administration, A2.b138).

20 '"Reports of the Irish College, [letters] to the most reverend archbishops and bishops of Ireland et Claims" (relié), 1874–89' (CCI Archive, Collège: administration, A2.b111).

21 Ibid.

22 '"Collège calendar" (manuscrit, incomplet), année 1873' (CCI Archive, Collège: administration, A2.b109).

23 '"Reports of the Irish College, [letters] to the most reverend archbishops and bishops of Ireland et Claims" (relié), 1874–89' (CCI Archive, Collège: administration, A2.b111).

A Day in the Life

The education of the students at the Irish College Paris was multidisciplinary and diverse. It was also highly demanding. Weekdays brought a range of subjects and expectations. Morning lectures on dogma, philosophy and rhetoric were followed by afternoon sessions of moral theology, scripture and sacred history. Classes on *les belles lettres*, introductory history and the French language chequered an otherwise overly familiar weekly schedule. An optional Irish language class was made available on Fridays at 17.30 for the most voracious students.[24] Though no formatted schedule for evening activity could be located within the archives, the 'Rules of the Irish College' (1863) attest to the continuation of study beyond the daily routine of class time. Several articles refer to student behaviour during evening study. The first item states 'strict silence during study class and all other time except the time allocated for speaking'.[25] Students, moreover, were not permitted to move or communicate within the room.[26] Weekends were an opportunity to reinforce concepts learned. Saturday morning began with classes on canon law, philosophy and rhetoric and was followed in the afternoon with dogma, philosophy and rhetoric. Sunday opened with discussion of sacred scripture, the Old Testament and the Council of Trent, and came to a close in the evening with the weekly devotional ceremonies of benediction and the rosary. A continued emphasis on scholarship was also instituted during the vacation months, with private study and attendance at special lectures an integral part of the evening programme at Arcueil.[27]

Students and Staff

The educational development of students was closely monitored by the college authorities. The performance of each student during their time at the college was observed across the subjects of rhetoric, philosophy and theology.

24 '"Collège calendar" (manuscrit, incomplet), année 1873' (CCI Archive, Collège: administration, A2.b109).

25 '"Usages of the Irish College Paris, written by D [octor] Lynch, October 1863". Rules of the college towards the end of the book" 1863' (CCI Archive, Collège: administration, A2.b71). A revised version of the College rules was issued in 1933. See 'Règlement du college: "Rules of the Irish College" (cahier manuscrit et exemplaire dactylographié), 1933' (CCI Archive, Collège: administration A2.b232).

26 '"Usages of the Irish College Paris, written by D [octor] Lynch, October 1863". Rules of the college towards the end of the book" 1863' (CCI Archive, Collège: administration, A2.b71).

27 '"Collège calendar" (manuscrit, incomplet), année 1873' (CCI Archive, Collège: administration, A2.b109).

Eligibility for the priesthood was denoted by both 'talent' and 'conduct'. In the first category, the student aspired to the status of 'premium'. This was infrequently awarded. Students' 'conduct' was also carefully gradated. *Optimus*, according to the College register, indicated that the individual's behaviour was 'most regular and edifying' while at the opposite end of the spectrum students could be ascribed the status of *levis* ('tending to immorality'), *malus* ('very bad') or *minus* ('not manifesting the clerical character although quiet and orderly').[28] An analysis of student competency and comportment was a central feature of the rector's annual report to the bishops of Ireland. The evaluation provided for the academic year 1875–76 was representative of the period. 'We are happy to be able to report favourably of the conduct of the Students during the year', advised Thomas McNamara, 'the reports from the several classes, the monthly examinations, and the examinations in the middle and end of the year furnished satisfactory evidence, on the whole, of assiduity in the various departments of our Seminary Curriculum'.[29] To members of the Catholic hierarchy, who observed student engagement with education at close quarters during their annual visit to Rue des Irlandais, this intensive learning experience was ideal preparation for the future priesthood. Bishop Moriarty of Kerry lauded the approach taken by the Irish College in his testimony to the Royal Commission in 1854:

> The system begets a habit of politeness towards superiors, and at the same time engenders in the students a more manly bearing. I have observed the Irish character under that system in the Irish College, Paris and I have always observed that that system produced the most beneficial results.[30]

Students attending the Irish College in Paris, thus, experienced a formal education which was intense of calendar, daily life and expectation.

Reading the Outside World

How did the college library fit into this learning environment? In terms of its organising structure, student engagement and thematic scope, the library sat adjacent to the core religious educational programme at the Irish College. The

28 'Registre des élèves entrés au college entre 1858 et 1938' (CCI Archive, Collège: administration (registres) A2.c4).

29 '"Reports of the Irish College, [letters] to the most reverend archbishops and bishops of Ireland et Claims" (relié), 1874–89' (CCI Archive, Collège: administration, A2.b111).

30 Patrick Boyle, *The Irish College in Paris*, pp. 85–86.

administration of the library was carried out largely by its students but was overseen by the college staff. Its governing executive consisted of a president, typically a director of the institution, a treasurer, a secretary and a librarian appointed by the college rector.[31] As a functioning entity within the financially besieged Irish College, the library was an economic and effective organisation. Its finances were ring-fenced within the college ledgers and were always balanced.[32] Membership to the college library, which was entirely voluntary, was one franc per quarter. According to its constitution, the president was to meet the other executive members at the beginning of every quarter to examine the accounts, authorise the purchase of books and address any other concerns.[33] The surviving minutes of this body, however, are limited in both content and chronological range. The librarian was the key official, being solely responsible for cataloguing volumes, documenting members and admitting students into the repository. The college archive contains oblique references to the creation of what Erving Goffman has termed 'frames' of analysis.[34] This was particularly important to a Catholic Church preoccupied with educational respectability. The inventory of items in the Irish College Library for the academic year 1890–91 establishes seven key themes/genres within the collection: biography, personal statements, history, current affairs, religion and spirituality, literature, and travel.

Biography

Biography is the dominant form of printed item in the listings. Of the many biographical subjects addressed in the collection, including George Washington and Napoleon, one held particular prominence: Daniel O'Connell. There were no fewer than three biographical sketches of O'Connell in the library's collection: *Select Speeches* (1862), edited by his son John O'Connell, *Life and Times of Daniel O'Connell, with Sketches of his Contemporaries* (1864) by C.M. O'Keeffe and *The Life and Times of Daniel*

31 'Catalogue manuscrit des livres appartenant à l'Historical Society of the Irish College Paris, 1859–1891. Contient également les "rules of the students (sic) library"' (CCI Archive, Documentation: histoire, E12.a1).

32 'Livre de comptes : "College accounts, Walsh Fund, crédit foncier emprunté, résumé des dépenses de nourriture", avec quatre notes manuscrites, 1883–1922' (CCI Archive, Collège: administration, A2.d21).

33 'Catalogue manuscrit des livres appartenant à l'Historical Society of the Irish College Paris, 1859–1891. Contient également les "rules of the students (sic) library"' (CCI Archive, Documentation: histoire, E12.a1).

34 Erving Goffman, *Frame Analysis: an Essay on the Organisation of Experience* (Cambridge, MA: Harvard University. Press, 1986).

O'Connell (1847–48) by William Fagan. All three works present O'Connell as both a political and spiritual Irish figure. His campaign for repeal of the Union is paralleled with that of Catholic emancipation, his engagement with the Catholic Church is documented as an essential catalyst to the realisation of civic activism among the mass population, while in his repudiation of violence, secularism and division, he is put forward as an exemplar to future community leaders. The twin peaks of late nineteenth-century Ireland, faith and fatherland, were recurring tropes in the biographical works on Daniel O'Connell acquired by the Irish College. Hermione Lee, in her treatment of biography as analytical text, has presented a dichotomous framework within which to interpret the historical content and cultural context for the writing of biography: 'autopsy' or 'portrait'. The former approach to the writing of biography is forensic, clinical and devoid of sentiment, presenting the individual as historical character. The latter approach, conversely, 'suggests empathy, bringing to life, capturing the character'.[35] The accounts held within the Irish College library lean heavily towards the portrait canon of biographical writing. This suggests a careful, coherent arrangement of this category of book. In the recreation of lives lived, these biographical accounts provided tangible contexts for students at the Irish College in which to understand the application of piety, devotion and spirituality, with the view to their return to Ireland as socio-religious leaders.

Personal Statements

A second discernible category was collections of speeches and writings. The discourses of Henry Grattan, late eighteenth-century Irish constitutional politician, were available for consultation in the library through the 1847 volume: *The select speeches of the right Hon. Henry Grattan*. This edited collection presents Grattan's views on an array of subjects from Irish independence to the Corn Laws but is dominated by discussion of the Catholic question. Grattan, a member of the Church of Ireland, was relentless in his support for Catholic emancipation across a 40-year political career, preserved in these speeches and statements. The overarching theme suggested by this collection is the centrality of the Catholic question within debates on Ireland's constitutional status. This argument was given greater weight through the library's acquisition of the *Speeches of the Right Hon. Richard Lalor Shiel*, published in 1847. As one of the founding members of the Catholic Association in 1823 and a leading campaigner

35 Hermione Lee, *Biography: a Very Short Introduction* (Oxford: Oxford University Press, 2009), p. 3.

for Catholic emancipation, the bound volume of Shiel's speeches might have been expected to represent this political focus. However, while those issues are addressed in this work, Shiel's speeches also attest to a public figure determined to improve wider society through a progressive, scholarly and outward looking Catholicism. His rhetoric deals with subjects such as Orange Lodges, the Church of Ireland, tithes, the Corn Laws and electoral reform. This volume underlines the virtues of a Catholic education by presenting Shiel as articulate, well read, and mature of thought.

This theme was developed further through the acquisition of *Letters and Speeches* of the Rev. D.W. Cahill, published in 1852. Cahill's illustrious career as a professor of natural philosophy in Ireland and the United States is well represented in this collection. However, perhaps its most coherent argumentative thread lies in placing Irish Catholicism and Irish questions more widely within a broader European context. Cahill's public addresses and private correspondence reaffirm the strength of the Catholic Church in the aftermath of the French revolution, the rise of secularism and the rule of hostile governments. His eloquent critique of Ireland through the lens of wider Europe was an apt selection for the library catalogue at the Irish College in Paris.

History

History books are heavily represented in the inventory of 1890–91. Particularly noticeable are the number of books about military history. Three particular titles evidence the broader thesis maintained within these volumes. *The Rise and Fall of the Irish Nation* by Jonah Barrington, published in 1833, takes as its key concept the militarisation of Irish life by the British state. Focusing on the events which led to the Act of Union, Barrington chronicles the fall of Grattan's parliament, the rise of the Irish Volunteers, the repressive legislation imposed on Ireland by the parliament at Westminster and the course of the 1798 rebellion. A former Volunteer, Barrington presents the insurrection as an inevitable consequence of British misrule in Ireland. The transgression of Ireland's right to self-government meant that the Irish people could no longer be assumed to fulfil their role in maintaining a 'peaceable kingdom'. Edward Hay's *History of the Insurrection of Co. Wexford, A.D. 1798*, published in 1803, also discusses this outbreak of violence. Hay contends that the rebels were brave, clean fighters who compared favourably to royalist soldiers in Co. Wexford. Hay had taken part in the uprising on the side of the United Irishmen, but also mediated with local gentry during the conflict. Though concluding his book with an air of optimism for peace and stability under the Union, Hay's volume highlights the centrality of violence in the Irish nationalist narrative of the late eighteenth century, attributing it a semi-legitimate quality, at least in terms of military behaviour, when compared with crown forces.

William Fitzpatrick's book, *'The Sham Squire' and the Informers of 1798*, meanwhile, complements these two volumes. Published in 1866, Fitzpatrick's work is a winding chronicle of the political events, personnages and loyalties (or rather disloyalties) of the final decade of the Union. Fitzpatrick centres his work on British misgovernment of Ireland during this period, arguing that it was largely through clandestine intelligence networks that the country was ruled. In an uncompromising, and often incongruous account, of the circumstances surrounding 1798, Fitzpatrick adheres to the thesis that militarism, in this case covert operations, was the key approach to British governance of Ireland. The rebellion of 1798, this work implies, was a proportionate response to an already militarised country.

Current Affairs

The college library inventory for the academic year 1890–91 evidences a reading collection which was current. This is true at least of periodicals on religious and spiritual affairs. Students could avail of a wide number of Catholic journals including the *Dublin Review*, the *Catholic University Gazette*, and the *Rambler*. Perhaps the most consistently subscribed to of these periodicals was the *Irish Ecclesiastical Record*. The *Irish Ecclesiastical Record*, founded in 1864 by Paul Cullen, was a monthly periodical. Each issue contained articles on spiritualism and official Church documents, while questions from concerned clergy on the application of Catholic dogma in the modern world were frequent in its letter pages. Each edition also contained reviews of recent publications. Although several reviewers critiqued new French books and commented on current trends in Parisian literature and culture, these pieces were only signed with initials making it impossible to discern if staff or students of the Irish College had written them. However, according to Patrick Boyle, Father McNamara frequently contributed reviews for the journal under the pen name 'Veteran practitioner'.[36]

During the period between 1870 and 1900, the *Irish Ecclesiastical Record* closely followed the interests and inquiries of the Catholic Church. The increased secularism of the French state, further, was the subject of a considerable number of articles: 'The Revolution' (1884), 'French Schools and Republican Rulers' (1887), 'Church and State in France' (1896), 'The Modern Reign of Terror in France' (1900). The journal evidenced an almost

36 Patrick Boyle, *The Irish College in Paris*, p. 109.

self-reflexive capacity to discuss religious and political matters, with the same cycle of contributors frequently re-appearing in issues, although its essays, book reviews and letter pages evinced a Catholic Church concerned over the diminution of its power after the First Vatican Council and its place in the new order of the late nineteenth century. As a Catholic periodical published during the rise of secularism across Europe, the *Irish Ecclesiastical Record* was an integral part of the Irish College's reading collection

Religious and Spiritual

Theological works were at the heart of the library's holdings. Printed series of lectures were prominent on the shelves. Nicholas Wiseman was the principal author of such tracts. The collection of his writings held in the Irish College library include *Four Lectures on the Offices and Ceremonies of Holy Week* (1834), *Twelve Lectures on the Connection between Science and Revealed Religion* (1853) and *Lectures on the Principal Doctrines and Practices of the Catholic Church* (1855). As a celebrated speaker renowned for his ability to address core Catholic issues with originality of thought, clarity of vision and rhetorical élan, Wiseman's works read as an engaging educational experience. Education and religion were themes addressed by other scholars also. John Henry Newman's *Discourses on University Education: Addressed to the Catholics of Dublin* (1852), *A Letter Addressed to his Grace the Duke of Norfolk on Account of Mr. Gladstone's Recent Expostulation* (1875) and *The Idea of a University Defined and Illustrated in Nine Discourses* (1881) presented his interpretation of a religious-based education which could create good Catholics and good citizens.

Literature and the Arts

Although not part of the curriculum at the Irish College and not intrinsic to the spiritual life, the reading of literature was evidently deemed beneficial for its students. The library inventory for 1890–91 contains a myriad of literary pieces ranging from *The Poetical Works of Lord Byron* (1852) to historical novels such as Mary Anne Sadlier's *The Confederate Chieftains: a Tale of the Irish Rebellion of 1641* (1868). A particular theme of interest, judging by the library's holdings, was music. Thomas Potter's *Legends, Lyrics and Hymns*, published in 1862, was aimed at entertaining young people. However, its preface, which dedicated the volume to the 'holy religious', indicated that its primary audience was Catholic clergy whose educational remit extended to imparting a sense of religious piety to Irish children through the medium of song and verse. Hymns such as 'The Sacred Heart of Jesus', 'The Nativity of our Lord' and 'The Most Holy Crown of Thorns' reinforced this cultural connection, and can be seen to form a manual of spiritual instruction through music. A different field of interest was folklore. The library's holdings contain a number of volumes which deal with Irish tales, mythology and storytelling such as Henri d'Arbois de Jubainville's *Le cycle mythologique irlandais et la mythologie celtique* (1884) and L. Tachet de Barneval's *Histoire légendaire de l'Irlande* (1856). These books advanced the view that Ireland held a unique historical heritage, integrating Celtic myths and legends into their narrative as quasi historical accounts. Their presence on the shelves of the Irish College library, further, indicates that an interest in the study of research into antiquity, as espoused by the Gaelic and Irish literary revivals respectively, had indeed percolated into the Irish College in Paris. Classical works, meanwhile, were well maintained in the collection. William Dodd's edited collection *The Beauties of Shakespeare: Regularly Selected from Each Play*, published in 1839, contained eloquent passages from the full catalogue of Shakespeare's staged works including *A Midsummer Night's Dream*, *Hamlet* and *Macbeth*. The careful selection of excerpts from Shakespeare's works demonstrates the importance attached to the aesthetic in composition. Other items relating to Shakespeare contained within the Irish College collection by 1890–91 included the eight volume set *The Plays of Shakespeare*.

Travel

Travel writing was a notable feature of the library catalogue in the late nineteenth century. This surge in popularity has been attributed to a number of intersecting politico-cultural factors including the end of the Napoleonic wars, the improvement in transport infrastructure, the growth of literacy, and the connectivity of information networks through structures such as the British Empire. A small number of the arranged titles constituted formal reports or personal narratives of Irish topography, population and antiquities. All, however, carried political baggage. As Glenn Hooper has commented, 'each travel narrative was a response to, or attempt to understand, quite specific political and economic circumstances, rather than a mere record of wanderings by various routes across the country'.[37]

A. Atkinson's *Ireland Exhibited to England in a Political and Moral Survey of her Population*, published in 1823 for example, offered a somewhat jaundiced commentary on Ireland in the early nineteenth century. Atkinson's argument

37 Glenn Hooper, *Travel Writing and Ireland, 1760–1860* (Basingstoke: Palgrave Macmillan, 2005), p. 3.

centred on a belief that Ireland's natural disposition towards political disorder could only be remedied through greater British state intervention and the religious unity of the Christian churches in Ireland. John Carr's *The Stranger in Ireland or a Tour in the Southern and Western Parts of that Country*, published in 1805, conversely, provided a more balanced portrayal of Irish society, from impressive reactions to the efficiency of Irish public bodies to a negative assessment of its infrastructure and communications. Samuel Lewis's two volume *A Topographical Dictionary of Ireland*, published in 1837 meanwhile, provides a heavily statistical analysis of Ireland's people and places. Given the annual influx of freshmen to the Irish College and the potential for summer sojourns to their home dioceses, it is unlikely that these works would have substantially informed students as to conditions in Ireland or impressed upon them the nature of the Irish mind. Travel writings on foreign countries, however, would appear to have had considerable appeal in this regard. The wanderlust of some within the Irish College, realised or imagined, was evident from a copy of *Harper's Handbook for Travellers in Europe and the East*, deposited on the library's shelves. The apparent fascination with international travel seems incongruous with the students' immediate commitments at the Irish College in Paris and the lengthy periods of isolation involved in studying for the priesthood. Yet perhaps in that very 'otherness, lay the attraction of books which documented experiences of international travel, foreign lands, and cultural exchanges.

Washington Irving's *Astoria: or Anecdotes of an Enterprise Beyond the Rocky Mountains*, was one such title. Published in 1836, Irving's account provided an insight into the experiences of those who worked for the great North-West Fur Trading Company in modern day Canada. This work, based on his diaries, the recollections of workers and the journals of fellow travellers, presents a graphic image of the exigencies of employment in the precarious Rocky Mountain wilds. As such it provided a striking reminder of the potential exposure of man to the extremes of the natural world and the need for protection from the unknown world beyond God's humanity.[38]

Another celebrated writer of such travelogues was Alphonse de Martine. His *Travels in the Holy Land or a Visit to the Scene of our Redeemer's Life*, published in 1837, exhibited the beautiful landscapes, excitable characters and alternative customs of the Middle East. He paid particular attention to the vitality of Christianity amid the welter of conflicting faiths in contemporary Palestine. This was a travel book with a subtle moralistic message. Indeed the religious undertones of these travel works formed part of a wider trope within the library's holdings: the essentiality of Christianity to

38 Washington Irving, *Astoria, or, Anecdotes of an Enterprise Beyond the Rocky Mountains* (London: Richard Bentley & Co., 1839).

the global civilising mission. This subject had been examined for the early modern period in the form of Patrick Moran's *Early Irish Missions: Fruits of Irish Piety in the British Church* (1877). However, a substantial collection of books held at the Irish College charted the expansion of the Catholic Church beyond Europe and into the eighteenth and nineteenth centuries. These included William Strickland's *Catholic missions in Southern India to 1865* (1865), Mary Elizabeth Herbert's *Abyssinia and its apostle* (1867), and Mary Cecilia Caddell's *A History of the Missions in Japan and Paraguay* (1862). Each of these books impressed upon the reader the difficulties of establishing and maintaining the Catholic faith in unchartered and often hostile territory. Central to these works, nevertheless, was the enduring spiritual conviction of those missionaries who travelled the world to convert native populations to the word of God. The presence of the illustrated volume, *Pictures of Missionary Life in the Nineteenth Century: the Western World, on the Shelves of the College Library* (1858), meanwhile, provided a vivid visual representation of Catholicism as international experience.

The Weekly Library

Unlike the college's daily schedule of classes, ceremonies and conferences, the library was only opened on every second or third day, usually in the evening. Its regulations explicitly limited students to borrowing one book at a time while each volume loaned had to be retained by that member for at least three days. Books could be kept for a maximum of two weeks.[39] The significance of these regulations lay in their further imposition by the college authorities of reading practices and rhythms on students. Three runs of book borrowing are preserved in the college archive: 20 October–5 November 1885, 14 October–18 November 1886 and 16 January–2 April 1888. Although these records do not document when volumes were returned, the frequency of members' borrowing strongly suggests the prevalence of prolonged reading cycles. The majority of the class of 1888 spent up to a week with a single book. Michael Brennan, from the diocese of Elphin for example, borrowed *The Confederate Chieftains: A Tale of the Irish Rebellion of 1641* for the maximum of five days before taking out a copy of C.M. Aladel's *The Miraculous Medal: Its Origin, History, Circulation*. Similarly, John Prendergast, a student from the diocese of Tuam, consulted the Catholic monthly *Dublin Review* for up to five days before borrowing *The Edited Speeches of Daniel O'Connell*. The typical

39 'Catalogue manuscrit des livres appartenant à l'Historical Society of the Irish College Paris, 1859–1891. Contient également les "rules of the students [*sic*] library"' (CCI Archive, Documentation: histoire, E12.a1).

reading time allocated to these volumes suggested a reading experience that encouraged an intensive focus on individual texts.

Who joined the Irish College Library? The document series referred to above contain a number of membership lists for the period under review, although these are largely undated and, at times, provide only the surnames of those involved. However, through a systematic cross-referencing of data with other archive collections, notably the college registers, student lists and annual reports, it is possible to identify who used the library, when they used the library and to suggest how they used the library.

What is most striking about the extant membership records is the limited number of students who became members of the library. This idea is reinforced by a comparison of library membership figures with records of student enrolment for specific years. October 1885: 36 students (40 per cent of the population). October 1886: 21 students (24 per cent of the population). October 1887: 40 students (44 per cent of the population). October 1889: 18 students (20 per cent of the population). The second set of data relates to the latter half of the 1890s but further evidences the declining interest in the library among the students. October 1896: 15 students (27 per cent of the population). October 1897: 17 students (28 per cent of the population). 1899: 8 students (12 per cent of the population). 1900: 12 students (17 per cent of the population).

How can one account for such low investment in the Irish College Library? It might be argued that the decrease in membership corresponded with a fall in the overall student population in the late nineteenth century. In April 1892, the Bureau Gratuit imposed a limit of 50 free bourse (scholarship) students at the Irish College per year in order to pay off the institution's heavy debt.[40] In effect no new boursiers could be admitted for at least two years. This had a significant impact on student numbers at the College, the student population almost halving from 88 in 1889–90 to 46 in 1894–95. The absence of new freshmen would evidently have an impact on the financial potential of the library. Indeed the largest percentage of members in any first quarter of the academic year was newly registered students. Between 1885 and 1900, new arrivals constituted between 48 per cent and 100 per cent of first-term members. However, the drop off in membership in the 1890s belied a deeper, long-standing problem. The library simply could not sustain the interest of students. A handful of second and third quarter membership lists can be isolated within the college archives, evidencing a sharp drop off in membership between September, January and April of the academic year. In January 1888, for example, only 20 students had paid subscriptions to the library. Of those who had become members three months earlier a mere 45 per cent remained.

40 'Annual reports, 1890–1917' (CCI Archive, Collège: administration, A2.b138).

By April, four students were still borrowing books. Similarly, in January 1898, seven students registered with the library, with only 35 per cent of members from October continuing their interest. 6 remained library users in April 1899. Writing concernedly to the Irish bishops that year, College rector Patrick Boyle explained the leakage as 'an inclination shown to avail of necessary visits to the city, to procure periodicals, and other literature, which, if not discouraged, would prove an obstacle to study'.[41] Reading from the shelves of the Old College library was primarily an autumn experience.

Membership of the Irish College library did not necessarily liberate the student. Reading items within its collections was restrained by its schedule, holdings, rules and the intensity with which one consumed a volume. The exploration of a text had rhythms which were highly subjective and could also depend on the type of item being read. It is also clear from the membership lists attached that the library was neither the educational nor the social focus of life at the Irish College. The library, therefore, did not necessarily transform the views of its residents, although it still maintained the power to influence the committed reader.

The Irish College library, as assembled between 1870 and 1900, was indeed a room with a view. However, that view was not uniquely Irish nor indeed uniquely nationalist in outlook. There was certainly ample print material with which to read Ireland. A number of these works were overtly nationalistic and a strong emphasis on the military past is noticeable. However, the more recent pieces available on Ireland tended to be less explicitly partisan or indeed political. Biography, collections of personal statements, and travel writings, all had political connotations but also contained more human narratives and ideas. The holdings of the Irish College library, Paris, during this period, suggest a much greater emphasis on educating students to be spiritually reflective members of the Catholic Church, politically engaged citizens, and public intellectuals, prepared to contribute to Irish society at the turn of the century.

41 Ibid.

7

'May God Bless You and All at Home': Mid-Nineteenth Century Irish Views on Italy through the Letters of Albert Delahoyde, 1860–1870

Florry O'Driscoll

Born in Dublin in 1841, and later educated at Clongowes Wood College in County Kildare, Albert Delahoyde was not yet 19 years of age when he volunteered to fight with the Papal Battalion of St Patrick in Italy in 1860. His story provides an interesting case study on increased literacy levels in nineteenth-century Ireland, told through the surviving correspondence of an Irish migrant and member of the diaspora. The letters of Delahoyde are particularly instructive about mid-nineteenth century Irish interactions with Italy, as they tell of the difficult relations between the Irish and the Italians, the level of Irish nationalism and patriotism among Irishmen abroad, and the influence of the Catholic faith amongst Irishmen in Italy at the time. Delahoyde's letters also showcase another effect of improved literacy in Ireland, as they reveal his ability with languages. It appears that he was already proficient in German and French when he left Ireland, and he later learned Italian and Spanish, while not neglecting Irish. Overall, the writings of Albert Delahoyde are an example of the practical effect of improved literacy in Ireland, as his correspondence reveals much about the links between writing, identity, and nationalism. This chapter begins by briefly relating the background to the arrival of the Irish soldiers in Italy in 1860, before recounting the short conflict that followed, as well as Delahoyde's service in the Papal Battalion and the Papal Zouaves. It then focuses on Delahoyde's letters, in order to ascertain what they tell us about him, the Irish soldiers in Italy, Irish-Italian relations in this period, and wider literacy in nineteenth-century Ireland.

The experience of the Papal Battalion of St Patrick in Italy was relatively neglected in historical scholarship until 2005. Thus, little is known on the thoughts and beliefs of the Irish soldiers of the Papal Battalion. Many of them were only in their late teens or early twenties when they arrived in Italy, and for the majority it was the first time not only outside of Ireland, but also outside the immediate area in which they had been born. Between 1929, when G.F.H. Berkeley published the most comprehensive account of Irish Papal soldiers – *The Irish Battalion in the Papal Army of 1860* – and 2005, the only significant general work on Ireland's contribution to Italian unification was Robert Dudley Edwards' edited collection *Ireland and the Italian Risorgimento* (1960).[1] Since 2005, there has been a growing, though still limited, amount of new scholarship. Charles A. Coulombe's *The Pope's Legion* (2008), Mary Jane Cryan's *The Irish and English in Italy's Risorgimento* (2011), and journal articles by Anne O'Connor, Jennifer O'Brien, and Robert Doyle, have all advanced our knowledge on this topic.[2] Other works such as Ian Kenneally's *Courage and Conflict* (2010) and book chapters by Ciarán O'Carroll have also focused on the Papal Battalion.[3] This chapter follows in the footsteps of these recent works, using the writings and language skills of an ordinary Irishman who opposed the quest for Italian unification to assess the wider significance of the Irish experience in Italy in an interesting example of transnational history.

Italy at mid-nineteenth century was a patchwork of states and territories, one of which was the Papal States. In Ireland, the notion that the Papal States and the Pope were surrounded by enemies in Italy had been growing since the late 1840s. There was some truth in this assertion, and throughout the 1850s the rift between Italian nationalism and the Catholic Church continued to deepen. By early summer 1860, the Kingdom of Piedmont-Sardinia, under Prime Minister Count Camillo Cavour, had annexed the territories of Tuscany, Parma, Modena and Romagna, thereby unifying a

1 G.F.H. Berkeley, *The Irish Battalion in the Papal Army of 1860* (Dublin & Cork: Talbot Press, 1929); R. Dudley Edwards (ed.), *Ireland and the Italian Risorgimento: Three Lectures* (Dublin: Italian Institute, 1960).

2 Charles A. Coulombe, *The Pope's Legion: The Multinational Fighting Force that Defended the Vatican* (New York: Palgrave Macmillan, 2008); Mary Jane Cryan, *The Irish and English in Italy's Risorgimento* (Viterbo: Archeoares, 2011); Anne O'Connor, 'Triumphant Failure: The Return of the Irish Papal Brigade', *Journal of the Cork Historical and Archaeological Society* 114 (2009): 39–50; Jennifer O'Brien, 'Irish Public Opinion and the Risorgimento, 1859–60', *Irish Historical Studies* 34.135 (2005): 289–305; Robert Doyle, 'The Pope's Irish Battalion, 1860', *History Ireland* 18.5 (2010): 26–29.

3 Ian Kenneally, *Courage and Conflict: Forgotten Stories of the Irish at War* (Cork: Cork University Press, 2009); Ciarán O' Carroll, 'The Papal Brigade of Saint Patrick', in Dáire Keogh and Albert McDonnell (eds), *The Irish College, Rome and its World* (Dublin: Four Courts Press, 2008), pp. 167–87; Ciarán O' Carroll, 'The Irish Papal Brigade: Origins, Objectives and Fortunes', in Colin Barr, Michele Finelli and Anne O'Connor (eds), *Nation/Nazione: Irish Nationalism and the Italian Risorgimento* (Dublin: UCD Press, 2013), pp. 73–95.

significant portion of northern and central Italy. As Pope Pius IX's territory now bordered the enlarged Kingdom of Piedmont-Sardinia, the Pope feared that the Papal States and possibly Rome itself would be next to be attacked. Pius IX believed that it was a matter of conscience to preserve intact the Papal States, and hand them on to his successor. To protect what he saw as his divinely ordained right, the Pope sent out a call for help to many of the Catholic nations in Europe in January 1860. Priests in countries such as France, Belgium, Spain and Austria preached the Pope's request from the pulpits, encouraging young men to travel to Italy to contribute to the military defence of their spiritual leader.[4]

To this end, in late 1859 and early 1860, the Catholic Church in Ireland launched a campaign, called 'The Last Crusade' by some, to assist Pope Pius IX in his fight against the forces working to unite the Italian peninsula. This campaign developed in three distinct stages. Firstly, the Catholic Church attempted to make Irish Catholics aware of the Pope's situation. The Catholic hierarchies did this by organising large gatherings at which petitions were signed in favour of Pius IX and his rule over the Papal States, and also by emphasising the fact that, in the eyes of the Irish Catholic Church, the Pope's spiritual authority depended on his temporal sovereignty. In other words, the Papacy needed to be politically independent to ensure its spiritual independence. Secondly, the Irish bishops began a fundraising effort that eventually produced the impressive sum of £80,000, most of it channelled to the Vatican via the Pontifical Irish College in Rome.[5] The final phase in this campaign involved raising an army, which included the individual at the centre of this story: Albert Delahoyde.

Thus, many of the local Irish clergy throughout the country became unofficial recruiting officers, preaching a message about the need for young Irish Catholic men to volunteer to support the Papacy in the upcoming struggle. A wave of patriotic articles, pamphlets and poems also appeared in the national press, which could now be read by more potential soldiers. From early 1860 on, there were many young men utilising their increased literacy and language skills in writing from Ireland offering their support to Tobias Kirby, rector of the Irish College in Rome.[6] Kirby and the Irish College played a major role in coordinating the Papal Battalion throughout its existence, corresponding with Irishmen in Ireland as they volunteered to serve, channelling the money

4 Cryan, *The Irish and English in Italy's Risorgimento*, pp. 18–35; O'Carroll, 'The Irish Papal Brigade', pp. 73–95.

5 On a similar topic, see Darragh Gannon, 'Room with a View: Reading Ireland in the Irish College Old Library, Paris *c*.1870–1900', this book, chapter 6.

6 Michael Olden, 'Tobias Kirby (1804–1895): The Man Who Kept the Papers', in Dáire Keogh and Albert McDonnell (eds), *The Irish College, Rome and its World* (Dublin: Four Courts Press, 2008), pp. 131–48.

raised at home to the men in Italy, and generally serving as the focus of Irish support for the Pope. In the end, about 1,300 Irishmen were recruited for the Papal Army, and formed a unit known as the Papal Battalion of St Patrick. Many more volunteered, but the Papal authorities were unwilling to accept more recruits than they believed they could equip and train in time. The men, travelling in groups of 20 or 30, began to arrive in Rome from May 1860. On reaching Italy, they officially enlisted in the Papal Battalion, as part of the wider Papal Army, under the overall command of General Louis Christophe de Lamoricière.[7]

By July 1860, meanwhile, Italian nationalist Giuseppe Garibaldi and his 'Thousand' had succeeded in taking control of the island of Sicily.[8] Crossing over to mainland Italy, Garibaldi and his men fought their way up the peninsula, overwhelming the Kingdom of the Two Sicilies by September.[9] These actions added to Garibaldi's already immense popularity in both Britain and the USA, but left him despised in Ireland, as 'Garibaldi aimed to secure the liberation of the south and the unification of Italy' with the ultimate aim of liberating Rome from the Pope.[10] Garibaldi declared his intention to march on Rome, which was defended by French soldiers, and therefore this was an act that could have triggered a wider European war. On 11 September, troops of the Kingdom of Piedmont-Sardinia invaded the Papal States to prevent Garibaldi's attack on the Pope's territories. The Piedmontese also aimed to take control of the south of Italy, thereby uniting the peninsula.[11]

The Papal Army volunteers' first engagement with the Piedmontese enemy occurred on 13 September 1860 at Perugia. The Papal Army, including about 150 Irishmen under the command of Captain James Blackney, was vastly outnumbered, since the Piedmontese comprised around 12,000 men. Some of the city's residents opened one of the gates to admit the Piedmontese soldiers, thereby revealing their support for Italian unification, in contrast with the Irish soldiers' belief that they would be welcomed as heroes by the citizens of the Papal States. According to Patrick Keyes O'Clery, the Irish soldiers, 'true to their national character ... did what they could to secure

7 O'Carroll, 'The Papal Brigade of Saint Patrick'.

8 Garibaldi's group of volunteers was known as the Expedition of the Thousand.

9 For more on these events, see especially Lucy Riall, *Garibaldi: Invention of a Hero* (New Haven, CT: Yale University Press, 2007), pp. 207–24; Lucy Riall, 'Garibaldi and the South', in John A. Davis (ed.), *Italy in the Nineteenth Century 1796–1900* (Oxford: Oxford University Press, 2000), pp. 132–53.

10 Marcella Pellegrino Sutcliffe, 'British Red Shirts: A History of the Garibaldi Volunteers (1860)', in Nir Arielli and Bruce Collins (eds), *Transnational Soldiers: Foreign Military Enlistment in the Modern Era* (Basingstoke: Palgrave, 2013), pp. 202–18.

11 Lucy Riall, *Risorgimento: The History of Italy from Napoleon to Nation State* (Basingstoke: Palgrave, 2009), pp. 32–36; Riall, *Garibaldi*, pp. 207–268; Riall, 'Garibaldi and the South', pp. 132–53.

a continuance of the defence, but it was in vain. Sixteen of them cut their way out, rather than surrender'.[12] The rest of the garrison was forced to capitulate, and the Papal troops were taken prisoner. Four days later, the Papal Army, including 350 Irishmen under Major Myles O'Reilly, fought against Piedmontese troops at Spoleto.[13] The soldiers withstood repeated attacks for 14 hours, but were eventually forced to surrender. The most important engagement of this brief conflict took place at Castelfidardo on 18 September. The Papal Army attempted to reach its base at Ancona, but was intercepted and subsequently defeated by Piedmontese troops under the command of General Enrico Cialdini.[14] After a brief siege of Ancona, the entire Papal Army surrendered. Subsequently, the Piedmontese marched south, avoiding Rome and its French contingent, and Garibaldi yielded the territories he had conquered to King Victor Emanuel II in October at Teano, near Naples.[15] At this point, the Italian peninsula was unified, with the exception of Rome and the province of Venetia, both of which became incorporated eventually into the Italian kingdom at a later stage.

As regards the Irish soldiers, the majority of them were marched to Genoa and held there as prisoners. On 20 October, a Papal owned ship, the *Byzantine*, began to transfer the men from Genoa to Marseilles. From here, they made their way to Paris and on to Le Havre, where eventually a ship took them back to Ireland. Most of the men of the Papal Battalion eventually arrived back through Queenstown in Cork (modern day Cobh). On their return, they received a hero's welcome. Alexander Martin Sullivan of the *Nation* felt that 'had those men been victors on a hundred fields they could not have been welcomed with more flattering demonstrations'.[16] Trains took the men from Cork City to their various places of origin in Ireland. At every stop along the way, large groups of people turned out to see them. In the eyes of George Berkeley 'they had made sacrifices not only for the Papal cause, but also for the cause of nationality in Ireland'.[17]

Albert Delahoyde however, was not amongst them. Delahoyde had arrived on the Italian mainland in the early summer of 1860. On his way to Italy, he spent some time in Belgium, putting his linguistic skills to good use as an interpreter for many of the recruits gathering there from the various Catholic countries. Delahoyde was garrisoned in Ancona throughout the brief conflict between the Papal Army and the Kingdom of Piedmont-Sardinia, spending

12 Patrick Keyes O'Clery, *The Making of Italy* (London, 1892), p. 192.
13 Cyril P. Crean, 'The Irish Battalion of St Patrick at the Defence of Spoleto, September 1860', *The Irish Sword*, Vol. 4 (1959–1960), pp. 52–60, 99–107.
14 Doyle, 'The Pope's Irish Battalion, 1860', pp. 26–29.
15 Riall, *Garibaldi*, pp. 207–24.
16 A.M. Sullivan, *New Ireland* (New York, 1878), p. 285.
17 Berkeley, *The Irish Battalion in the Papal Army of 1860*, p. 220.

his nineteenth birthday under heavy fire in his first experience of battle. After the fall of Ancona, Delahoyde was captured with his comrades and later transferred from Genoa to Marseilles in anticipation of a return to Ireland. He chose, however, to return to Rome for the foreseeable future, along with approximately 40 other Irish soldiers.

Delahoyde continued his military career in the service of the Papacy in Italy, joining the newly formed Papal Zouaves, and eventually becoming a Second Lieutenant in October 1862. The Zouaves had evolved from the Papal Army as part of the ongoing defence of the remnants of the Papal States. Delahoyde became a commissioned officer in 1864 and, as a result, he was able to witness some of the later events in Italian unification. He fought at the Battle of Mentana in November 1867, as part of the victorious Franco-Papal forces, which included roughly 200 new volunteers from Ireland, against Italian volunteers under Giuseppe Garibaldi who made a new attempt to take Rome. At this battle, Delahoyde was slightly wounded and was later made a Captain in acknowledgement of his bravery. Delahoyde was also one of the leading individuals involved in the defence of the Porta Pia gate in Rome in 1870, commanding a company in the battle where the Italian Army finally took full possession of the city, signalling the completion of Italian unification.[18]

With his literate nature and command of language, Delahoyde was a prolific letter writer during his ten years in Italy, and a number of his letters have survived.[19] I now turn to these letters in order to assess what they tell us about the Papal Battalion and the Papal Zouaves, the contacts between Ireland and Italy at mid-nineteenth century, the Irish soldiers' sense of Irish Catholic nationalism, and Delahoyde's linguistic ability. They are an excellent primary source, being liberally sprinkled with quotes in foreign languages, a longing for Ireland, religious references, and interesting observations about the Italians. Therefore, they are extremely illuminating on the connections between writing, identity, and nation at mid-nineteenth century. Delahoyde's letters also served a more political purpose, however. In 1911, six years after Albert's death, his brother John wrote to historian George Berkeley, informing him that Albert had told him that he had intended his letters as a record of events in order to 'confound the Garibaldian liars'. In other words, Delahoyde wished to use his high level of literacy and education to counteract what he saw as an Italian, and to a certain extent British, propaganda, which had attempted to discredit the Irishmen who fought in Italy.[20] Using the power of

18 'Delahoyde, Albert (1841–1905)', *Ainm.ie*, http://www.ainm.ie/; Berkeley, *The Irish Battalion in the Papal Army of 1860*.

19 On a similar topic, see this book, Gannon, 'Room with a View'.

20 Danilo Raponi, *Religion and Politics in the Risorgimento: Britain and the New Italy, 1861–1875* (Basingstoke: Palgrave, 2014).

his language, Delahoyde acted, in essence, as a public relations officer for the Irish cause in Italy.

One of the most interesting aspects of Delahoyde's letters is how they showcase his ability with languages. Delahoyde was not only a highly literate man in English, but even at the tender age of eighteen, he was already multilingual. In his first letter to his mother on 14 July 1860, he claimed to speak both German and French, the former a little more fluently.[21] He also wasted no time in acquiring a knowledge of the Italian language on arrival at his ultimate destination. In July 1860, he spoke of the fact that 'I have had no time to learn Italian but my ear is becoming familiarised'. Only a couple of months later, on 12 September 1860, he wrote to a friend named Ned, that 'the time for study is small; I'm afraid t'will be some time till I get a command of it'. At this point, Delahoyde had already started the habit of adding random Italian phrases to his letters, and this became more common as the decade progressed.[22] Throughout the 1860s, he received letters in other languages, not just in Italian, but also in Spanish and French. Delahoyde even communicated entirely in Spanish with the family of a colleague in the Papal Zouaves during the 1860s, and it was clear from his letters that he had spent time with the man's family in Spain. He also made mention of his native Irish language; he was the treasurer of an Irish language class that Irish nationalist John Devoy attended on Abbey Street in Dublin from 1858 on, and the latter claimed that Delahoyde spoke Irish quite well.[23] In later life, Delahoyde took an even keener interest in the Irish cultural revival of the late nineteenth century. When he moved to England in the 1870s, he joined the London Gaelic League and continued to study the language.

Therefore, it is fair to say that Delahoyde used his literacy in English to practical effect from a young age in order to facilitate his learning of other languages that would help him through his military career and later life. His proficiency allowed him to communicate effectively in German, French, Spanish and Italian, both in writing and verbally. In his linguistic ability, however, Delahoyde seemed to have been more the exception than the rule, as, apart from a few individuals, the majority of the Irishmen who travelled to Italy in the summer of 1860 could only speak English or Irish. Delahoyde was aware of the problems caused in the Papal Army by the fact that the different national groups could not communicate with each other, or at least struggled to do so. There were at least nine nationalities involved in the Papal

21 Albert Delahoyde to his mother, Ancona, 14 July 1860, '24 Letters from Albert De La Hoyde 1860–70', National Library of Ireland (NLI), MS13280.

22 Delahoyde to Ned, Ancona, 12 September 1860, '24 Letters', NLI MS13280.

23 John Devoy, *Recollections of an Irish Rebel: A Personal Narrative* (New York: Chase D. Young, 1929).

Army, including Belgians, French, Austrians, Swiss, Poles and Italians. For example, Delahoyde told his mother that 'with the Swiss we agree well but the men cannot talk the language'.[24] This exacerbated the difficulties that the Irish had in understanding the other ethnicities with which they came in contact. The ordinary citizens of the Papal States had similar issues understanding the Irish in their midst. There are examples in the letters of Delahoyde and others of the puzzlement of Papal State residents both at the Irish decision to join their enemy the Pope, and also, in general, at Irish culture and behaviour. These differences and misunderstandings were to lead to a mutual antagonism.

Delahoyde's education does not appear to have imbued him with much tolerance, as his attitude towards the people with whom he came in contact seems to have been quite prejudiced, even taking into account nineteenth-century racial prejudice. In many of his letters, Delahoyde compared Ireland and the Irish people with Italy and the Italians he encountered, both citizens of the Papal States and Piedmontese soldiers. An intense dislike of the Italians who lived in the Papal States shows through from one of his first letters home. Delahoyde wrote that 'the people are dirty looking and lazy, the lower class cheat you if they can, indeed I think that there is a great want of principle amongst the Italians comparatively with other countries, and Ireland in particular'.[25] He stated that he did not find the local women attractive, and instead missed the complexion of Irish girls. Writing in September 1860, Delahoyde stated further that 'our native Coleens they have genuine hearts but here there seems to exist a treachorous undercurrent'.[26] Another Dubliner in the Papal Battalion, Richard A. O'Carroll, propagated similar sentiments, claiming that

> you may imagine Rome is a grand place but I can tell you Ireland is far in preference to it. There is not a town I have ever seen yet equal to Ireland. The only thing I see is that this is a fine country for growing fruit, clear sky, very warm, and magnificent chapels ... as for the people they are of a slovenly, lazy race, scarcely ever work.[27]

Delahoyde and O'Carroll's attitudes were partly caused by the effects of living in a state of conflict, and by bitterness towards the perceived enemies of the Pope. Delahoyde described his regiment having rotten fruit thrown at them by the locals and claimed that 'we are anything but liked by the lower class'.[28]

24 Delahoyde to his mother, Ancona, 24 July 1860, '24 Letters', NLI MS13280.
25 Delahoyde to his mother, Ancona, 14 July 1860, '24 Letters', NLI MS13280.
26 Delahoyde to Ned, Ancona, 12 September 1860, '24 Letters', NLI MS13280.
27 Richard A. O'Carroll to his mother, Rome, 27 June 1860, 'Letters to his Mother [in Francis Street, Dublin] from Richard A. O'Carroll', NLI MS21522.
28 Delahoyde to his mother, Ancona, 24 July 1860, '24 Letters', NLI MS13280.

For Delahoyde and O'Carroll, as indeed for other young Irishmen of the Papal Battalion, the unwelcoming reception that they received in the Papal States seems to have come as a shock. This was apparently exacerbated by the fact that it was the Italian people of the Papal States who expressed this belligerence. In the eyes of Delahoyde and many other Irish soldiers, they had come to protect these people from the invading Piedmontese, but the citizens of the Papal States felt differently.

The letters of Delahoyde and his fellow soldiers give us an idea of the links between identity and nation in the minds of some in the Irish diaspora of the middle of the nineteenth century. The mutual contempt between the Irish and the Italians of the Papal States highlights that soldiers such as Delahoyde identified themselves in opposition to a foreign 'Other', in this case the Italians. They eulogised Ireland and the Irish as good and pure, whilst they gave the enemy various negative attributes. Delahoyde's letters are evidence of the lack of mutual understanding and strained relations between the Italians and the Irish in this period, not only in the Papal Battalion and the Papal Zouaves, but also in the wider world. Clearly, the cultural differences between the Irish and the citizens of the Papal States, and by extension between the Irish and the Italians, were exacerbated by the bitterness of a military campaign. Parallel to this antipathy arose also a growing sense of Irish patriotism and national pride, another topic on which Delahoyde's letters are informative.

Delahoyde's writings are revealing in regard to mid-nineteenth-century Irish attitudes to patriotism and nationalism, as he wrote proudly on numerous occasions about the Irish soldiers who served in Italy. In July 1860, he claimed that 'when properly organised ... I hope we will show, if necessary to Garibaldi and Co., that his chasseurs are no match for Erin's hardy sinews'.[29] Delahoyde later stated that the Irish soldiers received praise for their performance in the battle at Perugia. In a letter written in September 1860, and published in the nationalist newspaper the *Nation* the following month, Delahoyde told that 'the General regrets extremely the want of Irishmen, he was astonished at their conduct yesterday ... he has even said he'd give all his Swiss and natives for 5,000 Irish'.[30] Two years after the end of the brief conflict, writing to his brother Joe from Rome in January 1862, Delahoyde made the claim that 'the King of Naples I believe is resolved to have Irish troops if ever he gets his states again'.[31] Delahoyde's letters show that he was proud of his fellow Irishmen in the Papal Army and Papal Zouaves, and especially of the positive image that they bestowed upon the country.

29 Delahoyde to his mother, Ancona, 14 July 1860, '24 Letters', NLI MS13280.

30 Delahoyde to his mother, Ancona, 19 September 1860, '24 Letters', NLI MS13280.

31 Delahoyde to his brother Joe, Rome, 11 January 1862, 'Letters of a Papal Zouave', NLI MS13280/2.

It is clear from Albert Delahoyde's writings that he believed that he represented Ireland abroad. Participation in the movement against Italian national unification for him, as for many Irish soldiers, fostered Irish national pride, as it allowed the establishment of a de facto, though limited, Irish army. The events of the 1860s were an expression of this national sentiment and identity, not just for the Irish soldiers who fought in Italy, but also for many of the Irish people at home. This showed in the letters of Delahoyde through his use of language, his expressions of patriotism and pride in his fellow soldiers, but most of all in his Catholic faith. Time and again, he wrote of his strong religious beliefs and his willingness to lay down his life for the Pope. These strong religious beliefs were shared not only by a large number of Delahoyde's fellow Irish soldiers, but also by those in Ireland who had supported the endeavour from the outset.

Of all the topics discussed in the letters of the men of the Papal Battalion, by far the most prevalent was religion. Delahoyde's writings provided ample proof of his strong Catholic faith. They were littered with religious references, and he spoke often of praying for himself and other members of his family. In a letter written to his mother from Ancona, he enclosed a set of rosary beads, which he had used himself. He also informed her that he had received, from an unknown source, 'a coral rosary blessed by the Holy Father, with a cross having attached a plenary indulgence if kissed at the hour of death'.[32] Delahoyde regularly attended Mass during his time in Rome, on one occasion, in 1861, to commemorate the first anniversary of the battle of Castelfidardo. Writing to his brother Joe from Rome, in January 1862, Delahoyde told him that 'I will try for the piece of the true cross and I am almost certain of getting it'.[33] As there was no further mention of this relic in his letters, however, we must conclude that he was unsuccessful in his quest.

Delahoyde's tone remained religious throughout the 1860s, but became increasingly more fatalistic as the decade progressed. In 1860, he stated that he was fearful for his safety, 'however God's will be done ... may God bless you and all at home'.[34] His tone unsurprisingly became more depressed as the battles continued, and, writing again to his mother in September 1860, he stated that 'I fear few of us will live to tell the tale'.[35] In a document that George Berkeley named the Mentana Letter, Delahoyde wrote again to his mother, on 8 November 1867. He described the scene in a church in Rome which had been ravaged by the Italian Army – 'everything plundered, the altar

32 Delahoyde to his mother, Ancona, 24 July 1860, '24 Letters', NLI MS13280.
33 Delahoyde to his brother Joe, Rome, 11 January 1862, 'Letters of a Papal Zouave', NLI MS13280/2.
34 Delahoyde to Ned, Ancona, 12 September 1860, '24 Letters', NLI MS13280.
35 Delahoyde to his mother, Ancona, 19 September 1860, '24 Letters', NLI MS13280.

furniture, crucifixes too, smashed and burned, a scene which brought tears to all our eyes … God send us happier times for indeed his hand has been heavy on us'.[36] Later, writing to his sister Mary from Monte Rotondo in 1868, he stated simply that 'Death is busy everywhere'.[37] Before the final battle for Rome in 1870, Delahoyde's tone became extremely fatalistic, and it appears that he felt he would not survive. Writing to his mother, he stated that

> I cannot say if Divine Providence will spare me in this my third campaign but I am quite resigned to accept death, if such be the Divine Will … even should I be called I shall be happier above than here, and God knows we have not much reason to regret this world which for us has not been one of pleasure.[38]

The positive and upbeat young man of 1860 had been replaced by a mature man, cognisant of his own mortality and sensing his impending doom after ten years of intermittent warfare.

Contemporaries of Delahoyde also exhibited a strong religious tone in their communications. Fellow Irish soldier Richard O'Carroll wrote of a scene in Spoleto where the local priest celebrated mass for the soldiers. He described a shrine 'and in it was a splendid figure of the Blessed Virgin interceding for all sinners to heaven, it is a splendid sight'. He visited only Catholic sites during his time in Rome, and proudly described seeing Pope Pius IX in person on a number of occasions. O'Carroll was confident that 'God will bless our undertaking with success'.[39] Aloysius Howlin, who fought at Perugia, stated that 'we had tried as well as we could to defend the rights of the Church, in one word we had fought for the Pope and for Catholic Ireland, that was enough'.[40] In a letter reprinted in the *Nation* in October 1860, another Irish soldier, Patrick Clooney, claimed that 'by the help of God all we have gone through for Pius the Ninth will yet be told you'.[41] Writing about the Papal Battalion over half a century later, another veteran, Michael Smith, was very defensive of the cause he had fought for. In a letter to historian George Berkeley, he stated

36 Delahoyde to his mother, Rome, 08 November 1867, 'Letters of a Papal Zouave', NLI MS13280/1.

37 Delahoyde to his sister Mary, Monte Rotondo, 14 February 1868, 'Letters of a Papal Zouave', NLI MS13280/1.

38 Delahoyde to his mother, Rome, 12 September 1870, '24 Letters', NLI MS13280.

39 Richard O'Carroll to his mother, Rome, 27 June 1860, 'Letters to his Mother', NLI MS21522.

40 Aloysius Howlin, 'Narrative of Brother Aloysius Howlin', NLI MS13282.

41 Patrick F. Clooney, 'Letters, Photographs, Notes and Drafts, Being Materials for G.F. Berkeley's Studies of the Irish Brigade in the Papal Service, 1860', NLI MSS13280–13287.

that 'I regret to learn at this late date that any reflection should be cast on any of the Papal Brigade who fought for God and right ... I was fighting to defend my faith and to uphold the temporal power of Pope Pius IX'. He described the Papal Battalion as 'that noble band of men who fought for their religion and expected no recompense for their services on this side of the grave'.[42] Other writings by men of the Papal Battalion expressed similar sentiments.

Clearly, Irish Catholic identity was one of the main reasons why Irishmen such as Albert Delahoyde travelled to Italy in 1860 to join the Papal Battalion. It was also an important reason why a number of Irish soldiers, including Delahoyde, subsequently spent many years in the service of Pope Pius IX as part of the Papal Zouaves. Yet, this was not the only reason. Faith did not rule out other motivations for enlisting. The aid given by the same Pope to the starving Irish during the Great Famine of the 1840s left many of them grateful and feeling that they owed him their lives. The fact that the Irish had a long and proud tradition of fighting on foreign fields was another reason for volunteering. Anger towards Britain also played its part, exacerbated by anti-Catholicism and anti-Papal sentiments in the British press, along with the British support for Garibaldi.[43] It is possible that Delahoyde included the British in his list of 'Garibaldian liars' to be combatted through his writings. Some British newspapers, such as *The Times,* described the soldiers in the Papal Army as gullible and naïve, often celebrated the defeats of the Papacy, and even claimed that the Irish were cowards who had readily surrendered. In fact, the British, eager to weaken the Catholic powers of France and Austria, unofficially backed the movement for Italian unification. They appeared neutral, but in reality supported Garibaldi's invasion of Sicily and southern Italy with their navy.[44]

Catholicism, though, was certainly the most important factor for many of the Irishmen who joined the Papal Battalion, and later the Papal Zouaves. Even though the opponents of the Irish during the brief conflict in Italy were also Catholics, however, this fact did not cause the Irishmen to doubt the legitimacy of their endeavour, and neither did this lead Irish people in Ireland to support fellow Catholics in the Kingdom of Piedmont-Sardinia or in the Papal States who wished to be part of a united Italy. It is clear from the widespread show of support at home, including the raising of £80,000 less than a decade after the Famine had ended, that Irish Catholics were concentrated almost exclusively on helping Rome and the Papacy. Yet, whilst this was

42 Michael Smith to F.D. Hackett, Brooklyn, 1912, 'Letters, Photographs, Notes and Drafts', NLI MSS13280–13287.

43 Raponi, *Religion and Politics in the Risorgimento.*

44 Manuel Borutta, 'Anti-Catholicism and the Culture War in Risorgimento Italy', in Lucy Riall and Silvana Patriarca (eds), *The Risorgimento Revisited: Nationalism and Culture in Nineteenth-Century Italy* (Basingstoke: Palgrave, 2012), pp. 191–213.

predominantly for a spiritual reason, there was also a political motive. This was the protection of the Pope's temporal sovereignty, as many Irish soldiers believed that the earthly power of the Papacy was linked to its political independence.

The fall of Rome in 1870 was the final act in the long and complicated process of Italian unification and it also signalled the end of Delahoyde's soldiering career. Soon after, he left the Papal Zouaves and returned to Ireland. Delahoyde later received a position in the Indian mail service, with the duty of travelling with the post from London to Brindisi. At this time in the nineteenth century, mail for India would leave London by train, cross the channel by ferry, and then continue by train across France and Italy until it reached the heel of Italy. Here, at Brindisi, it would be loaded onto a ship bound for Bombay. Delahoyde travelled this route helping to guard the mail until his retirement. It appears that he married at some point and had at least two children, but again, as with many of the events of Delahoyde's life, details are sketchy. After retiring in 1890, he lived quietly in London until his death at the relatively young age of 63, in 1905.[45]

Ultimately, Albert Delahoyde was representative of the hundreds of young Irishmen who volunteered to fight in Italy. His youthful sense of adventure, his patriotism, his views on the Italians, and, most of all, his strong sense of Irish Catholic identity, were characteristics that many soldiers of the Papal Battalion of St Patrick and the Papal Zouaves possessed. Furthermore, even though individuals such as Delahoyde belonged to the middle class and therefore were relatively well off, their writings are representative of the increased levels of literacy among young Irish people. Many participants in the conflict in Italy in the 1860s left a revealing record of their experiences, and therefore show how the improved literacy in Ireland was beneficial for their sense of identity and nationality. Letters written by some of them found their way into the newspapers at home, and influenced others with their rhetoric. They also provided an Irish viewpoint on an endeavour that was often viewed with suspicion abroad. Furthermore, the soldiers who wrote these letters brought a new feeling of Irishness home with them after their experiences. Ultimately, serving in the Papal Battalion and the Papal Zouaves led to a strengthening of a sense of Irish identity for many of its veterans, and provided a rallying cry for an Irish Catholic nationalist sentiment, which would become increasingly important in the coming years. This shows clearly through the written record and the literary ability of Albert Delahoyde.

45 'Delahoyde, Albert', Ainm.ie.

8

'Good Translations' or 'Mental Dram-Drinking'? Translation and Literacy in Nineteenth-Century Ireland

Michèle Milan

'We have some experience in the art of rendering'

Nation, 13 October 1855

This chapter offers insights into the development of English-language literacy and publishing in nineteenth-century Ireland from the perspective of translation history. Making use of bibliographical surveys and nineteenth-century paratextual and metatextual materials, it touches upon the ideas of acceptability and selectivity in translation. Translation is considered not only in its relation to language learning, but above all in its relation to the political, religious and cultural currents of the age. In Ireland, translation contributed to the growth and dissemination of religious literature and children's fiction in English, as well as to the development of cultural nationalism.[1] This essay considers translation within the social and cultural dynamics that contribute to mass mobilisation and the formation of a national identity, such as education, literacy and print culture. Notwithstanding the importance of commercial practices

1 Michèle Milan, 'Found in Translation: Franco-Irish Translation Relationships in Nineteenth-Century Ireland'. PhD thesis. (Dublin City University, 2013), http://doras.dcu.ie/17753/, pp. 54–55. A monograph developing these ideas is forthcoming, *Translation in Nineteenth-Century Ireland: Cross-Cultural Encounters* (Oxford: Peter Lang, 2019). For translation from Irish and cultural nationalism in Ireland, see Maria Tymoczko, *Translation in a Postcolonial Context: Early Irish Literature in English Translation* (Manchester: Jerome Publishing, 1999).

and interests that underlie the circulation of reading materials in the period under study, this contribution is especially concerned with the ways in which the production, circulation and reception of translations interconnect with questions of education, empowerment and moral reforms. The *Nation*, organ of the Young Ireland movement, offers worthwhile examples for this study, and this chapter makes use of several articles published therein. With a rise in English-language translations, the perpetual debate on 'good' vs 'bad' books increasingly involved discussions on 'good' vs 'bad' translations. In particular, attitudes towards French literature, above all French fiction, were extremely ambivalent. Translation occupied a critical, ambiguous place in the contemporary debates. Throughout the nineteenth century, various agents of translation contributed to the dissemination of what they identified as 'good reading' – an undertaking which also involved a selection of 'good translations'. Translations are therefore situated within a set of discursive practices that encouraged reading and the acquisition of knowledge and moral virtue from books – but not from just any book. While the range of views and motivations expressed by translators, editors, publishers and journalists on the subject of translation at the time should certainly not be reduced to a mere binary, translation nevertheless lay at the heart of a debate on the morality of literature, and on 'good books' vs 'poison literature', a debate which proceeded unabated for decades, even centuries.

Translation and Literacy in Nineteenth-Century Ireland

Various scholars have noted that, owing to a number of socio-cultural and economic factors, the acquisition of reading and writing skills in English rather than in Irish is a key feature of the history of literacy in nineteenth-century Ireland.[2] There was undoubtedly a certain amount of translation into Irish. This includes, for example, Archbishop John MacHale's religious and literary renderings, various Irish-language verse translations published in the *Nation* from about 1858, as well as those translations which were spurred by the Gaelic Revival later in the century.[3] But the growth of literacy and publishing

2 These factors include the national education system, emigration, the Famine, and the lack of support from political and religious institutions. See Niall Ó Ciosáin, *Print and Popular Culture in Ireland, 1750–1850* (New York: St Martin's Press, 1997b), p. 6, p. 154; Michael Cronin, *Translating Ireland: Translation, Languages, Cultures* (Cork: Cork University Press, 1996), p. 106.

3 Philip O'Leary, *The Prose Literature of the Gaelic Revival, 1881–1921: Ideology and Innovation* (Pennsylvania: Pennsylvania State University Press, 1994); Ailbhe Ní Ghearbhuigh, *An Fhrainc Iathghlas? Tionchar na Fraince ar Athbheochan na Gaeilge, 1893–1922* (PhD dissertation, NUI Galway, 2013).

in Ireland was paralleled by an increasing availability of English-language translations. The landmark studies produced by Welch (1986), Cronin (1996) and Tymoczko (1999) offer in-depth historical analyses of translation from Irish into English. Cronin's work also provides ample documentation of the history of translation in Ireland from medieval to modern times, including language pairs other than Irish–English.[4]

If we consider translation on a large scale across texts and genres that include literary, religious, didactic, historical, political and scientific writings, the range of source materials and languages expanded during the period under study. French, German, and the classical languages remained the dominant source languages from a quantitative point of view.[5] Accordingly, the impact of continental languages and writings requires special attention in order to broaden our understanding of literacy and translation in Ireland beyond the Irish–English pair, thereby also widening our knowledge of the history of Irish print culture in English. While Irish newspapers and magazines such as the *Nation* and the *Dublin University Magazine* featured a variety of both original and reprinted translations, a number of Irish printers and publishers also contributed to the dissemination of translated works. Various actors thus played a role in the process: the translators themselves, as well as a number of other 'agents of translation' such as critics, editors, printers, publishers, booksellers and so forth.[6]

Irish individuals whose translations found their way into print in the nineteenth century came from a variety of religious and political backgrounds. For obvious socio-economic reasons, however, only a small percentage came from the poorer classes. They include various figures closely associated with the *Nation* newspaper, for example, Thomas Davis, John Blake Dillon, William Smith O'Brien, Mary Eva Kelly (later O'Doherty) and Jane Elgee (later Wilde) – Eva and Speranza of the *Nation* respectively – as well as numerous obscure and often anonymous figures.

4 Robert Welch, *A History of Verse Translation from the Irish 1789–1897* (Gerrards Cross: Colin Smythe, 1988); Cronin, *Translating Ireland*; Tymoczko, *Translation in a Postcolonial Context*.

5 To date, my surveys of nineteenth-century translations and translators from which this essay draws cover about 7,000 books – a figure which continues to expand on an ongoing basis – and numerous periodical publications. This study has not yet, however, fully incorporated biblical translation.

6 Together with the above-mentioned surveys, several hundred Irish translators have thus far been entered in a bio-bibliographical list which I have been compiling since 2009 for future publication. This also includes the systematic listing of printers, publishers, and periodicals involved in the circulation of translations. On the use of the term 'agents of translation', see John Milton and Paul Bandia (eds), *Agents of Translation* (Amsterdam: John Benjamins, 2009).

Translation was used and advocated as a means of learning languages. In 1891, in the Preface to his *Introduction to the Study of the Irish Language*, Rev. William Hayden advised students in the Irish language to use translation as a means of improving their skills; he recommended that the student

> should endeavour to understand each section by the help of the adjoined translation, and of the Glossary. When he has made himself familiar with the meaning of the section he should endeavour to put the English into Irish … If he does this several times he will find that his translation will gradually approximate to the text of the author, and the degree in which it does so will serve to gauge his own progress in the tongue he is learning.[7]

This passage clearly shows that the use of translation for linguistic and literary study was a recommended practice. Arguably, the consistent use of masculine pronouns might also be symptomatic, or at least reminds us of the gendered distinctions operative in Irish society at the time.[8] Although many Irish women engaged in translation throughout the nineteenth century, women were largely excluded from wider intellectual, scientific and political discussions. Gender patterns in translation are directly linked to women's restricted educational opportunities and, above all, to the male monopoly on most aspects of cultural, social and political authority throughout the period. Largely stemming from the belief that women's essential role was in the domestic sphere, as a wife and a mother, women's education was a subject to be treated separately, the notion of moral virtue being an important feature. It is also worth noting that between the translations from Irish by Charlotte Brooke in the late eighteenth century and those by Lady Gregory in the late nineteenth, there were in fact few published translations from Irish into English (and vice versa) under a woman's name throughout that period.

Translation from classical languages was still largely a male preserve. However, women, at least in the middle and upper classes, were acquainted with continental languages, particularly French and German.[9] When the *Weekly Irish Times* ran a series of translation exercises and translation competitions over several years in the 1890s and 1900s, women's participation was significant, and it was not uncommon to see the first prize go to a female

7 William Hayden, *An Introduction to the Study of the Irish Language, Based Upon the Preface to Donlevy's Catechism* (Dublin: Gill & Son, 1891), p. v.

8 And, needless to say, not limited to Irish society.

9 See also Michèle Milan, 'A Path to Perfection: Translations from French by Catholic Women Religious in Nineteenth-Century Ireland', in D. Raftery and E. Smith (eds), *Education, Identity and Women Religious, 1800–1950: Convents, Classrooms and Colleges* (London: Routledge, 2015), pp. 183–98.

translator.[10] In this regard, it is worth suggesting that despite the traditional view of translation as a subordinate, second-hand activity, translation could therefore offer possibilities as a tool of learning and empowerment for women.[11]

Translation, Literacy and Empowerment

> To impose another language on such a people is to send their history adrift among the accidents of translation – 'tis to tear their identity from all places – 'tis to substitute arbitrary signs for picturesque and suggestive names – … 'tis to corrupt their very organs, and abridge their power of expression.[12]

These words from Thomas Davis, one of the three founders of the *Nation* newspaper, and probably the best remembered Young Ireland figure, anticipated by nearly 150 years the writings of postcolonial thinkers Frantz Fanon, Eric Cheyfitz, and in translation studies, Maria Tymoczko. In other words, and by way of defining the effects of English imperialism on the Irish language, Davis hereby eloquently articulates a link between conquest and translation which these scholars would explore years later – that is, the idea of conquest and colonisation as a process of translation of a people.[13] Yet it must be admitted that the *Nation*, as most periodicals in Ireland at the time, addressed mainly an English-speaking readership.

Further, Davis left us with some telling examples of discourse in which translation is loosely or closely associated with questions of empowerment and knowledge acquisition. In regard to classical literature, Davis encourages the reading of translations from Greek and Latin because, he argues,

10 For example, Miss Louie Halpin from Foxrock, Co. Dublin was the prize winner in December 1907: 'French Prize Competition', *Weekly Irish Times*, 7 December 1907, p. 17.

11 For space constraints, this discussion is necessarily terse. On gender and translation, and for detailed discussions of women, translation and empowerment, see for example Sherry Simon, *Gender in Translation: Cultural Identity and The Politics of Transmission* (London: Routledge, 1996); Lorna Hardwick, 'Women, Translation and Empowerment', in Joan Bellamy, Anne Laurence and Gillian Perry (eds), *Women, Scholarship and Criticism: Gender and Knowledge, 1790–1900* (Manchester: Manchester University Press, 2000), pp. 180–203.

12 Thomas Davis, *Thomas Davis: Selections from his Prose and Poetry*. T.W. Rolleston (ed.) (Dublin: Talbot Press [1914]), p. 172.

13 Frantz Fanon, *The Wretched of the Earth*, trans. Constance Farrington (New York: Grove Press, 1963), p. 270; Eric Cheyfitz, *The Poetics of Imperialism: Translation and Colonization from the Tempest to Tarzan* (Oxford: Oxford University Press, 1991), p. 11; Tymoczko, *Translation in a Postcolonial Context*, p. 19, p. 62.

> it is preferable to read well a good translation, than to stumble through the original; and any fair man, considering how much of the spirit of classic lore can be translated, will confess the folly of expecting one man out of a hundred to learn so much from the originals as from good translations.[14]

A direct relationship is hereby established between learning and translation. While some believe that texts should be read in their original language, for Davis, 'good translations' – on the face of it, those which succeed in conveying the 'spirit' of classical literature – open up a world of classical and foreign literature to readers. Similarly in the *Irish Examiner,* the anonymous review of Henry Cary's English translation of Herodotus claims that the influence of classical literature on the mind is both *refining* and *liberalising,* and translations are *a boon* to those who cannot read in the original:

> So long as a knowledge of Greek and Latin, and a consequent acquaintance with the great poets, historians, orators and dramatists, is confined to a few, so long must good translations into a living language be of the utmost value and importance, in refining the mind, forming the taste, and enriching the memory.[15]

The *Nation* newspaper as a whole is known for its initial support to the Repeal campaign and for its unremitting deployment of cultural nationalist rhetoric. Much has already been said about the importance of the repeal reading rooms in regard to Young Ireland's educational programme.[16] While the *Nation* writers are noted for their own rousing ballads, they also largely drew their inspiration from foreign sources. For Davis and the *Nation,* translation can go a long way in bringing knowledge to the wider public, and knowledge will then help liberate the Irish people from foreign rule. The *Nation*'s outlook, we argue, may be regarded as a legacy of the Enlightenment's belief in the power of knowledge and education, and of its cosmopolitan ethos. But for Young Ireland, the effect sought is not only enlightening and educational, it may also be radicalising to some extent.

The following passage suggests that the empowering effect of translation is part of the *Nation*'s cultural-political programme. Indeed this article was prefixed to one of their very first translations, published in their second

14 Thomas Davis, Lecture delivered to the Historical Society, *Nation,* 22 January 1848.

15 *Irish Examiner,* 2 February 1848, p. 2. Cary's translation was published by one of the key English publishers, Bohn, in what purported to be a cheap edition.

16 Róisín Higgins, 'The *Nation* Reading Rooms', in James H. Murphy (ed.), *The Irish Book in English, 1800–1891* (Oxford: Oxford University Press, 2011), pp. 262–73; James Quinn, *Young Ireland and the Writing of Irish History* (Dublin: UCD Press, 2015).

number under the main heading of 'Continental Literature' – thereby setting the tone for many issues to come. The *Nation* thus provides a rationale for launching a series of translations from continental authors:

> The literature of the continent has been hitherto a sealed book to the Irish public … It may be stated as a general truth, that the more intimately acquainted the people of any country are with the sentiments, the actions, and the condition of their neighbours – the more aspiring, the more liberal, and the more intolerant of oppression, that people will be.[17]

A connection is here established between knowledge of continental literature and empowerment, which fits within the larger framework of using the printed word as a means towards political awakening and large-scale mobilisation. What is of interest to us in this example is that these words introduced the translation of a contemporary French text. No doubt the product of translation was intended as a tool for empowerment and resistance, and the article continued then by laying stress on patriotism. Translation and all its paratextual and metatextual devices were often used to foster Irish patriotic sentiment by importing or emphasising foreign patriotic ideas. Although this initial transnationalist perspective was not always followed to the letter,[18] it was nevertheless a crucial feature of the *Nation*'s agenda, and translation offered a natural medium through which transnationalism could be developed.

Furthermore, as various scholars have pointed out, it was not just the political, liberal or patriotic sentiment which was fostered in the *Nation*, but there was also a moral dimension to the Repeal movement, notably through its close connection with the Temperance movement.[19] The high ideals of nationality for which they laboured were closely linked with the idea of both a political and a moral regeneration; literature was seen as a means towards social and moral improvement. Translation could support that too, and emphasis on the educational and moral utility of reading certain types of literature was, moreover, not limited to the nationalist press.

For example, translation was a means of highlighting social and moral implications of events occurring abroad. Dublin-born Frances Sarah Cashel Hoey, who stands out as one of the most prolific nineteenth-century translators

17 *Nation*, 22 October 1842, p. 26. For a more detailed discussion of this article and the accompanying translation from the French of Lamennais, see my forthcoming, Milan, *Translation in Nineteenth-Century Ireland*.

18 The editor introduced one of Speranza's translation from German, 'The Holy War', with the counter-productive comment 'We have no idea how a crusade of the nations would work', *Nation*, 21 February 1846, p. 296.

19 Ó Ciosáin, *Print and Popular Culture in Ireland* (1997a), p. 185.

in any language pair, provides a 'view from the agent'.[20] Also known as a novelist and a journalist, she translated over 35 books from the French, either on her own or in collaboration.[21] While most of her writings were published in London, her *1794, a Tale of the Terror,* translated from the French of Charles d'Héricault, was published by Dublin-based M.H. Gill & Son in 1884. In the preface to her translation, Hoey describes the effects of the French Revolution upon the middle classes as 'the gravest moral effects', because the result was a generation of French people who 'grew up without a religion'.[22] Furthermore, she uses the infectious disease analogy to describe the wider context and social implications:

> Contagion of another kind had long been doing its work: the contagion of loss of faith, loss of respect, loss of modesty, the dislocation of family ties, the corruption of good manners by evil communications, the drying up of the sources of compassion, the unsexing of women.[23]

'These evils', she argues, 'had an important share in the moral deterioration of France'.[24] It seems that Hoey's translation – and, possibly, her paratextual commentary – made an impact on a number of critics in Ireland and Britain. A review of her work appeared in the *Irish Ecclesiastical Record,* stating that d'Héricault's account of 'the worst stage of the First Revolution' is 'written in a good spirit, and is safe and instructive reading'.[25] What is more, while reporting a couple of solecisms in the English version, the critic reckons that overall, 'the translation is really so good that it looks not at all like a translation'. With this additional dimension factored in, a good translation is not only one that should be morally commendable, if not even morally instructive, but it does not draw attention to itself – and ultimately hides its own nature.[26]

With translators working outside Ireland such as Hoey, the interplay of foreign and domestic production, and the circulation and reception of reading materials need to be seen within a wider, transnational framework. The wider,

20 See Daniel Simeoni, 'Translating and Studying Translation: The View from the Agent', *Meta: Journal des traducteurs / Meta: Translators' Journal* 40.3 (1995): 445–60.

21 See also Frances Clarke, 'Hoey, Frances Sarah (Mrs Cashel Hoey) Johnston', in James McGuire and James Quinn (eds), *Dictionary of Irish Biography* (Cambridge: Cambridge University Press, 2009), pp. 735–36.

22 Frances Cashel Hoey, 'Translator's Preface', *1794, a Tale of the Terror* (Dublin: M.H. Gill & Son, 1884), pp. vi–vii.

23 Hoey, 'Translator's Preface', viii.

24 Ibid.

25 *Irish Ecclesiastical Record,* Vol. 7, 1886, p. 767.

26 For a detailed discussion of translation and invisibility, see Lawrence Venuti, *The Translator's Invisibility: A History of Translation.* 2nd ed. (London and New York: Routledge, 2008).

complex socio-cultural configurations within which translation operates needs to be taken into account, and the role played by Irish publishers in the process, moreover, deserves some attention.

Some Key Irish Publishers of Translations in the Nineteenth Century

Throughout the nineteenth century, various Irish printers, publishers, booksellers and circulating libraries contributed to the dissemination of translated works. There are among them some well-known firms, such as Dublin-based Hodges, Smith & Co., who brought out scholarly and classical translations. A fair number of printers and booksellers in Dublin and in the main Irish towns around the country also played their role as 'agents of translation'. Furthermore, while the lines between nineteenth-century publishing, printing and bookselling are often blurred, there were occasional occurrences of what I may venture to call 'crossover' activity between these business occupations and the task of translating or editing translations. Early in the century, Dublin-based printer/publisher/bookseller Richard Cross stepped into this crossover territory when he ventured to edit an already existent translation before bringing it out. With much integrity towards the readers, Cross wrote a preface to justify his approach, arguing that the original, anonymous English translation from the French contained a number of linguistic and grammatical errors requiring correction:

> The printer finds it necessary to inform the Reader that he re-prints this work under some disadvantages; … The Translator whoever he was, seems to have understood the French language but imperfectly, for the copy abounds with Gallicisms not at all, or incorrectly translated.[27]

From the 1840s onward, three Irish publishers played a key role in the circulation of translations from continental languages: Simms and McIntyre, James Duffy and M.H. Gill and Sons.[28] Based in Belfast, Simms and McIntyre contributed to the mass-marketing of continental fiction in the middle years of the century. By 1844, they had opened a London office. They included a number of translations, mostly from well-known contemporary authors, in their catalogue and in two particular series, 'The Parlour Novelist', and 'The Parlour Library'. The latter gained a reputation of being more instructive and literary in tone, and was in fact initially titled The Parlour Library of

27 'Preface to this Edition', in Jean Bernières de Louvigny, *The Interior Christian: in Eight Books*, trans. anon (Dublin: printed by Richard Cross, 1804), pp. xi–xii.

28 For space constraints, other, possibly equally significant, publishers were omitted.

Instruction. They played a role in the circulation of Alexandre Dumas's novels in English, which were published in the Parlour Novelist series, and that included the all-time popular *The Count of Monte Cristo* (1846). In the same series also appeared translations from Eugène Sue and George Sand. As part of their Parlour Library, they encouraged locally-based translation work by bringing out some of Jane Elgee (later Lady Wilde)'s productions, including *Pictures of the First French Revolution, being Episodes from the History of the Girondists* (1850) from the French of Lamartine, and her better-known translation from the German of Meinhold, *Sidonia the Sorceress* (1849).

An advertisement for the Parlour Novelist series articulates their objective: 'To produce a series of Novels and Tales, by the most distinguished Authors, at a price which will really place them within the reach of the whole reading public'.[29] It is also worth noting that several translations from Dumas and Sue were at the time listed in the *Catalogue of Books Contained in The People's Library…Belfast* (1847), which again indicates a link between translated continental writings and literacy, inasmuch as it suggests a movement towards widening access to books and information for the people.[30]

Catholic publishing was a significant source of translation in nineteenth-century Ireland. The period under study saw the emergence of two key publishers of continental Catholic writings in translation: James Duffy and M.H. Gill and Sons. In this area, translations were not only encouraging literacy, but they were also intended to foster 'good conduct', as well as piety and religious devotion. The translated corpus includes much devotional literature, as well as Catholic fiction for children and young readers. There was an active involvement of male and female Irish translators, both lay and religious – Catholic nuns as well as numerous clergymen to include, for example, Christian Brothers, Jesuits and Redemptorists – and of printers, booksellers and publishers. In this respect, the translation landscape in nineteenth-century Ireland is particularly symptomatic of the strengthening of Catholic publishing and Catholic education during that period.[31]

James Duffy is the best-known Irish publisher in the nineteenth century, probably most noted for his role in disseminating Young Ireland writings at

29 'Advertiser', *Dublin University Magazine*, February 1847.

30 On the notion of 'the people' and its significance for an understanding of nineteenth-century translation in Ireland, see for example Michèle Milan, 'For the People, the Republic and the Nation: Translating Béranger in Nineteenth-Century Ireland', in Ben Keatinge and Mary Pierse (eds), *France and Ireland in the Public Imagination* (Oxford: Peter Lang, 2014), pp. 79–98.

31 On this we should stress that there were certainly also translations of non-Catholic religious writings being produced in Ireland, and which this article cannot discuss specifically for space constraints; but as regards non-Biblical continental literature, the trend in Catholic writings appears conspicuous in many ways.

cheap prices, as well as a large number of Catholic writings. As suggested by MacCarthy,[32] despite his close association with Young Ireland and the *Nation*, James Duffy's overall motives were not necessarily and unequivocally political, but above all a mixture of commercial, religious, didactic and moral motives. That said, anyone who may think that Duffy rejected all that came from abroad would only need to look at his book advertisements to see that there consistently was a fair selection of continental writings, mostly translations from French, Italian and German. By 1878, James Duffy and Sons were able to advertise a set of 16 volumes of Saint Alfonso Maria de Liguori's writings in the English language, some of which written by Irish translators. Moreover, Duffy's own magazines carried a certain amount of translated and serialised Catholic stories. Dublin-based bookseller Patrick O'Byrne, whose adverts for cheap books would sometimes occupy an entire page in the *Nation*, worked as an associate in Duffy's business ventures; but he also contributed a number of translations from French in *Duffy's Fire Side Magazine* in the mid-1850s. Appearing under the rubric 'Flowers from Foreign Fields', his stories were translated from French contemporary authors. O'Byrne's texts are probably best described as 'Episodes' or 'Historical Anecdotes'. They are illustrative of a strong vogue for historical novels and tales in nineteenth-century translation, with a particular interest in the French Revolution. He claimed to have received £19 10s for these, also admitting to one of his friends that he was only just about learning French when he started to produce these translations.[33]

Another example of crossover activity between publishing and translation can be found in the publishing house M.H. Gill and Sons, who were equally active in spreading Catholic literature in translation. Gill and Sons carried a fair number of devotional titles translated from various languages, mainly French, German and Italian, and often by Irish translators. They were particularly active in the dissemination of translations in the last decades

32 Anne MacCarthy, 'A Catholic Literature for Ireland: James Duffy and Duffy's *Irish Catholic Magazine*', in, M.ª Luz Suárez Castiñeira, Asier Altuna García de Salazar and Olga Fernández Vicente (eds), *New Perspectives on James Joyce: Ignatius Loyola, Make Haste to Help Me!* (Bilbao: Deusto University Press, 2009), pp. 65–75.

33 'W.L.' 'Anonymities Unveiled. IX. Contributors to "Duffy's Fireside Magazine"', *Irish Monthly* 20.228 (1892), p. 323. There appears to have been a trend towards the use of evocative expressions such as 'Flowers from Foreign Fields' for translated materials. In the *Nation*, translations of continental poetry appeared under the rubric 'Flowers from Foreign Lands'. Another series was titled 'Echoes of Foreign Song'. O'Byrne also claimed that his own rubric title took Duffy's fancy, so that when they afterwards published Charles P. Meehan's translations of French Catholic tales, they gave the book series the same title, 'Flowers from Foreign Fields'. In the *Dublin University Magazine*, 'M.E.M.' contributed numerous translations under the series title of 'Leaves from the Portuguese Olive'.

of the nineteenth century. Their catalogue included stories aimed at young readers, for example, *The Coiner's Cave*, translated from the German of Wilhelm Herchenbach by Josephine Black, and *The Ferryman of the Tiber: an Historical Tale*, from the Italian of Madame Antonietta Klitsche de la Grange.[34] The very telling title *Good and Pleasant Reading for Boys and Girls … Selected, Edited, and in Parts Translated from the French, German, &c. by the Late H. J. Gill, M.A.* is a compilation of translations by a member of the Gill family. Henry Joseph Gill is an example of what I may thus venture to call a 'crossover agent of translation', who created a close link between the two crucial fields of publishing and translating.[35]

Good versus Bad Books

Translation thus contributed to the expanding market for fictional writings produced with children and young readers in mind. Edifying and instructive stories in translation were rather popular. One of the finest examples is *Elizabeth; or, the Exiles of Siberia: a Tale Founded on Truth*, translated from the French of Madame Cottin, i.e. Sophie Cottin, née Ristaud. Reprinted many times across the English-speaking world, and across Ireland, Elizabeth offers an illustration of Christian fortitude and virtue, particularly filial virtue and piety. This story of an exemplary life appealed across denominational lines. The educational society the Kildare Place Society claimed sales of 65,000 copies between 1817 and 1824,[36] and there is evidence that the translation was used in the Christian Brothers' schools in the 1830s.[37]

On the basis of various paratextual and metatextual commentaries such as translators' prefaces or book reviews, we can, however, sense a form of dichotomous discursive pattern, a polarised discourse about 'good' versus 'bad' books, and translations often lay somewhere at the heart of that debate. Definitive lists of 'best books' were becoming a regular feature of the

34 Interestingly, the author's preface to this story discusses good and bad books, showing that this was not only a trend in Ireland or Britain, but also elsewhere in Europe and beyond.

35 Another key Irish translator in this area was Mary Anne Sadlier (1820–1903), who married into a successful Catholic publishing business in North America, D. & J. Sadlier. Denis and James Sadlier were of Irish birth too. For more on Sadlier, see Michèle Milan, 'Mary Anne Sadlier's Trans-Atlantic Links: Migration, Religion and Translation', *Atlantic Studies* 15.3 (2018): 365–82.

36 Charles Benson, 'The Dublin Book Trade', in James H. Murphy (ed.), *The Oxford History of the Irish Book, Vol. IV: The Irish Book in English, 1800–1891* (Oxford: Oxford University Press, 2011), pp. 27–46, p. 33.

37 Barry Coldrey, *The Educational Ideas of Edmund Rice and Other Essays* (Thornbury: Tamanaraik Press, 2001), p. 33.

day, often including a number of translations. The notion of good reading embraced writings such as those mentioned thus far: instructive, historical or literary translations, as well as edifying and pious translated stories for young readers.

At other times, Irishness was presented as an added criterion for good literature. For example, in 1852 the *Nation* claims that

> [t]he nature of our people demands that their education shall appeal not merely to the intellect, but to their highest moral emotions. And the poisonous stimulants imported from London and Paris can only be successfully counteracted by a literature addressed to the memory and imagination of the country.[38]

This type of foreign literature – 'imported from London and Paris' – was frequently charged with undermining the nation's morals, in contrast to a locally produced literature. Although it is not really clear here what these imported 'poisonous stimulants' are, it is very likely that novels and serials were at the heart of this accusation. The Explanatory Address in James Duffy's *Catholic Guardian* denounces, too, 'the mass of poisonous and offensive thrash which is everywhere to be met with'.[39] Yet at the same time, Duffy's periodicals carried a number of 'good' translations as we noted earlier. The aim was explicitly to supply an antidote to the poison.

When it comes to nineteenth-century discourse on 'poison literature', principally that which was deemed immoral and licentious, we are spoiled for choice. The following quote from a Catholic priest who felt a need to sound the alarm is not untypical: 'I have reason to know that tens of thousands of Catholic readers weekly regale themselves with draughts of this poisonous literature'.[40] The discourse is replete with allusions to drink and intoxicating liquor. Furthermore, the author of this letter uses a dramatic comparative mode when he argues that

> [i]f a mother would weep to find her child near a house of questionable fame, why not keep her offspring from the contagion of questionable literature? If an employer fear a libertine or a drunkard in his concerns, why not endeavour to keep his people from the libertinage and the sottishness of the story, or atheistical essay?[41]

38 *Nation*, 24 January 1852, p. 328.
39 *Catholic Guardian*, 1 February 1852.
40 Letter by Rev. R.B. O'Brien [repr.], *Nation*, 7 November 1857.
41 Ibid.

It is clear from this quote that the letter carries additional connotations of sexuality and religion, bringing the notion of questionable literature closer to that of questionable sexuality as well as irreligiousness.

The 'French Invasion'

Although the trope of contagion and pervasive influence is not limited to the reception of translations, it is important to emphasise how translations were at times directly targeted. The 'French invasion' which we are about to discuss is of course not of a military nature; rather, it was the title of an article published in the *Nation*, which was itself part of an ongoing debate in that paper about French novels and *feuilletons*. One of the most articulate spokesperson at the time for those who stood against French serial novelists and writers such as George Sand was the *Nation* editor, Charles Gavan Duffy, who embarked on a passionate tirade against translations from French. While this rant was also against French novels in the original, translations of these originals were simply the worst enemy. Translations presented a greater danger because they were accessible to a wider readership – they were cheap and in English.

While Duffy later remarks that he has little time for puritanical and alarmist observations, his article begins ominously thus:

> Cheap translations from the French are rapidly increasing amongst us. In the pettiest circulating library whole volumes of extravagant sentiment, and ill-concealed obscenity, either in the original, or done into English, can be read at the cost of a few pence. We have looked on silently at Eugene Sue, Dumas, and brotherhood, shoving out Shakespeare and Walter Scott, though not without a vague sentiment that we were betraying a duty in permitting such fiery stimulants to become habitual to our readers, without, at least, saying our say about it.[42]

Duffy presents French fiction as a conspiracy. He believes that these authors are first introduced in their most innocent appearance, through their 'least objectionable books', and then appear in all their most indecent splendour. He is particularly worried about the effect such literature would have on women, a concern which rests on ideals of female morality and virtue. Ultimately for Duffy, 'if you would drive out the impure and atheistical but sensational literature borrowed from the French, you must replace it by stimulating stories

42 Anon [Charles Gavan Duffy], 'A French Invasion', *Nation*, 22 September 1849, p. 58.

of our own land', thereby, again, promoting home-grown, untainted, literature as the ideal counter-agent to perceived immoral – and godless – influences from abroad. [43]

'Mental dram-drinking'

The source of the term which was adopted for the title of this essay, namely, 'mental dram-drinking' appeared in the *Nation* in a review of the *Celt*.[44] This article provides a crucial example for it gathers together various strands of nineteenth-century ideology and critique. First, the review is overall in the cultural nationalist vein. Second, it shows an increasing tendency in the *Nation*, as in other papers, to locate Catholicism as somewhat coterminous with the national interest by praising a literature which is 'thoroughly national in spirit and Catholic in tone'.[45] Of greater interest to this chapter, however, is the author's stress on the literacy element, the educational benefit of literature and the need to make the printed word more widely accessible, while also advocating the development of a native literature which would have Ireland as its main focus and subject:

> The general diffusion of education throughout the country has now rendered literature an essential to life and happiness; and it has been solely from the want of a cheap literature, devoted to the illustration of Ireland, past and present, that the people have been driven to such resources as the London press offered. Not to mention the numerous penny papers which come from the other side of the water containing exclusively rehashes of French Novels – the perusal of which is analogous to a sort of mental dram-drinking, the higher class, such as Chambers's, and other British journals, are filled with matter which has no reference whatever to Ireland, her history, race, or resources, together with their being but too frequently offensive in their treatment of political and religious questions.[46]

43 Charles Gavan Duffy, *The Revival of Irish Literature* (London: T. Fischer Unwin, 1894), p. 49. It must be stressed that the stance against French novels was not confined to the *Nation* and to Catholics. John Wilson Croker, for example, an Anglican, reputedly a Tory politician, and a literary critic who wrote for the *Quarterly Review*, is probably the most famous detractor of French literature in the early middle decades of the century.

44 The expression was, however, in use before; see, for example, the *Mechanics Magazine*, 20 (1834), p. 159.

45 *Nation*, 3 October 1857.

46 Ibid. The *Nation* relentlessly advocated the need for books of a historical interest; on this see James Quinn, *Young Ireland*.

This article makes a clear statement that cheap translations of French novels have a degenerating impact on Irish society. In addition, and this may be open to interpretation, the term 'rehashes' can also imply that the translations are poorly done, that there seems to be a lack of skill. In other words, this suggests, they really are not 'good translations'.

It is hoped that this paper has shed light on the relevance of translation to the history of the book and of literacy in Ireland. The nineteenth century saw a rise in importation of translations, but there were also some important local publishing initiatives in Ireland. This study seeks to further construct a more comprehensive socio-cultural framework of translation in the nineteenth century. On the basis of the powerful language used in the foregoing examples, and the widespread nature of this type of discourse, we could arguably speak of some form of 'moral panic', for which translations of French novels had become the bogeymen in the nineteenth century.[47]

A sentiment of contempt and distrust towards the very act of translation could sometimes even occur, as illustrated in a review of Denis Florence MacCarthy's translations from the Spanish of Calderón in the *Dublin University Magazine*. Using a vivid travel metaphor, the author of the review argues that '[u]nless from sheer love of errantry, Mr. M'Carthy has no call to wander off to Spain'. And, what is more, '[m]uch less do we approve of a poet of really original powers, descending to the useful but subordinate labour of a translator'.[48]

Accordingly, this chapter has touched on ideas of acceptability and selectivity insomuch as they are crucial to the production, circulation and reception of translations. The notion of 'good translations', overall, emerges as an ambivalent term. It can be understood in terms of texts fitting a model of instructive, morally and politically empowering, and even virtuous and pious literature. At times a 'good' translation may also simply refer to a translation which is well done, though the criteria upon which such statements were made are not always clear. Some commentaries discussing aspects of translation processes were more explicit than others. Richard Cross's preface, written as a printer-cum-translation-editor, certainly offers a glimpse into such discourse. But this essay seeks to demonstrate above all that translation in nineteenth-century Ireland needs to be considered in the light of wider societal discourses and socio-cultural dynamics that include, for example, religion, literacy, gender construction, nation-building and the formation of a national and/or cultural

47 See forthcoming Milan, *Translation in Nineteenth-Century Ireland*, for a discussion on how the concept of translation and the morality of novels can also be understood in terms of hospitality.

48 Anon, 'Denis Florence M'Carthy's Calderon', *Dublin University Magazine*, 59 (April 1862), p. 440. Note that this inhospitable remark is not, however, representative of the magazine as a whole, for it contained a significant amount of verse translation.

identity, and even the temperance movement. Translations, and the discourses surrounding them, contributed to the cultivation of moral and social values in nineteenth-century Ireland.

The link with literacy is explicit. 'Good' translations are intended for both practical and moral instruction; they are tools of improvement. Furthermore, throughout the nineteenth century we see an increase in cheaper publications, thus making translations more accessible to a growing readership in English. In addition to ideologies of reading, nineteenth-century publishing economics would need to be taken into account, as well as the role played by readers in the selection of texts, and their impact on both the production and the circulation of translations.[49] It seems, however, difficult to gauge the *real* extent of that impact. Reversely, it would be difficult to fully gauge the impact of book selection on the wider socio-cultural features of a society, and on the habits and manners of the reading public.[50]

The *Nation* is a particularly interesting example for this study because it used the medium of print, including translations of literary and non-literary writings, to appeal to a mass audience and cultivate a politicised readership. It also provided a space for readers to become writers and translators, and express their opinions through published correspondence. There is no doubt, however, that translations lay somewhere at the heart of a debate which proceeded unabated for decades, and far beyond the pages of the *Nation*; a debate which emphasised moral earnestness, and in which translation represented on the one hand a means toward moral improvement and/or towards political or religious ends, and on the other, an invasive, corrupting influence undermining the nation's morals – indeed some mental dram-drinking.

49 The economics of translation in nineteenth-century Ireland, a nebulous and under-researched area, will be the subject of future discussions. Additionally, a transnational approach will add important insights. Indeed, while a number of matters discussed in this essay are certainly specific to nineteenth-century Ireland, similar patterns of reception and self-censorship occurred in other cultures, countries and at other times. See for example Denise Merkle, Carol O'Sullivan and Luc van Doorslaer (eds), *The Power of the Pen: Translation & Censorship in Nineteenth-Century Europe* (Berlin: LIT Verlag, 2010).

50 The question about the ethical and practical effects of reading books is certainly not new. It may be worth considering this in terms of interconnectedness and a mutual impact between print culture and society, for instance building upon the work of book historians such as David Finkelstein (the 'sociology of texts') and Robert Darnton (the 'communication circuit').

Section 4
Visual Literacies

9

From Dublin to Dehra Dun: Language, Translation and the Mapping of Ireland and India

Nessa Cronin

Historical narratives of cartographic surveys conducted in nineteenth-century Ireland and India have been well documented individually within the context of their own national formations and, albeit to a much lesser degree, in a comparative colonial light.[1] Yet, while similarities and points of contact between Ireland and India in the formation of imperial geographical knowledge has often been recognised, relatively little scholarly work has been devoted to unearthing the interconnected history of cartography between these two countries. In recent years, there has been a growing body of work that has interrogated the relationship and influence between Ireland and India in terms of a critique of empire, literary influences, ideas of 'internationalism', and transnational histories of famine, to name but a few areas that have come under increased scrutiny.[2] As Jill Bender observes, S.B. Cook's historical scholarship in this area set the stage for subsequent studies that would examine the 'relations between Ireland and India in terms of a two-way traffic mediated through distinct but analogous experiences of British rule'.[3] More recently, in *Irish Imperial Networks*, Barry Crosbie

1 For the history of the Ordnance Survey in Ireland see John H. Andrews, *A Paper Landscape: The Ordnance Survey in Nineteenth-Century Ireland*. 2nd ed. (Dublin: Four Courts Press, 2002). This is still the key text, while Matthew Edney's *Mapping an Empire: The Geographical Construction of British India, 1765–1843* (Chicago: University of Chicago Press, 1997) charts the geopolitical construction of India through English surveys and cartography in the period.

2 Gauri Viswanathan, 'Ireland, India, and the Poetics of Internationalism', *Journal of World History* 15.1 (2004): 7–30.

3 Jill Bender, 'The Imperial Politics of Famine: The 1873–74 Bengal Famine and Irish Parliamentary Nationalism', *Éire-Ireland* 42.1–2 (2007): 132–56, 134.

argues that one needs to further nuance the history of the Irish experience of empire ('the multiplicity of communities'), as he writes: 'To the detriment of empire studies in Ireland, nationalism during this period was generally equated with anti-imperialism and as a result the role that Ireland played in British overseas expansion was largely omitted from the Irish history books'.[4] This lack of attention is all the more surprising given that 'during the late eighteenth and early nineteenth centuries Irish scientific institutions and Irish people played an increasingly prominent role in Britain's attempts to expand the boundaries of empire eastward'.[5] And, as Cóilín Parsons observes, 'the historical fact of empire and the development of geographical knowledge and cartographic practices cannot be disaggregated'.[6] It is argued here that British maps produced for state administration in this period (most notably with the Ordnance Survey in Ireland and the Great Trigonmetrical Survey in India) were very much embedded within a discourse coloured by scientific positivism, where the language of maps and science was seen to 'faithfully' and objectively depict the 'real' world. Used in conjunction with demographic and household information, statistical data, and within the parameters of the increasingly powerful discourse of political economy, official state-produced maps would fast become the dominant visual language of the territory under scrutiny and provide a standardised baseline for cartographic literacy in the modern period.

While literary and historical scholars have offered important insights into the interconnections between Ireland and India in this period, very little work has explored the transnational points of contact, the *spaces* where the making of empire met. This chapter argues that the history of the making of empire is inextricably bound to the histories of science and cartography in the nineteenth century. As a visual language of space, cartography is distinctly positioned as a practice that translates and articulates not only the mastery of territory but also, through information gleaned from survey and ethnographic accounts, the populations that live there as well. If we consider translation not just as a linguistic act, but one that is also 'a cultural political practice',[7] then we need to attend to the various ways in which the idea of translation (whether it is translating languages, landscapes, populations) can operate across a variety of media. This is not just a rhetorical or discursive movement, but is a recursive and dialogical shift that highlights how translation *creates* new epistemological and empirical sets of subjects as part of its own internal

4 Barry Crosbie, *Irish Imperial Networks, Migration, Social Communication and Exchange in Nineteenth-Century India* (Cambridge: Cambridge University Press, 2012), p. 4.

5 Crosbie, *Irish Imperial Networks*, p. 103.

6 Cóilín Parsons, 'The Archive in Ruins', *Interventions: International Journal of Postcolonial Studies* 13.1: 464–82, 465.

7 Lawrence Venuti, 'Translation as Cultural Politics: Regimes of Domestication in English', *Textual Practice* 7 (1993): 208–23, 209.

logic and cultural practices. As Michael Cronin writes: 'Translation implies in both a geometrical and linguistic sense, movement, a resistance to fixity. Its momentum is dialogical'.[8] This dialogical momentum of translation is therefore what lends it a transformative power and so, by extension, the map as translation of the landscape is never just a faithful rendering of the 'real', but has to be seen as an ultimate *construction* of the 'real' in its own right. It is argued here that the visual literacy of national territory and colonial space was accented and accelerated through the national surveys of Ireland and India undertaken in this period. In particular, it will be shown that the discourse and practice of mapmaking was shaped by the introduction of instruments known as 'Colby's Compensation Bars' which were used to accurately measure baselines under challenging climatic conditions. The techniques and language of science were translated in this instance from Dublin with their use in the Irish Ordnance Survey to Dehra Dun where they would be used by George Everest in his baseline survey of India in the 1830s.

Nineteenth-Century Ireland and India

Postcolonial critic Kapil Raj has argued that the colonial or imperial relationship is not one of a simple transference of cartographic knowledge from the administrative centre to the colonial periphery, but that one needs to understand 'the complex reciprocity involved in the making of science within the colonial context'.[9] While Irish postcolonial scholars such as Heather Laird have pointed to the dangers inherent in applying Indian models of postcolonial critique to an Irish space, the question arises how do we read such comparative and sometimes 'reciprocal' histories without reducing one to the other, when their links were at times explicitly made by British and East India Company administrators in the expansive period of empire in the nineteenth century?[10] The arguments surrounding the reading of Ireland as a colonial laboratory or site for colonial experimentation are at this stage well rehearsed. Indeed, the central concern of S.B. Cook's pivotal study, *Imperial Affinities: Nineteenth Century Analogies and Exchanges between India and Ireland*, is to explore 'how Ireland served as a colonial prototype, a provider

8 Michael Cronin, *Translating Ireland: Translations, Languages, Cultures* (Cork: Cork University Press, 1997), p. 6.

9 Kapil Raj, 'Colonial Encounters and the Forging of New Knowledge and National Identities: Great Britain and India, 1760–1850', *Osiris*, 2nd Series, 15 (2000): 119–34, 119.

10 See Heather Laird's analysis of the application of the insights from Indian Subaltern Studies to an Irish context in *Subversive Law in Ireland, 1879–1920: From 'Unwritten Law' to the Dáil Courts* (Dublin: Four Courts Press, 2005), especially pp. 129–70.

of policy precedents that the British drew upon in governing India and other parts of the empire they perceived were somehow similar to Ireland'.[11] Similarly, T.G. Fraser opens his essay 'Ireland and India' by arguing that throughout the British period 'service in India provided the mechanism for young men of education and ambition, but no great connections, to rise in the social hierarchy, and in this the Irish proved to be no exception'.[12] It was no accident, he continues, that Kipling chose 'O'Hara' to be the surname of his hero *Kim*.[13] Fraser notes that the Irish were also 'well represented among the rank and file of the British garrison in India' where such men acted as the 'steel frame' around which the Raj was built.[14] Christopher Bayly notes that emigration to India in terms of demographics and timescale 'differed in fundamental aspects from Irish emigration to other parts of the Empire and to America'. Irish emigration to India was, he observes, of a different order in that it 'was generally neither seasonal migration, nor permanent, but of ten or twenty years duration'.[15] While a large number of young men went to India with a view to developing a career otherwise unavailable to them back home (as soldiers, administrators or priests), 'a substantial number of Irish recruits into the Company's armies were from poor peasant families in the West and South of Ireland'.[16] Keith Jeffrey cites the statistic that between 1825 and 1850, '48 per cent of all recruits for the Bengal army were Irish'.[17] This is, however, only one-half of the gendered story of emigration to India. The history associated with Irish women in the subcontinent is one that has yet

11 S.B. Cook, *Imperial Affinities: Nineteenth Century Analogies and Exchanges between India and Ireland* (New Delhi: Sage Publications, 1993), p. 7.

12 T.G. Fraser, 'Ireland and India', in Keith Jeffery (ed.) *'An Irish Empire?' Aspects of Ireland and the British Empire* (Manchester: Manchester University Press, 1996), p. 77.

13 On reading Rudyard Kipling's character Kim (in the novel of the same name) as an Irish boy involved in the mapmaking endeavours and espionage of British India, see Nessa Cronin, 'Monstrous Hybridity: Kim of the "Eye-rishti" and the Survey of India', in Tadhg Foley and Maureen O'Connor (eds), *Ireland and India: Colonies, Culture and Empire* (Dublin: Irish Academic Press, 2006), pp. 131–39.

14 Fraser, 'Ireland and India', p. 78.

15 C.A. Bayly, 'Ireland, India and the Empire: 1780–1914', *Transactions of the Royal Historical Society*, 6th Series, 10 (2000): 377–97, 389.

16 Ibid.

17 Keith Jeffrey, 'The Irish Military Tradition and the British Empire', in Keith Jeffrey (ed.), *'An Irish Empire?' Aspects of Ireland and the British Empire* (Manchester University Press, 1996), pp. 94–122, p. 94. Jeffrey goes on to argue that in the late nineteenth century 'emigration and recruitment varied in inverse proportion ... It may be, therefore, as Peter Karsten has observed, that "when emigration opportunities look bad (due to recession in the British, Australian and North American economies) the queen's shilling looks good"', p. 103. For more on the Connaught Rangers, see also John Morrissey, 'A Lost Heritage: The Connaught Rangers and Multivocal Irishness', in Mark McCarthy (ed.), *Ireland's Heritages: Critical Perspectives on Memory and Identity* (Aldershot: Ashgate, 2005), pp. 71–87.

to be fully examined both in its own terms and in conjunction with its male narrative.[18] Fraser concludes with the observation that, 'Ireland and India touched at many points. Irish participation in the administration of India was so extensive as to help justify the claim that it was an "Irish" as well as a "British" empire, offering advancement and often fame, to young Irishmen of relatively humble background'.[19]

In 'Ireland, India and the Empire: 1780–1914', Bayly comments on what can be gained in drawing comparisons and distinctions between the two countries, 'We can learn much from connective and comparative histories, even from the interconnections of histories so distant in space and cultural form as those of Ireland and India'. He maintains that in 'some parts of the older agenda of empire, nation and class are still valid. Ireland and India bear comparison not only because they were "othered" in similar patterns of imperial discourse or because they were zones of hybridity for shifting subjects'. In terms of reading one country's experience alongside that of another, Bayly points out that

> [w]hat has happened more recently, though, is that the critique of orientalist knowledge has made a considerations [*sic*] of these comparisons and connections easier by undermining the stark distinction between East and West. It has also re-established the history of Eurasia as in [*sic*] overlapping terrain of communities, powers and lines of commerce.[20]

Such Saidian 'overlapping terrains' of East and West crossed over both in terms of the joint nomenclature of the geographical space known as 'Eurasia', and with the alignment of Europe and Asia in terms of a shared historical timeline.[21] The areas that are of primary concern to Fraser and Bayly are those of nation-building, landowning, agrarian disturbances, administrative, and religious connections and the hybridity associated with such colonial spaces. While Bayly makes reference to the cartographic projects undertaken in both countries, the opportunity to make a sustained examination of the

18 See Maina Singh, 'Political Activism and the Politics of Spirituality: The Layered Identities of Sister Nivedita/Margaret Noble (1867–1911)', in Tadhg Foley and Maureen O'Connor (eds), *Ireland and India: Colonies, Culture and Empire* (Dublin: Irish Academic Press, 2006), pp. 39–57; and Fiona Bateman, 'Ireland's Spiritual Empire: Territory and Landscape in Irish Catholic Missionary Discourse', in Hilary M. Carey (ed.), *Empires of Religion* (Basingstoke and New York: Palgrave Macmillan, 2008), pp. 267–87.

19 Fraser, 'Ireland and India', p. 91.

20 Bayly, 'Ireland, India and the Empire', pp. 377, 378, 379, 382.

21 As the physical embodiment of such 'overlapping terrains', Kipling's *Kim* consciously plays with concepts of identity by continually crossing lines drawn by nation, religion, 'race' and language.

connections between the two mapping projects in this period is left for others to explore.[22]

As outlined above, scholars across various fields have contributed greatly to a broader understanding of the interconnections between Ireland and India in terms of the nation-building and empire (and especially to 'soldiers and cannons' in terms of Irish military history), with the essential role that cartography played in the power-geometries being too often kept off-stage. The appropriation and subsequent management of colonial and imperial spaces must be read not only in geographical and economic terms, but also in terms of the struggle over geography as articulated by Edward Said. Such geographic 'struggles' bear testimony to the contested sites of the overlapping terrains of colonial and imperial spaces, terrains that are in fact inhabited places shaped and demarcated by different languages, histories, and traditions.[23] Bayly's analysis of the 'overlapping terrain of communities, powers and lines of commerce', is predicated on knowledge of the individual terrains in the first instance of nineteenth-century Ireland and India. David Livingstone has argued 'the sites where experiments are conducted, the places where knowledge is generated' are central to our understanding of the construction of scientific cultures.[24] As 'scientific knowledge bears the imprint of its location', we therefore need to be cogniscent of the material factors that shape scientific discourse and so re-examine the domestic and imperial *spaces* of where, when, and how such discourses are seen to unfold.[25] While arguments for colonial comparative histories have been well made, it is also worth bearing in mind David Lloyd's emphasis that one might look to 'differential' rather than 'comparative' histories, in order to retain the openness of nuance and avoid the possible trap of collapsing singular experiences into sameness. As Lloyd argues, '[t]here are no identical colonial situations, so that in place of comparative we should in fact employ the term "differential", marking the ways in which quite specific cultural forms emerge in relation to a universalizing process'.[26] While the particularities of historical and geographical contexts were different in Ireland and in India, what was similar was the imagined end-game of such colonial spaces, but to create a map of empire one had to have the idea of it first.

22 Bayly writes in regard to late eighteenth-century Ireland that the 'Irish parliament disappeared and the apparatus of British rule with its resident magistrates, garrison towns and trigonometrical surveys was imposed'. Bayly, 'Ireland, India and the Empire', p. 386.

23 This is the argument made in Edward Said's opening chapter 'Overlapping Territories, Intertwined Histories', in *Culture and Imperialism* (London: Vintage, 1994), pp. 1–72.

24 David N. Livingstone, *Putting Science in Its Place: Geographies of Scientific Knowledge* (Chicago: University of Chicago Press, 2003), pp. 4–5.

25 Livingstone, *Putting Science in Its Place*, p. 13.

26 David Lloyd, *Ireland After History* (Cork: Cork University Press and Field Day, 1999), p. 3.

Mapping the Nation

The structures of empire and colonialism are embedded in, and dependent upon, the development of certain hierarchies of knowledge while being simultaneously engaged in incorporating or delegitimising others (most notably tacit and indigenous knowledge formations). One mode in which this was achieved in the early nineteenth century was with the commissioning of national surveys and the production of detailed, standardised, national maps that drew on historical predecessors. The rationale of trigonometrical surveying was that it was possible to conceive of the map as the territory but on the proviso that the map would take legal precedent over that geographic space. As cartographic historian Matthew Edney writes: 'Triangulation defines an exact equivalence between the geographic archive and the world ... Not only would this be the same size of the territory it represents, it would *be* the territory'.[27] The map was therefore an image that could easily morph into 'fact' (a disinterested unit of naturalised objectivity). This was enabled through the scientific positivism of nineteenth-century Europe that was married to a representational view of language where language (mathematical, instrumental) is seen to represent the way the world actually 'is', rather than being a second-order construction of that world. The map thus becomes the literal embodiment of empirical space and the space of empire; it is ready and waiting to be unfolded and utilised by its patrons, viewers and readers.[28] The literacy assumed in the reading of the modern map is a literacy that enables an authoritarian vision of how the world 'is', i.e. often singular, monolingual and definitively scripted in black and white.

The Ordnance Survey of Ireland was firmly grounded in the *ratio* and *telos* of the Enlightenment project and was the natural heir to the 'New Science' that helped shape William Petty's Down Survey (1656–1658) and the regional boom in road and estate maps of the eighteenth century. In *A Paper Landscape:*

27 Edney, *Mapping an Empire*, p. 21. Emphasis as in original.

28 The best explanation of the principles behind triangulation and the trigonometrical survey is that by Edney: 'What triangulation offered was a systematic technology whereby geographic information could be made truly certain and comprehensible. Its principles are relatively simple. The surveyor first imagines a series of straight lines joining the tops of hills or tall buildings. The hill-tops are selected so that the lines form either a long chain of triangles or a network of interlocking triangles spread out across the landscape ... The surveyor determines the geometry of the triangles by measuring their interior angles. The actual size of the triangles is determined by the very careful measurement on the ground of the length of one side of a triangle; the lengths of all other triangle sides are calculated from this one "baseline" by means of trigonometry. The later Enlightenment term for a triangulation was therefore a trigonometrical survey. The result is a rigorous mathematical framework in which all points are defined with respect to each other.' Edney, *Mapping an Empire*, p. 19.

The Ordnance Survey in Nineteenth Century Ireland, John H. Andrews stresses that the rationale for the Survey was not primarily a military one, but that it was intended as a necessary aid for the purposes of land valuation and reform of the Irish land taxation system. In terms of computation and utility, advances in mapping technologies also aided such spatial liberations. The Euclidean language of geometry conceived space as abstract and empty, a space upon which the Cartesian subject could be objectified and inscribed. Such a framework, being knowable and universal, provided the grid upon which the co-ordinates of truth could later be engraved with the fixity and permanence of lithographic and copperplate technologies. As Brian Harley notes: 'Accuracy became the new talisman of authority'.[29] The abstraction of the world, its classification into the mutually exclusive polarities of subject and object, resulted in a mastery of the subject over its assumed corollary, the object.[30] To legitimate the land through the veracity of cartography was in turn a confirmation of the Anglo-Irish power geometries that constructed that map. The Irish Survey maps acted as a 'cartographic expression of the two kingdoms' and as such embodied a singular vision of a unified body of empire in the latter half of the nineteenth century.[31] As a direct result of the work conducted in Ireland, Andrews stresses that 'the whole character of the Ordnance Survey was transformed, as a result of its Irish experience, from glorified military reconnaissance party to universal cartographic provider'.[32] This tenet of cartographic and, by implication, scientific universalism would also extend its geometry of power to encompass the Indian subcontinent.

A Compensatory Science: Cartographic Innovations in Ireland and India

In December 1799 Colonel William Lambton put forward a proposal to conduct a geographical survey of India under the auspices of the East India Company. In February of the following year orders were issued for the commencement of work on the survey. The measurement of a baseline near

29 J.B. Harley, 'Maps, Knowledge, and Power', in Paul Laxton (ed.), *The New Nature of Maps: Essays in the History of Cartography* (Baltimore, MD: Johns Hopkins University Press, 2001), p. 77.

30 As discussed by Theodor W. Adorno and Max Horkheimer in 'The Concept of Enlightenment', in *Dialectic of Enlightenment*, trans. John Cumming (London: Verso, 1997), p. 13. In a related vein see also, Michel Foucault, 'Classifying', *The Order of Things: An Archaeology of the Human Sciences* (London: Routledge, 1994), pp. 125–65.

31 Andrews, *A Paper Landscape*, p. 24.

32 John H. Andrews, *History in the Ordnance Map: An Introduction for Irish Readers* (Kerry, Wales: David Archer, 1993), p. 3.

Madras began from which a series of triangles would be drawn out and mapped up to Mysore, and a second baseline was measured near Bangalore. Having connected the two sides of the peninsula, Lambton measured an arc of the meridian and the series of triangles that were measured for this later became known as the 'Great Arc Series'. The Great Arc would form the basis for the mapping of all of India, as it would serve as the baseline or benchmark from which all other subsequent surveys could proceed. As the influence of the Raj spread in early to mid-nineteenth-century India, the mapping of the country symbolised the spread of the East India Company, and so geography and politics progressed across time and space. The survey was later re-named the Great Trigonometrical Survey (GTS) of India in 1817 and was largely completed by 1890.[33] Everest commenced work with Lambton in 1818 and in 1823 became the superintendent of the GTS of India.[34] In 1830 Everest was additionally appointed to the post of surveyor general of the GTS, a position from which he retired 13 years later. Where the Indian cartographic tradition placed an emphasis on routes (and, in particular, on Buddhist pilgrimage routes), the British concentrated on 'area and fixed scales in a way that the Indians did not'.[35] In addition to the GTS working its way through India, there were many other revenue (cadastral) surveys from 1822 on that would later give rise to large-scale maps for much of the subcontinent.

When Everest took up the position in the GTS in 1823, the instruments that had been used in the Indian Survey had been badly damaged and were in desperate need of repair. He later became ill and returned to England to work on the mathematical observations and on the calculations for the Great Arc that had been thus far made. In the following years, until his return to India, Everest worked on improving and modelling his instruments for the specific needs of the Indian Survey. As Crosbie notes: 'He [Everest] wanted to see the new theodolites, heliotropes, modern lamps and night-lights all used regularly in Ireland applied for use in India'.[36] In particular, he worked on a

33 Jeremy Black, *Visions of the World: A History of Maps* (London: Mitchell Beazley, 2003), p. 103.

34 For an account of George Everest's life see James R. Smith, *Everest: The Man and the Mountain* (Caithness, Scotland: Whittles Publishing Services, 1999).

35 Black, *Visions of the World*, p. 103.

36 Crosbie, *Irish Imperial Networks*, p. 115. See also, J.E. Insley, '"Instruments of a Very Beautiful Class": George Everest in Europe, 1825–1830', in James R. Smith (ed.), *Colonel Sir George Everest CB FRS: Proceedings of the Bicentenary Conference at the Royal Geographical Society, 8th November 1990* (London: Royal Geographical Society and Royal Institute of Chartered Surveyors, 1990), pp. 23–30. Also, Patrick Duffy in a recent Heritage Week lecture at the Royal Irish Academy, Dublin, 22 August 2016, made reference to the connections between Everest and the Ordnance Survey of India. See Siobhán Fitzpatrick, 'The Maps That Keep on Giving', *Royal Irish Academy*, 26 August 2016, https://www.ria.ie/news/library-blog/maps-keep-giving (accessed 25 January 2017).

smaller version of the cumbersome Cary theodolite which would be smaller and cheaper than its predecessor. In addition, he would also recommend that the East India Company should use this model in place of its other small theodolites to ensure both instrumental and computational uniformity. At the same period in Ireland, the director of the Ordnance Survey, Colonel Thomas Colby, was also working on improving and standardising the measuring instruments for his national survey. In 1825 a preliminary survey of the Irish baseline site at Lough Foyle was carried out.[37] However, Colby wanted to improve on the steel chains that were the standard instrument of ground measure at this time. The problem with the chains was that the metal was susceptible to variations in temperature, and with additional wear and tear of the links, the readings obtained from a single site were not always regular, and thus opened the way for scientific error in later positional calculations.[38] As Andrews writes of the chains, 'although their temperature may be taken in a rough and ready fashion and a correction made for expansion and contraction, their precise lengths remain unknowable as long as there is no way of applying the thermometer to every point along the line'.[39] This minor discrepancy in chain readings would have major implications when final measurements and positions were being reckoned.

Scottish engineer and army officer Thomas Drummond joined the surveying party in Ireland in 1824.[40] Mistakenly credited for 'inventing' what would become known as the Drummond Light, he improved the lamps used for night work at field stations where he recognised the utility of limelight lamps in 1825. This was work he developed upon attending lectures on the subject by Michael Faraday and learning of the inventions of surgeon, chemist and gentleman scientist, Sir Goldsworth Gurney, who developed the Bude Light to improve light in operating theatres. Drummond's contribution was that his heliostat or reflector 'took the mirror principle a stage further'.[41] Both instruments were tested in Ireland in 1825 and the reflector 'was greeted with a "shout of exultation" by a crowd of sightseers' when it was first detected at Knocklayd, 40 miles from Divis Mountain near Belfast.[42]

37 The main account of this survey is that of William Yolland, *An Account of the Measurement of the Lough Foyle Base, with its Verification and Extension by Triangulation; together with the various methods of computation followed on the Ordnance Survey, and the Requisite Tables* (London: Palmer and Clayton, 1847).

38 My account here of the Irish Survey is indebted to Andrews's *A Paper Landscape*.

39 Andrews, *A Paper Landscape*, p. 45.

40 For more on Thomas Drummond see M.Á.G. Ó Tuathaigh, *Thomas Drummond and the government of Ireland, 1835–40*. O'Donnell Lecture (Dublin: National University of Ireland, 1977).

41 Andrews, *A Paper Landscape*, p. 42.

42 Ibid. Drummond later made the 66-mile connection between Slieve Snaght and Divis on the night of 9 November 1825. See also Thomas Drummond, 'On the Means

Drummond would later write up and circulate an account of this in his paper, 'On the Means of Facilitating the Observation of Distant Objects in Geodetic Operations', published in the *Royal Society Philosophical Transactions* in 1826. As previous methods of baseline measurement were deemed as being unacceptable to Colby, in the spring of 1826 Drummond was charged with the task of initiating experiments to resolve the problem of gaining accurate baseline readings. A series of experiments were conducted in London where the inventor Charles Babbage was in regular correspondence with Colby. Once the experiments were completed in the London workshop of Troughton & Simms, the measuring bars (made of iron and brass) were ready to be used in the field.[43] Using what would become known as Colby's 'compensation bars', measuring work on Lough Foyle recommenced in September 1827, and by 1829 every line measured in Ireland depended on the original baseline measured at the Lough Foyle baseline conducted with the aid of Colby's bars.[44]

While Everest is known to have visited Colby in Ireland in the late 1820s and acquired a double set of six bars for the GTS which he practiced in Greenwich, he was not entirely happy that the two bars accurately compensated each other and thought it still necessary 'to take their temperature and make the necessary allowances for expansion and contraction'.[45] He later wrote that he 'learned the use of them … when … trying those made for the E.I. [East India] Company on Lord's Cricket Ground, St. John's Wood Road'.[46] As James R. Smith notes, Everest's experiments with Colby's compensation bars at Lords was arranged

of Facilitating the Observation of Distant Objects in Geodetic Operations', *Royal Society Philosophical Transactions* Part 2 (1826): 324–37. I am grateful to Dr Peter Collier for his discussion of Drummond's limelights with me in personal conversation.

43 On the South African context see, Tomasz Zakiewicz, 'The Cape Geodetic Standards and Their Impact on Africa', Unpublished paper, FIG Working Week 2005, Cairo, Egypt 16–21 April (2005), pp. 1–19, https://www.fig.net/resources/proceedings/fig_proceedings/cairo/papers/wshs_03/wshs03_02_zakiewich.pdf (accessed 30 November 2016).

44 The compensation bars also migrated south of the equator where they were subsequently used to measure bases in the Cape of Good Hope as used by Lieutenant Alexander Henderson, and one bar remains in the Ordnance Survey in Dublin. *An Illustrated Record of the Ordnance Survey in Ireland* (Dublin: Ordnance Survey of Ireland, 1991), p. 17 and Andrews, *A Paper Landscape*, p. 47.

45 Andrews, *A Paper Landscape*, p. 51. George Everest, 'Memoir', in 'Papers Relating to the Survey of India 1807–1838', BL Add MS 14,380, f. 77. This MS is catalogued as 'Memoir by the same, containing an account of the Irish Survey, and a comparison of the same with the system pursued in […] 1829'. Also noted in, George Everest, *An Account of the Measurement of Two Sections of the Meridional Arc of India … conducted under the orders of the Honourable East India Company* (London: Wm. H. Allen, 1847), xciii, xcviii–xcic.

46 Everest, quoted in R.H. Phillimore, *Historical Records of the Survey of India, Vol. IV, George Everest (1830–43)* (Dehra Dun, India: Survey of India, 1958).

> not only to show the equipment to dignitaries and scientists who so wished, but also to allow Everest to practice use of the bars under the guidance of two who had worked with Colby in Ireland. Three weeks' hire of the ground cost £24, with another £106 in expenses. The results were encouraging; over a 567 feet length there was agreement between two measures to 3/40th inch or 1 in 90000.[47]

Both Colby and Everest were aware that the scientific validation of any survey lay with its instruments, and Everest was sufficiently impressed with Colby's bars that he later used a modified bar system in India.[48] Significantly, in terms of the transmission of ideas, the first published reference to Colby's bars was in a report of a lecture given by Everest in Calcutta as published in *Asiatic Researches* in 1833, as Everest had used a version of the bars in creating a baseline for his survey near Dehra Dun.[49] On the connections between Ireland and India, Edney writes: 'After 1824, the proponents of the GTS looked to the Ordnance Survey of Ireland as the epitome of what they hoped to achieve in India'.[50] As Crosbie also observes, 'Ireland was considered an important site where new technologies, methods of scientific practice and organization were being developed and could be used in other parts of the Empire'.[51] And so, while Lord's Cricket Grounds may be regarded as the site for cartographic tests, the Irish project was seen to operate as the key reference point. Indeed, India would not be the only country to follow Ireland's example. In 1838 upon the recommendation of the Astronomer Royal, Sir George Airy, authority was given for the construction of 'two iron 10-feet bars, similar in size and general arrangement to those used by Colonel Colby, for reference in his measurement of the base near Lough Foyle, in Ireland' to be used in Africa.[52] The bars were produced once again by Troughton & Simms and dispatched to Sir Thomas Maclear the following year in 1839 to the Cape Colony for his verification work on the Geodetic Survey of South Africa. Following the success of the Survey's scale of six inches to the mile in Ireland, it was argued that a similarly detailed scale should also be adopted in England. In 1840 the Treasury 'authorised the

47 James R. Smith, 'Sir George Everest, F.R.S. (1790–1866)', *Notes and Records of the Royal Society of London* 46:1 (1992): 89–102, p. 96.

48 Andrews, *A Paper Landscape*, p. 51.

49 George Everest, 'On the Compensation Measuring Apparatus of the Great Trigonometrical Survey of India', *Asiatic Researches* xviii.2 (1833): 189–214, as cited in Andrews, *A Paper Landscape*, p. 50.

50 Edney, *Mapping an Empire*, p. 35.

51 Crosbie, *Irish Imperial Networks*, p. 105.

52 As cited in, Zakiewicz, 'The Cape Geodetic Standards', p. 7.

mapping of northern England and Scotland on the six-inch scale', with work beginning the following year in Lancashire.[53]

Everest made constant references to the methods and work being done by his colleagues in Ireland throughout his work in India, comparing and modifying them in light of his own experiences in the field. On 18 August 1831 he wrote:

> It was the opinion of Lieut. Colonel Lambton that ... one party in the field would in the course of 4 months furnish matter for 8 months computation, but ... under his system there was no office in the field, so that not even the angle-books were regularly brought up, and this, I believe, is also the practice in the Great Trigonometrical Survey of Ireland.[54]

Later, in October of the same year, Everest was beginning to tire of the increasing demands being made of his time from the military department, with their requests for more discussion and more details concerning his work. Comparing the methods in Ireland to that in India in order to further his case he wrote:

> The Superintendent of the Great Trigonometrical Survey of Ireland has hardly any official correspondence save with the officers under his authority, and that he curtails as much as possible. When I was ... in England, many propositions were submitted by me to the Court of Directors, but written explanations were hardly in any case required of me, and viva-voce communications with the Chairman were deemed to answer all purposes.

However, Everest's problems did not end there as, 'His Honor in Council has himself assured me that my explanations are never understood, in spite of the ... efforts which I make to divest them of all obscurities'.[55] The measurement and computation of the Great Arc would be completed by 1843, after which Everest retired from the Survey.

Everest was not the only officer to make a personal connection between the Irish and Indian Surveys. Born in Ceylon, Henry Montgomery Lawrence had attended Foyle College in Derry with his two brothers, where his uncle Reverend James Knox was headmaster, from January 1815 to June 1819.[56]

53 Catherine Delano-Smith and Roger J.P. Kain, *English Maps: A History* (Toronto University Press, 1999), pp. 220–21.
54 Everest cited in Phillimore, *Historical Records*, Vol. IV, p. 338.
55 Everest cited in Phillimore, *Historical Records*, Vol. IV, pp. 343–44.
56 Phillimore, *Historical Records*, Vol. IV, p. 452.

The Lawrences were joined by Robert Montgomery who later 'was to become a close collaborator in India and give his name to a Punjabi district'. In 1828 Henry Lawrence 'spent some months with OS in Ireland' and returned to Calcutta in February 1830.[57] Thomas Jervis, a surveyor on the Survey of India, believed that an education in surveying was singularly important and in 1837 wrote as to 'the easy and unexceptionable introduction of useful science, and industrious habits where they are most wanted: amongst the Natives of India', as this was one method 'of introducing to the notice of the people of India generally the advantages of a good education, and habits of order, regularity, industry and moral rectitude'.[58]

This was written two years after the famous 1835 education minute by Thomas Babington Macaulay (instituting English as the primary language of instruction in Indian schools) and, more interestingly, Jervis was aware of Colby's system of coordinating the Survey in Ireland and hoped to introduce the same regime of practice in India. Of Colby's system, he commented that it was 'a sort of Fellenberg School on the grandest scale ... Promptitude, regularity, and cheerfulness are the essentials of such [a] system, and here their effects are displayed in every individual of the establishment as in the parts of a steam engine'. Philipp Emanuel von Fellenberg, as Edney notes, was a Swiss educator 'whose educational system was intended to elevate the lower orders of society and weld them more closely to the higher orders'.[59]

As many engineers already had a history of training in Ireland before leaving for the field in India, Jervis's suggestion in his letters of December 1837 recommends that all future engineering cadets should be trained in Ireland with the Ordnance Survey before being dispatched to India. And in many instances, such recommendations were adhered to.[60] Thus, the role of education (and scientific military training in this instance) was tightly bound up with the progress of cartographic science and map literacy. Such cartographic literacy had a twofold impact; in developing new scientific methods and instruments with which to 'read' the landscape, while also calibrating an anglophone construction of space. With one endeavour serving the interests of the other,

57 Fraser, 'Ireland and India', p. 81. Fraser writes that the Lawrence brothers identified their position in India with their previous home in Ireland, and argues that there is 'ample evidence that the Lawrences saw themselves as steeled in the "No Surrender" tradition in the siege of Derry, which they transposed to the equally contested space of India'.

58 Thomas Jervis, as cited by Edney, *Mapping an Empire*, p. 313.

59 Ibid.

60 Phillimore notes the training of two engineer officers, Waugh and Thomas Renny, who went through 'a short course with the trigonometrical survey of Ireland'. Phillimore, *Historical Records*, Vol. IV, p. 3. Renny spent 'a few weeks with the OS. in Ireland' prior to his arrival in India in 1831. Ibid., p. 462.

they could both be harnessed to mutually produce and motivate the scientific and moral cogs of the wheel of an empire that was moving and mapping its way through the Indian subcontinent.[61]

Ireland then, as Tony Ballantyne notes, 'provided intellectual capital for the Raj as well as raw man-power. This was particularly the case with surveying which was, of course, essential in the construction of imperial authority'.[62] The collection and collation of geopolitical information in the form of the colonial cartographic archive 'would facilitate the exploitation of resources and revenue reserves, improve strategic planning and speed up the movement of troops'. In this, Ireland provided one 'key reference point' for the surveying of India.[63] While questions such as the transmission of scientific ideas in light of surveying and field operations in Ireland and India are highlighted here, it also is worth bearing in mind the wider questions of the development of professions including surveying, civil engineering, and cartography in terms of the wider scientific projects of the charting of nations and empire. This broader point is made by Jacinta Prunty who stresses the multiple roles and functions of the map. The map itself, Prunty maintains, 'bears testimony to changing technology, political priorities, artistic fashions, and the mobility of skilled personnel; by purposely focusing on the local level, cartography can provide new openings into the wider world of ideas and ambitions within which the local is embedded'.[64]

The changing technologies and cartographic activities in Ireland, England, Africa and India resulted in the manufacture, development, training and transmission of scientific instruments (both in terms of techniques and ideologies), and the mobility of personnel from place to place. In the instance of Colby's compensation bars, the instruments of empire were tested in the

61 The celebrated and most geographically famous instance of such a marriage of education and geography in the Indian context is the role that Indians (known as 'pandits') later played in mapping High Asia between 1863 and 1885. Edney comments that the 'most important reason for the historiographic privileging of the pandits is that throughout the period of British hegemony in India, the pandits were the only Indians ever to be fully accredited by the British as autonomous field surveyors in their own right', Edney, *Mapping an Empire*, p. 309. See also Kapil Raj, 'When Human Travellers Become Instruments: Indo-British Exploration of Central Asia in the Nineteenth Century', in Marie-Noëlle Bourget, Christian Licoppe and H. Otto Sibum (eds), *Instruments, Travel and Science: Itineraries of Precision Form the Seventeenth to the Twentieth Century* (London and New York: Routledge, 2002), pp. 156–88.

62 Tony Ballantyne, 'The Sinews of Empire: Ireland, India and the Construction of British Colonial Knowledge', in Terrence McDonough (ed.), *Was Ireland a Colony? Economics, Politics and Culture in Nineteenth-Century Ireland* (Dublin: Irish Academic Press, 2005), p. 154.

63 Ibid., p. 155.

64 Jacinta Prunty, *Maps and Map-Making in Local History* (Dublin: Four Courts Press, 2004), p. 25.

imperial centre of London and finely tuned for application in the peripheries of empire, being transported from Dublin to the Cape Colony via Dehra Dun. The reciprocal triangulation between Ireland, England, and India in particular, was a necessary feature in the construction of the colonial, cartographic archive where the experiments in one were adopted and adapted to fit the needs of the other. This highlights one instance in which Irish history yields 'social documents deeply engaged on both sides of the colonialist struggle', showing the reflexive movements where ideas of 'centre' and 'periphery' can be seen to be constantly shifting and demand reconceptualisation.[65]

The translation of methodologies and cartographic literacy from Ireland to India also doubly marked the way in which Ireland acted as both subject and object of cartographic inscription of an imperial landscape. At the end of his essay on the cartographic construction of India, Raj highlights what he terms 'an apparent paradox'. He writes that while 'the material practices of the Survey of India differed in crucial ways from those of the Ordnance Survey of Great Britain and Ireland' that, yet, 'the knowledge produced out of these differing practices and protocols could be rendered commensurable and placed on the same map. How does the switch from these local practices to universal science operate?'.[66] In answering this question Raj suggests a distinction between two aspects of science, the 'material and social practices' on the one hand and, 'the knowledge to which they give rise', on the other.[67]

However, a third distinction could also be argued for (thus resolving the 'apparent paradox'), this being the positivist organisation of imperial space that was imagined and articulated, a priori, in the first instance, that provided a 'universal' grid upon which such localised knowledges and practices could be developed, transcribed, translated and mapped. In this scenario, what could be regarded as a doctrine of commensurability (as expressed through scientific equivalence) ensured from the outset that all data could be equally mapped, logged and registered. As Susan Bassnett and Harish Trivedi maintain: 'Translation has been at the heart of the colonial encounter, and has been used in all kinds of ways to establish and perpetuate the superiority of some cultures over others'.[68] Maps then can be seen to operate as one of those other ways in which colonialism is articulated and translated, across both verbal

65 Charles Orser, as cited in Terence McDonough (ed.), *Was Ireland a Colony?*, p. xiv.

66 Raj, 'Colonial Encounters', p. 133. It is of interest to note that while Raj focuses on the construction of a universal cartographic knowledge which he argues was dependent on measurement and calibrations, as noted with his discussion of Rennell's translation of tabular data, he makes no mention of Colby's compensation bars as adopted and adapted by Everest in India.

67 Ibid.

68 Susan Bassnett and Harish Trivedi (eds), *Postcolonial Translation: Theory and Practice* (London: Routledge, 1999), p. 17.

and visual registers. Conversely, while colonial space could be regarded, in one sense, as the (badly) translated 'copy' of the imperial original 'at home' in the colonial centre (the '0°' of the Greenwich Meridian), in this instance the Irish Ordnance Survey served as the 'original' project and practice, an original that would be 'copied' and 'translated' onto the other imagined spaces of empire, and finally back to Britain with its own triangulation and survey completed by the end of the century. With this, the map is somehow 'greater' than the land which it purports to represent, and so the 'copy' would override the 'original'. And so, in the ultimate act of colonial translation, space no longer actually matters – its representation on the map would replace the territory and be the key signifier in one visual frame of reference. The map would operate as a colonial shortcut to and, more importantly, proxy for colonial territory.

In her essay 'The Rani of Simur: An Essay in Reading the Archives', Gayatri Spivak describes the movement of a soldier who traverses across nineteenth-century India and partakes in a Heideggerian 'worlding' of native space, and in so doing recreates the domestic as something foreign, the *heimlich* as *unheimlich*.[69] In Brian Friel's play *Translations*, Lieutenant Yolland (the Royal Engineer employed in the Ordnance Survey of Ireland in the play) worries that his participation in the survey marks a similar sort of 'eviction of sorts', a displacement of the Irish from their native place, resulting in a Fanonian alienation of self where 'home' becomes unhoused through language.[70] In Spivakian terms the soldier 'is effectively and violently sliding one discourse under another', and as such can be read as the soldier-surveyor whose physical presence on such overlapping territories marks the partial erasure, if not closing down, of native space.[71] And so, the soldier-surveyors and civilians, local landowners and native informants, played an integral role in the material construction of empire, in the drawing and the marking out of the *graphos* of the map. Spivak's soldier could well have learned the slippery discourse of the *jurisdictio* in the training-ground of Ireland, which as we have seen served as the cartographic baseline for India in the nineteenth century.

69 Gayatri Spivak, 'The Rani of Simur: An Essay in Reading the Archives', in Francis Barker, Peter Hulme, Margaret Iversen and Diana Loxley (eds), *Europe and its Others, Vol. 1 Proceedings of the Essex Conference on the Sociology of Literature* (Colchester: University of Essex, 1985), p. 133.

70 Brian Friel, *Translations* ([1981] London: Faber and Faber, 2000), p. 52.

71 Spivak, 'The Rani of Simur', p. 241.

10

Reading the Hand: Palmistry, Graphology and Alternative Literacies

Stephanie Rains

By the end of the nineteenth century, it was estimated that 86 per cent of the Irish population were literate.[1] While more nuanced understandings of what that literacy might actually entail complicate this statistic, it was nevertheless the case that the overwhelming majority of the population – especially those of working or school age – could read and write with basic competency, and usually a great deal more than that. The resonances of literacy becoming an almost universal skill were profound in the everyday lives of many people, particularly perhaps those who were now significantly more literate than their parents or grandparents had been. Most obviously, it opened up new employment possibilities as literacy meant that working-class or lower-middle-class school-leavers could aspire to clerical and office-work which was probably more secure, better-paid and of higher status than previous generations of their family could have achieved. Particularly in Dublin, but also in other cities and even small towns, the army of clerks expanded rapidly during the late nineteenth century. Working alongside these clerks but performing a more highly-specialised form of literate work, the number of typists expanded even more rapidly. Where in 1901 there were 704 typists in Ireland, by 1911 there were 2,865, almost all of them women.[2] Often proficient in shorthand as well, their working lives were founded on a very particular kind of literacy – a skill of the hands which

1 Clare Hutton, 'Publishing the Irish Cultural Revival, 1891–1922', in Clare Hutton and Patrick Walsh (eds), *The Oxford History of the Irish Book, Volume V, The Irish Book in English 1891–2000* (Oxford: Oxford University Press, 2011), pp. 17–42, p. 19.

2 See 'Census of Ireland 1901/1911 and Census Fragments and Substitutes, 1821–51', *National Archives of Ireland*, for the Irish census returns of 1901 and 1911, www.census.nationalarchives.ie.

produced uniform, mechanised writing at greater speed than had ever been possible before.

This era in which more and more people were regularly writing as well as reading coincided with a popular fascination with the hand itself, and specifically with a belief that the hand was a way of gaining particular insight into its owner's identity and character, or even into their future. One publication claimed simply that '[t]he hand of man is the key to his character. The hand is the picture of the brain'.[3] This chapter will explore the intersecting forms this fascination with the hand took, from graphology (the interpretation of handwriting) and palmistry, to x-rays and the use of fingerprint technology in criminal cases. These diverse activities overlapped each other in a cultural landscape where scientific and occult practices often blurred into one in the public imagination. As well as examining the blurring of that line, this chapter will also discuss the ways in which the pseudo-sciences of graphology and palm-reading (often referred to as cheiromancy in order to emphasise its supposedly proven origins in Greek culture) operated as 'alternative literacies' in an era of mass literacy and rapid scientific and technological change. It will further argue that the popularity of these 'alternative literacies' was to a considerable degree grounded in the rising rates of actual literacy, as populations proud of their new-found skill in handwriting were drawn to claims that it was a unique reflection of their inner selves, and even that the hand itself was indeed a key to character.

In order to understand how the boundaries between science and the occult became so blurred, it is worth considering the broader cultural and scientific context of the period. That broader context requires us to consider the avalanche of new technologies and scientific discoveries the general public were being asked to assimilate, quite a few of which were specifically focused upon the hand in one way or another. That combination of new technology and the human hand was especially clear in the case of the x-ray. Invented by Wilhelm Roentgen in 1895, x-ray technology – as it was seen by the public in its first years – had a particular focus upon the hand. As Sylvia Pamboukian has noted, almost all of the x-ray images first seen by the public were of hands – the first published image circulated was of Roentgen's wife's hand wearing a ring in order to emphasise the hand's skeletal form.[4] Hands wearing jewellery, along with hands showing some kind of bone damage, were frequently published during the initial public enthusiasm for the new technology, and unsurprisingly (for practical reasons) the hand was the body part most frequently x-rayed for the public's entertainment at bazaars and fairs. For example, when an

3 'This Scientist Endorses Palmistry', *Sunday Irish Independent*, 30 May 1909, p. 4.

4 See Sylvia Pamboukian, '"Looking Radiant": Science, Photography and the X-Ray Craze of 1896', *Victorian Review* 27.2 (2001): 56–74.

x-ray machine was first exhibited in Ireland at the Cyclopia Bazaar (a charity fundraising event in aid of the Molesworth Street Eye and Ear Hospital) in 1896, the *Irish Times* reported that visitors 'may, if they wish, have negatives taken of the bones of their own hands', and very many did just that, as it proved one of the most popular entertainments at the entire event.[5]

As well as x-rays, fingerprint technology was (by definition) focused upon the hand, and during the 1890s it also rapidly captured the public imagination. Although it was not accepted into British courtrooms as evidence until 1901 (and the first Irish case to use fingerprints seems to have been a burglary trial in 1905), it received a great deal of press attention from 1892 onwards, when Francis Galton published his study *Finger Prints*, and it soon began appearing in the wildly popular and growing genre of detective fiction, most notably that of Arthur Conan Doyle.[6] Sherlock Holmes was an early devotee of fingerprints as a method of detection, first using them as early as 1890, in *The Sign of Four,* and it is striking that by the publication of 'The Adventure of the Norwood Builder' in 1903, Conan Doyle used fingerprint evidence as a key plot device with which the reader was presumed to be familiar.[7] The popular Irish writer Mrs L.T. Meade wrote at least two short stories in 1902 featuring Diana Marburg, a 'palmist detective' who uses her powers of divination to solve crimes. The stories are very clear in their expectation that readers take the heroine's palm-reading seriously, just as Conan Doyle expects readers to trust fingerprint technology.

As the enormous popularity of genres like detective fiction indicates, the new literacy of ordinary citizens resonated in their leisure activities as well as the workplace. It enabled the growth of popular publishing for that new readership, not only producing books, but also magazines and periodicals aimed at younger and less well-educated but nevertheless enthusiastic readers. Irish examples of these publications included the *Shamrock* (begun in 1875), *Ireland's Own* (begun in 1902), and the *Irish Packet*. The advent of 'new journalism', and newspapers such as the *Irish Independent* (begun in 1905) with its more informal and approachable style intended to appeal to less privileged readers, also encouraged those readers to 'write back' via letters pages, notes and queries columns and above all else competitions, which typically required readers to display their literacy by contributing poetry, limericks, jokes, stories or 'missing word' games.[8] All of these activities – at work and at home – were dependent upon the fact that the majority of the Irish population now operated

5 'Cyclopia', *Irish Times*, 15 May 1896, p. 5.

6 Francis Galton, *Finger Prints* (London: Macmillan and Co., 1892).

7 See James O'Brien, *The Scientific Sherlock Holmes: Cracking the Case with Science & Forensics* (Oxford: Oxford University Press, 2013) for a full discussion of Conan Doyle's use of fingerprints in Holmes stories.

8 See Karen Steele and Michael de Nie (eds), *Ireland and the New Journalism* (London:

within a culture of literacy. The more sophisticated practitioners of palmistry – such as William John Warner, an Irish 'society palmist' who worked as 'Cheiro' – deliberately blurred the lines between the scientific discoveries of x-rays and fingerprints, and the claims of palmistry. For example, in Cheiro's 1932 memoir, *Confessions: Memoirs of a Modern Seer*, he reproduced a purported x-ray of King Edward VII's hand alongside the standard palm drawings or photographs of other famous clients Cheiro claimed to have known – he did not explain the significance of the x-ray, nor draw from it any conclusions about the King's personality. But its mere presence, alongside apparently learned treatises on the ancient 'science' of palmistry, would have served to imply a connection between x-ray technology and palmistry. And elsewhere in the book he directly compared palmistry to the science of fingerprints, arguing that:

> If the ignorant prejudice against a complete study of the hand could be overcome, the police would be still more aided by studying the lines of the palm, and by a knowledge of what these lines mean, especially as regards mentality and the inclination of the brain in one direction or another.[9]

Other influential practitioners – such as Edward Heron-Allen, a friend of Oscar Wilde and the inspiration for his 1887 story 'Lord Arthur Savile's Crime: A story of Cheiromancy' – also made 'scientific' claims for palmistry.[10] He argued that the human hand was not only what separated mankind from other animals (an argument previously made by Aristotle, and much-cited by palmists), but that it was also the most important body part because it is 'essentially the organ of the mind, the medium of its expression, and the instrument whereby its promptings are carried into execution'.[11] Both 'Cheiro' and Heron-Allen also published books purporting to teach readers how to practice palmistry correctly. Cheiro's 1895 book *The Language of the Hand* claimed to instruct readers how to become palm-readers, using diagrams of palm lines, accompanied by much arcane discussion of the 'science' and 'ancient wisdom' of cheiromancy.[12] Their manuals were part of a small avalanche of late nineteenth century 'self-help' palmistry books which in effect traded upon

Palgrave Macmillan, 2014) for an overview of the ways that new journalism impacted Irish publishing.

9 'Cheiro', *Confessions: Memoirs of a Modern Seer* (London: Jarrolds, 1932), p. 25.

10 Joan Navarre, 'Oscar Wilde, Edward Heron-Allen, and the Palmistry Craze of the 1880s', *English Literature in Transition, 1880–1920* 54.2 (2011): 174–84.

11 Edward Heron-Allen, *A Manual of Cheirosophy* (London: Ward, Lock & Co, 1885) p. 24.

12 'Cheiro', *Cheiro's Language of the Hand* (London and New York: Transatlantic Publishing Company, 1897).

the expanded readership created by mass literacy in order to sell alternative literacy skills to those readers.

Graphology and Palmistry: Alternative Literacies

Where palmistry focused on 'reading' a person's character via their palm lines, graphologists claimed to be able to discern personality and behavioural traits by studying handwriting. By the late-nineteenth and early-twentieth centuries, graphology was extremely popular, perhaps because it had the particular benefit that it naturally lent itself to being conducted in print, as the exchange between customer and the 'expert' could take place at a distance, using the postal service and printed responses. Many popular Irish newspapers and magazines ran regular graphology columns, to which readers could submit a sample of handwriting under a pseudonym, and receive a few sentences of character analysis in the following week's issue. Some of these character descriptions were brutally frank. For example, in April 1900 the *Lady of the House* graphologist 'Scripto', told 'Violet' that she had a 'pretty, lady-like hand, showing great natural discretion, which rarely fails to be in evidence except when "Violet" is fired with enthusiasm over some topic which arouses her quick sympathy'. However, in the same issue 'Daisy' was counselled that 'there is a peevishness about your writing which is disagreeable to look upon ... If you restrained any display of peevishness for a whole fortnight I am convinced your calligraphy would reflect the improvement such a course of discipline would effect'.[13]

These less than complimentary readings were quite common in graphology columns, and may well have been an indication that readers were often submitting handwriting samples of other people's writing for character analysis – quite possibly that of potential suitors, especially given the prominence in graphologists' commentary of qualities such as reliability, trustworthiness and financial prowess, which seem to hint at an understanding by the graphologists working for women's papers that it is a future husband's character which they were assessing. In another example in 1895, *Irish Society*'s regular graphology column assured a reader that the handwriting sample they had submitted was 'a most untidy hand, indicating chiefly extravagance, an impetuous hasty temper, some aggressiveness and an extremely vivid imagination'.[14] Graphology was also well suited to the chatty and even intimate tone of interaction between readers and publications which was so crucial to 'new journalism', particularly

13 'Scripto', *Lady of the House*, April 1900, p. 36.
14 'Graphology', *Irish Society*, 6 July 1895, p. 843.

in its focus on 'personality', itself something of a late nineteenth-century phenomenon.[15] Its possible use as a technique for analysing a suitor's character is also a reminder of how extensive handwritten notes and letters were in everyday life by the end of the century, as widespread literacy and cheap postal services ensured that written communication was an almost universal experience. It may have been its very universality which contributed to the belief that handwriting was revealing of character traits, which graphologists were notably quick to judge according to expectations of gender and class behaviour, valorising 'restraint' and 'discipline' while criticising 'impetuousness' or 'extravagance'.

Palmistry had a much longer history than graphology, but appears to have enjoyed a particular currency in popular culture from the late nineteenth century until after the First World War. Palmistry did of course have a very ancient heritage, and has probably been constantly practiced in many parts of the world for centuries – in Europe it has traditionally been associated with Romany fortune-telling. However, its surge of popularity from the 1880s was very marked, as newspaper and magazine columns became filled with advertisements for palmists, self-help books claiming to teach palm-reading were published by the dozen, commentators noticed and discussed the practice, and eventually movements began to condemn it and prosecute its practitioners.

Fortune-telling for money was illegal in Britain and Ireland under the 1735 Witchcraft Act, although in fact practitioners were often prosecuted in lower courts under vagrancy legislation instead. Despite its illegality, by the start of the twentieth century no bazaar, fete or even high society party was complete without a palmist, and the classified advertisement columns of newspapers – even in smaller towns such as Omagh or Nenagh – were routinely full of palmists advertising the hours when they would be 'at home' to visitors.[16] The interest in palmistry – in Ireland as in other countries – seems to have stretched across all social classes, but its professional practice appears to have been mainly by working-class women, with a few exceptions for the 'celebrity' palmists who catered to high society. It seems to have been traditionally associated with older widows with no other resources, who

15 For example, see Deborah Cohen, *Household Gods: The British and their Possessions* (Newhaven: Yale University Press, 2006) for a thorough discussion of the ways in which women's magazines and advice books encouraged late-nineteenth century readers to think of their home décor as an expression of their individual personalities, as opposed to the older concept of it displaying moral character.

16 Cecil Tell, who claimed to be a 'French Palmist', advertised his 'consultation' hours in Omagh in the *Ulster Herald* on 2 December 1905, p. 4, and in 1910 the Ormond Bazaar and Fete in Nenagh advertised that it would feature both palmists and crystal gazers, *Nenagh Guardian*, 20 May 1910, p. 4.

turned to palm-reading as one of the few sources of income available to them. In 1915, for example, when Mrs Mary Kelch of Harold's Cross, Dublin was convicted of palmistry and fortune-telling under the name Carmen Sylvia, she told the court that her husband had died 15 years earlier and 'she had to do it for a living'.[17]

These were obviously very small-scale operations with no advertising, and it seems likely that most of their clients were friends and neighbours. More commercial operations ran from rented rooms and entertainment parlours in city centres, with a particular concentration around Henry Street in Dublin. One of these was the World's Fair Waxworks housed at 30 Henry Street from the 1890s until its destruction during the 1916 Rising. The Waxworks building is known to have housed a theatre and other 'entertainments', so fortune-telling (at the cost of one shilling) was a plausible addition to these activities, which were all aimed at the growing working-class leisure market. The palmistry phenomenon from the 1880s onwards however was also characterised by its popularity among the most privileged classes. This was so marked that the phrase 'society palmist' became a recognised descriptive term for the most successful practitioners. In Dublin, examples included 'Madame Celeste', 'Minerva' and 'Professor Leo', all of whom had rooms on Grafton Street and Stephen's Green in the early years of the twentieth century. These palmists advertised in 'society papers' such as *Irish Society* and clearly anticipated an upmarket (and wealthy) clientele, charging as much as five shillings per reading by comparison to their Henry Street competitors' one shilling fee.

The 1890s was a decade marked by the prevalence of charity bazaars in Dublin, usually organised by the mainly Protestant upper-middle classes, typically in aid of the city's hospitals, and held in venues such as the Royal Dublin Showgrounds and Earlsfort Terrace Exhibition Palace. These were large-scale and very fashionable events, sometimes drawing crowds of up to 80,000 visitors in a week, and they traded upon offering spectacle and novelty to the Dublin crowds. They therefore reflected the cultural trends of the period, and alongside stalls selling bric-a-brac, Turkish coffee palaces and displays of tightrope walking, these bazaars frequently employed palmists operating from exotically decorated tents, and who featured prominently in the bazaars' advertising. In 1896, for example, the Ishani Bazaar's newspaper advertisements promised the presence of no fewer than three palmists, Madames Cheiro, Esmeralda and Carmen Sylva, 'each of whom in return for the smallest of fees will lay bare the future, both grave and gay, of her patron'.[18]

17 'Fortune-Telling in Dublin', *Irish Times*, 6 November 1915, p. 3.
18 'Ishani Bazaar', *Freeman's Journal*, 6 May 1896, p. 3.

Palmists' penetration of Irish society's upper echelons was emphasised by the judge in a 1915 court case in Dublin. Considering sentencing, he remarked that when on a previous occasion he had sentenced an offender to prison (rather than a fine), she appealed directly to the Lord Lieutenant, and it had then emerged that she had previously read fortunes at a social event at Dublin Castle.[19] The relative impunity with which 'society' palmists operated, whether at charity events or from premises in fashionable areas, had been commented upon by the *Irish Times* in 1912, when they noted the contrast with 'humbler individuals who set up to tell fortunes', and who were regularly prosecuted.[20] Internationally, the most successful 'society palmist' was 'Cheiro', who (as was discussed above), monetised his high-society success by publishing advice books on practising palmistry. 'Cheiro' was an Irishman, born as William John Warner in Bray in 1866, and he would go on – via a range of names and careers – to become one of the era's most colourful charlatans. He published not one but two memoirs, in which he gave fanciful details of his origins as well as of the palmistry predictions he'd supposedly made for famous people – most of whom, such as Rasputin, Pope Leo XIII and Mark Twain, were conveniently dead by the time his 1932 memoir, *Confessions: Memoirs of a Modern Seer*, described his meetings with them. The memoir obscured his quotidian origins in Bray, instead claiming that his father's family were of Norman aristocratic ancestry, specifically descending from one 'Robert de Hamon' who sailed to England with William the Conqueror. Warner subsequently used the name Hamon, eventually styling himself 'Count Louis Hamon', or even 'Count Louis le Warner Hamon' during his career in London, Paris, New York and eventually California, where he died in 1936.[21]

A hint of his Irish background emerges in his story of meeting Charles Stewart Parnell in a train from Liverpool to London (both of them, this implies, having just arrived by boat from Ireland), and reading his 'destiny' from his hand. Parnell asks how 'the end' will come, and Warner replies '[a] woman, without a doubt ...You can see for yourself how the Line of the Heart breaks the Line of Destiny just below that point where it fades out'. Parnell responds with a 'low quiet laugh' and the statement that 'a man with my life has no time for women'.[22] By 1902 Warner was living in Paris, where he ran several newspapers, a champagne business and a bank based on investments by wealthy Americans living in the city. When the bank failed spectacularly in 1909 he fled to New York, although he was resident in Ireland again at the

19 'Fortune-Telling in Dublin', *Irish Times*, 6 November 1915, p. 3.
20 'Fortune Tellers', *Irish Times*, 18 September 1912, p. 6.
21 'Cheiro', *Confessions*.
22 Ibid., p. 25.

time of Independence, and was (rather incongruously) the owner of a peat works in Co. Offaly which was burned down by the IRA.[23]

Prosecutions for Palmistry in Dublin

In August 1901, the Catholic magazine *Irish Rosary* published an article specifically decrying palmistry and what it referred to as 'crystal gazing'. The unnamed author argued that these were 'superstitions' especially prevalent in England (apparently due to its Protestantism), and cited as evidence for this a recent complaint by the *Lady's Pictorial* that the 'superstition we deplore among the lower classes ... grows steadily and rapidly among the educated classes in England. Christian science, palmistry, crystal-gazing ... attract thousands of persons whom one would scarcely suppose to give way to such follies'.[24] This positioning of palmistry as particularly English was rather undermined however by the article's admission that palmistry was then so prevalent in Dublin that the Archbishop had been forced to specifically condemn it in his Lenten Pastoral address that year – the very fact that he'd felt obliged to issue this condemnation suggesting of course that palmistry's popularity was just as great in Ireland as it was in England.[25] The Archbishop's own denunciations were also undermined by the fact that not only he had opened the 1898 Columba Bazaar in Dublin (in aid of a parish school in Drumcondra) which like most charity bazaars of the time had featured a palmist, but also, two years after issuing this formal condemnation of palmistry, he and his wife would be among the patrons of the Isolde Bazaar in Chapelizod, which proudly announced palmistry as one of its main attractions.[26]

Quite aside from the doctrinal contradiction of the Archbishop's patronage of events which included palmists, it was of course also illegal, although there never appear to have been any prosecutions arising from palmistry at bazaars or other middle-class events. Instead, the authorities concentrated their attention upon the palmists who operated out of rented rooms in town and city centres and appealed mainly to working-class and lower-middle-class customers. These include cases such as 'Madame Eugenie' and 'Professor Mars', both of whom practiced palmistry from within entertainment parlours on Henry Street in Dublin, and both of whom were prosecuted in a concerted suppression of the practice in 1905. In Madame Eugenie's case it was not a

23 'Tale of a Crowded Career: Bray Man's Busy Life', *Irish Independent*, 28 June 1926, p. 8.
24 'Seancus', *Irish Rosary*, August 1901, p. 536.
25 'Lenten Pastorals', *Irish Times*, 18 February 1901, p. 5.
26 'Columba Bazaar', *Irish Times*, 27 April 1898 p. 6; 'Isolde Bazaar', *Irish Times*, 1 June 1903, p. 6.

first offence, and the prosecutor complained that she had previously '[given] his worship an undertaking that she would discontinue this foolish practice of deceiving servants, shop girls, and other young girls with these mysteries of the future. She was, however, at it again'.[27]

The usual method by which the authorities brought palmists for prosecution was by first sending an undercover policeman to have his fortune told. This of course was necessary in order to prove that the palmist was indeed foretelling the future in return for payment, a necessary condition for prosecution. It also meant however that the police officers later had to give fairly detailed evidence in court about the precise nature of the palmists' predictions. The contrast between the typically phlegmatic constable giving straight-faced evidence, and the high-flown and often wildly unlikely predictions he had been given for his future tended to cause particular amusement in court, not only from the public gallery, but often from court officials as well. At the trial of 'Professor Mars' in 1905, the constable who had visited the defendant reported that he had been assured, 'I cannot say that a woman will be your downfall, but there is a fair and dark-haired woman in your path (laughter)', to which the prosecuting solicitor responded 'Two of them, poor wretch', prompting more laughter from the public gallery. In 1909, even the presiding magistrate appeared to join in the gaiety in a case against 'Madame Charles', whose premises at 9 Upper Merrion Street were visited by Constable 125B in order to gather evidence for a prosecution. The constable's shilling fortune prediction included the information that '[y]ou had a tall, dark young lady at one time, but she seems to be gone away ... You will be married to her soon, but you will be happy together'. In response, the defendant's solicitor enquired 'Had you ever a dark young lady in your life?', but before the constable could reply, the magistrate interrupted to remind him 'You are not bound to incriminate yourself', to predictable laughter in court.[28]

Such moments of courtroom comedy were common, and probably the main reason why so many cases against palm-readers were reported in the national papers, often under headlines such as 'an amusing case'. It is clear that those laughing in court – from the public gallery to the magistrates – did not themselves take palmists' predictions seriously, and appeared to regard them as harmful only to the 'shop girls and servants' so often referenced by prosecuting solicitors and magistrates. In other words, like the romantic novels or risqué photographs which were also being rigorously policed by the growing social purity movement during the first decade of the twentieth century, palm-reading, crystal balls and all of the paraphernalia of fortune-telling were regarded as corrupting and dangerous mainly to the young, the

27 'Palmistry Prosecution in the Police Court', *Irish Times* 1 February 1906, p. 3.
28 'Lady Palmist: The Constable's Dark Young Lady', *Irish Independent*, 4 July 1909, p. 11.

female and the working class.[29] Just as it was presumed that those readers lacked discrimination and rational judgement with regard to their reading of novels or penny papers, so their consumption of palm-reading was also understood to be naïve and uncritical.

These differing implications of literacy (of any kind) also explain why charity bazaars – even those patronised by the Archbishop of Dublin – could openly advertise palmists and 'crystal gazers' as some of their main attractions, even as the Archbishop himself was formally condemning the practices, and indeed as other palmists were being prosecuted. The crucial difference between the palmists prosecuted and those listed as star attractions at charity bazaars was of course their clientele. The majority of visitors to charity bazaars were from the middle or upper classes, unlike the gullible servant girls who were constantly referenced in court cases as being 'duped' by palmists operating from rented rooms and entertainment parlours.[30] In 1899 one palmist, using the alias 'Madame Futura', was even convicted of a complicated double fraud resulting from having run both a fake servants' registry office and having done palm-readings from rooms on South Anne Street in Dublin.[31] The professional men laughing during prosecutions in the Dublin district courts obviously regarded themselves, their friends, neighbours and families as immune from the confusions sown by fortune-tellers of all kinds.

In this respect then, fortune-telling was subject to the same class and gender judgements as the other forms of popular entertainment which were being condemned or even suppressed with increasing frequency. It is telling, for example, that in the 1901 Lenten Pastoral in which he denounced palmistry, the Archbishop of Dublin had also singled out popular theatres in the city as showing a 'disregard of all moral restraint' in their staging of 'debasing performances and displays', along with wakes, the reading of immoral poetry and romances, and finally the 'display of pictures of a demoralising tendency' on advertising hoardings.[32] This places palmistry alongside the principal targets of the social purity movement in Ireland during the early-twentieth century – literature, advertising and many leisure activities popular with the

29 See Stephanie Rains, '"Nauseous Tides of Seductive Debauchery": Irish Story Papers and the Anti-Vice Campaigns of the Early Twentieth Century', *Irish University Review* 45.2 (2015): 263–80 for a discussion of the social purity movement in Ireland at this time.

30 It was very specifically 'servant girls' who were often named as the generic victims of palmists, as in the cases reported in 'Fortune Telling in Galway: Servant Girl Duped', *Irish Times*, 12 July 1910, p. 6; and 'Fortune Telling: "Gypsy" and Domestic Servant', *Irish Times*, 13 July 1917, p. 2.

31 'Extraordinary Charge of Fraud', *Irish Times*, 6 March 1899, p. 3.

32 'Lenten Pastorals', *Irish Times*, 18 February 1901, p. 5.

working class. Women, and in this instance especially working-class women, were perceived to be more at risk than male or middle-class consumers. The *Irish Rosary* article which condemned palmistry and 'crystal gazing' specifically gendered the risks involved, suggesting that

> 'such a man as will make headway on the Stock Exchange or in the Four Courts' was not likely to be fooled by the claims of fortune-tellers, but that some 'neurotically-deranged freaks' might take the practice seriously – and when giving an example of one of these 'neurotically damaged' individuals, it added that she was, 'a woman, of course'.[33]

Science Meets the Occult

The immunity of professional men from the charlatans of fortune-telling in all of its forms may not have been as complete as many liked to believe, however. While palmists' tendency to prey on 'shop girls and servants' was much emphasised in court and in editorials, the confusion about where science ended and the occult began appears to have been quite widespread. Sometimes even educated observers were prepared to contemplate the possibility that palm-prints could be expertly 'read' in order to divulge character and temperament, even as they contemptuously refused the idea that a person's future could also be read in this way. This sense of confusion between quackery and science was evident as early as 1887, when an *Irish Times* column asserted that:

> The enlightened folk who sweepingly condemn the fortune-teller as a liar and a cheat are probably no less mistaken than the ignorant rustics who blindly believe in her as an infallible oracle. Should not precisely the superior enlightenment of which we boast now-a-days be rather an argument for believing in the fortune-teller? If phrenology and graphology are permitted to take rank as acknowledged sciences, why should not the gipsy woman's power of divination be equally allowed to count as a shrewd deciphering of character, coupled with logical deductions as to the events likely to be evoked by the action of the passions, in combination with a given set of circumstances?[34]

And the *Irish Rosary*, in its lengthy condemnation of palmistry in 1901, went on to concede that 'if the "science" merely pretended to give a wide,

33 'Seancus', *Irish Rosary*, August 1901, p. 536.
34 'Belief in Fortune-Telling', *Irish Times*, 11 June 1887, p. 1.

general outline of a person's character – his temperament, disposition, qualities and so on – such an outline, for instance, as phrenology aims at giving, one might think there could be something in it'.[35] In 'Fingerprints', one of L.T. Meade's stories featuring Diana Marburg the palmist detective, she tellingly blends palm-reading and fingerprint evidence in a way which seems to reflect a widespread sense that the two were scientifically equivalent. Marburg solves the mystery of jewellery stolen from a country house safe and foils an attempt to frame an innocent man for its theft. Both a palm print and a set of fingerprints have been left by the thief in some wet furniture varnish at the crime scene. Having given readings for her fellow guests the previous night, Marburg instantly recognises the palm print as belonging to her friend's fiancé Jim Cunnyngham – but the fingerprints turn out to belong to their host, Sir Edward Granville, who had planted the palm print (taken from a cast he had been allowed to make) because he wanted to frame Cunnyngham in order to marry Marburg's friend. On first meeting Granville, Marburg had noticed 'the long and broad thumb of an iron will – the spatulate fingers of precision and determination. The man who has these characteristics sticks at nothing to obtain his ends'.[36] This was entirely typical of the language of palmistry, and was precisely the kind of pseudo-science to be found in manuals on the topic, such as Cheiro's *Language of the Hand*. Later in Meade's story however, when the fingerprints are discovered at the crime scene, Marburg displays an enthusiastically scientific knowledge of fingerprint technology, explaining that 'I remembered Professor Galton's well-known and exhaustive researches on finger-prints, the fact which he has abundantly proved being that no two persons in the world have the same skin ridges'.[37]

Its use in a detective story in order to reveal the identity of a criminal underlines the powerful appeal of equating palm-reading with fingerprint technology. The lines being blurred were not only those between science and the occult, but also those between the proof of an individual's identity and the revelation of their character. The willingness to equate embodied techniques for basic identification with claims to be able to read character, which are seen in the popular enthusiasm for both palm-reading and graphology, suggests a widespread desire for reassurance that the physical body (and specifically the hand) could be 'read' in order to reveal an individual's inner qualities, thus defeating possible attempts at disguise or deception. If fingerprints were accepted as unique to each individual, then even to supposedly expert

35 'Seancus', *Irish Rosary*, August 1901, p. 536.
36 Mrs L.T. Meade, 'The Dead Hand', *The Oracle of Maddox Street* (London: Ward Locke, 1904).
37 Ibid.

observers, the idea that palm lines or handwriting might also contain hidden revelations of character did not seem too far-fetched.

Conclusion

From graphology to x-rays, and palmistry to fingerprints, the hand was therefore perceived to be a revelatory body part, capable of revealing inner qualities otherwise invisible to the observer. If it was now possible to see through human flesh, then perhaps it was also possible to 'pierce the veil' to other planes of existence and see into the future or even communicate with the dead, and a great many people sought out methods which they hoped would allow them to do just that. As Henry Carrington Bolton put it in his 1895 exploration of fortune-telling in America: 'The intelligent and cultivated become students of psychology, hypnotism and psychical phenomena, while the unlettered and credulous dabble in cheiromancy, clairvoyance and astrology'.[38]

In 1909 Nicholas Vaschide published a book-length study entitled *Essai sur la Psychologie de la main*, in which he made a 'scientific' case for both palmistry and graphology as a guide to true inner character, arguing that handwriting's strokes and manoeuvres with a pen revealed aspects of its owner's temperament, character and morals, adding that 'graphology, or the study of handwriting, is nothing less than an experimental demonstration of the mental revelations made through the hand', while also asserting of palm-reading that 'lines of the hand develop, changing as the years pass and the character develops'.[39] In Ireland, the *Sunday Independent* published a lengthy and approving article reviewing the book and outlining its main arguments as proven scientific facts, which was hardly surprising given that unlike 'Professor Leo' who had advertised his palmistry service from rooms on Grafton Street, Vaschide was a genuine professor at the entirely reputable Laboratory of Pathological Psychology of the School of Higher Study in Paris.[40]

The mass literacy of the late-nineteenth century brought with it a world of 'alternative literacies' which co-existed and intertwined with conventional understandings of reading and writing. There was a great deal more to the culture of literacy which existed by the late nineteenth century than the expansion of a purely utilitarian ability to read and write. Especially for those who were among the first generations of their family to be fully literate, it brought with it new life chances in the form of clerical or typing work with

38 Henry Carrington Bolton, 'Fortune-Telling in America To-Day. A Study of Advertisements', *Journal of American Folklore* 8.31 (1895), p. 299.

39 Nicholas Vaschide, *Essai sur la Psychologie de la main* (Paris: Marcel Rivière, 1909).

40 'This Scientist Endorses Palmistry', *Sunday Independent*, 30 May 1909, p. 4.

better pay and conditions than previous generations could have aspired to. But it also brought access to the enormously expanded world of mass media, not only as readers but as writers too. The 'new journalism' of the period encouraged readers to write back and they did so, in many different contexts. And once entire families and communities were literate, then personal and intimate writing would also have become the norm – letters, telegrams, postcards and diaries which between them recorded everything from mundane family updates to important news and the most private of thoughts. It is therefore hardly surprising that handwriting itself – and the hand which produced it – should have been seen as something important, highly individual and deeply connected to its owners' sense of identity.

Graphology and palm-reading both traded upon this belief that the hand itself was uniquely revealing of the inner self, and that its movements or characteristics were in some way a reflection of the mind. Where graphology claimed that character and behavioural traits could be interpreted from a person's handwriting, palmistry went further again and suggested that as fingerprints were unique to each individual, so the very surface of the hand itself in the form of the palm lines could reveal not only their character but also their life story and even perhaps their future. While official narratives (especially during criminal prosecutions) spoke of amused 'men of business' and duped 'servants and shop-girls', in reality there were scientists prepared to consider that the 'hand is the picture of the brain', just as there must have been many shop girls who considered their shilling palm-reading on Henry Street to be merely a cheap amusement. In a world of rapidly developing scientific knowledge and new technologies, these 'alternative literacies' functioned as one of the most unstable borders between science and entertainment.

Select Bibliography

Primary Sources

Archives

British Library (BL)
Bureau of Military History (BMH), Military Archives, Ireland
Centre Culturel Irlandais (CCI), Paris, France
National Archives of Ireland (NAI). 'Census of Ireland 1901/1911 and Census fragments and substitutes, 1821–51'
National Library of Ireland (NLI)
Public Record Office of Northern Ireland (PRONI)

British Library (BL)

BL Add MS 14,380, f. 77. George Everest. 'Memoir, containing an account of the Irish Survey, and a comparison of the same with the system pursued in India, 1829', in 'Papers Relating to the Survey of India, etc.'

National Library of Ireland (NLI)

NLI MS13280	'24 Letters from Albert De La Hoyde 1860–70'
NLI MS13280/2	'Letters of a Papal Zouave'
NLI MS13282	'Narrative of Brother Aloysius Howlin'
NLI MS21522	'Letters to his Mother [in Francis Street, Dublin] from Richard A. O'Carroll, a sergeant in the Papal Brigade, containing descriptions of Rome, the battle of Loreto, and experiences as a prisoner of war, with associated items including certificate of presentation of Papal medals, June-Oct., 1860'
NLI MSS13280–13287	'Letters, Photographs, Notes and Drafts, being Materials for G.F. Berkeley's Studies of the Irish Brigade in the Papal Service, 1860'
NLI MSS G 1036–1048	Douglas Hyde Diaries
NLI MS 17,775	Arthur Hyde Diary

Journals, Magazines and Newspapers

Arminian Magazine
Belfast Evening Telegraph
Catholic Guardian
Christian Advocate
Dublin Penny Journal
Dublin University Magazine
Freeman's Journal
Ireland's Own
Irish Evangelist
Irish Independent
Irish Monthly
Irish Packet
Irish Penny Journal
Irish Rosary
Irish Society
Irish Times
Lady of the House
Mechanics Magazine
Methodist Times
The Nation
Nenagh Guardian
The Shamrock
Sunday Irish Independent
The Times
Ulster Herald
Watchman
Weekly Irish Times
Wesleyan-Methodist Magazine

Secondary Bibliography

Adams, J.R.R. *The Printed Word and the Common Man: Popular Culture in Ulster 1700–1900*. Belfast: Institute of Irish Studies, 1987.

Adorno, Theodor W. and Horkheimer, Max. 'The Concept of Enlightenment', in *Dialectic of Enlightenment*, trans. John Cumming. London: Verso, 1997, pp. 3–42.

Akenson, Donald H. *The Irish Education Experiment: The National System of Education in the Nineteenth Century*. London: Routledge, 1970.

Altholz, J.L. *The Religious Press in Britain, 1760–1900*. New York: Greenwood Press, 1989.

Altick, Richard D. *The English Common Reader*. Chicago: University of Chicago Press, 1957.

Anderson, Benedict. *Imagined Communities: Reflections on the Origins and Spread of Nationalism*. 1983; revised ed. London: Verso, 2006.

Andrews, Ann. *Newspapers and Newsmakers: The Dublin Nationalist Press in the Mid-Nineteenth Century*. Liverpool: Liverpool University Press, 2014.

Andrews, John H. *History in the Ordnance Map: An Introduction for Irish Readers*. Kerry, Wales: David Archer, 1993.

Andrews, John H. *A Paper Landscape: The Ordnance Survey in Nineteenth-Century Ireland*. 2nd ed. Dublin: Four Courts Press, 2002.

Arthur, William. *Ought Not the Two Methodist Bodies in Ireland to Become One?* Dublin, 1869.

Arthur, William. *The Householder's Parliament: A Word to the Electors of 1885*. London, 1885.

Ballantyne, Tony, 'The Sinews of Empire: Ireland, India and the Construction of British Colonial Knowledge', in Terrence McDonough (ed.), *Was Ireland a Colony? Economics, Politics and Culture in Nineteenth-Century Ireland*. Dublin: Irish Academic Press, 2005, pp. 145–61.

Barr, Colin. 'University Education, History and the Hierarchy', in Lawrence W. McBride (ed.), *Reading Irish Histories: Texts, Contexts and Memory in Modern Ireland*. Dublin: Four Courts Press, 2003, pp. 62–79.

Barr, Colin, Finelli, Michele and O'Connor, Anne (eds). *Nation/Nazione: Irish Nationalism and the Italian Risorgimento*. Dublin: UCD Press, 2013.

Barry, M.J. 'Ireland as she was, as she is, and as she shall be', in *Essays on the Repeal of the Union*. Dublin: James Duffy, 1845.

Bassnett, Susan and Trivedi, Harish (eds). *Postcolonial Translation: Theory and Practice*. London: Routledge, 1999.

Bateman, Fiona. 'Ireland's Spiritual Empire: Territory and Landscape in Irish Catholic Missionary Discourse', in Hilary M. Carey (ed.), *Empires of Religion*. Basingstoke and New York: Palgrave Macmillan, 2008, pp. 267–87.

Bayly, C.A. 'Ireland, India and the Empire: 1780–1914', *Transactions of the Royal Historical Society*, 6th Series, 10 (2000): 377–97.

Bebbington, D.W. *The Nonconformist Conscience: Chapel and Politics, 1870–1918*. London: George Allen & Unwin, 1982.

Benatti, Francesca. *A National and Concordant Feeling: Penny Journals in Ireland, 1832–1842*. Unpub. PhD diss., NUI Galway, 2003.

Bender, Jill. 'The Imperial Politics of Famine: The 1873–74 Bengal Famine and Irish Parliamentary Nationalism', *Éire-Ireland* 42.1–2 (2007): 132–56.

Benson, Charles. 'The Dublin Book Trade', in James H. Murphy (ed.), *The Oxford History of the Irish Book, Vol. IV: The Irish Book in English, 1800–1891*. Oxford: Oxford University Press, 2011, pp. 27–46.

Berkeley, G.F.H. *The Irish Battalion in the Papal Army of 1860*. Dublin & Cork: Talbot Press, 1929.

Bhreathnach, Edel and Bernadette Cunningham (eds). *Writing Irish History: The Four Masters and their World*. Dublin: WordWell, 2007.

Biagini, Eugenio F. and Mary E. Daly, 'Editors' Introduction', in Biagini and Daly (eds), *The Cambridge Social History of Modern Ireland*. Cambridge: Cambridge University Press, 2017, pp. 1–4.

Billington, Louis. 'The Religious Periodical and Newspaper Press, 1770–1870', in Michael Harris and A.J. Lee (eds), *The Press in English Society from the Seventeenth to Nineteenth Centuries*. London: Associated University Press, 1986, pp. 89–108.

Black, Jeremy. *Visions of the World: A History of Maps*. London: Mitchell Beazley, 2003.

Bolton, Henry Carrington. 'Fortune-Telling in America To-Day. A Study of Advertisements', *Journal of American Folklore* 8.31 (1895): 299–307.

Borutta, Manuel. 'Anti-Catholicism and the Culture War in Risorgimento Italy', in Lucy Riall and Silvana Patriarca (eds), *The Risorgimento Revisited: Nationalism and Culture in Nineteenth-Century Italy*. Basingstoke: Palgrave, 2012, pp. 191–213.

Boyle, Patrick. *The Irish College in Paris from 1578 to 1901*. London: Art & Book Co., 1901.

Bradshaw, D.B. 'The Irish Edition of the "Methodist Magazine"', *Proceedings of the Wesleyan Historical Society* 13.3 (1921): 56–60.

Brake, Laurel and Marysa Demoor (eds). *Dictionary of Nineteenth-Century Journalism in Great Britain and Ireland*. Gent: Academia Press, 2009.

Brantlinger, Patrick. *The Reading Lesson: The Threat of Mass Literacy in Nineteenth-Century British Fiction*. Bloomington: Indiana University Press, 1998.

Breathnach, Ciara. '"Indelible Characters": Tattoos, Power and the Late Nineteenth-Century Irish Convict', *Cultural and Social History* 12.2 (2015): 235–54.

Brown, Michael. *The Irish Enlightenment*. Harvard: Harvard University Press, 2015.

Callanan, Frank. *The Parnell Split, 1890–91*. Syracuse, NY: Syracuse University Press, 1992.

Census of Ireland, 1861. Dublin: Alexander Thom for Her Majesty's Stationery Office, 1863–64.

Census of Ireland, 1871. Dublin: Alexander Thom for Her Majesty's Stationery Office, 1873–76.

Census of Ireland, 1881. Dublin: Alexander Thom for Her Majesty's Stationery Office, 1882.

Census of Ireland, 1891. Dublin: Alexander Thom for Her Majesty's Stationery Office, 1892.

Census of Ireland, 1901. Dublin: His Majesty's Stationery Office, 1901–04.

Census of Ireland, 1911. Dublin: His Majesty's Stationery Office, 1912–13.

Chambers, Liam. 'Paul Cullen and the Irish College, Paris', in Dáire Keogh and Albert McDonnell (eds), *Cardinal Paul Cullen and his World*. Dublin: Four Courts Press, 2011, pp. 358–76.

Chartier, Roger. 'The Two Frances: The History of a Geographical Idea', in Chartier, *Cultural History: Between Practices and Representations*. Cambridge: Polity Press, 1988, pp. 172–200.

'Cheiro' [William John Warner]. *Cheiro's Language of the Hand*. London and New York: Transatlantic Publishing Company, 1897.

'Cheiro' [William John Warner]. *Confessions: Memoirs of a Modern Seer*. London: Jarrolds, 1932.

Cheyfitz, Eric. *The Poetics of Imperialism: Translation and Colonization from the Tempest to Tarzan*. Oxford: Oxford University Press, 1991.

Clarke, Frances. 'Hoey, Frances Sarah (Mrs Cashel Hoey) Johnston', in James McGuire and James Quinn (eds), *Dictionary of Irish Biography*. Cambridge: Cambridge University Press, 2009, pp. 735–36.

Clarke, Randall. 'The Relations Between O'Connell and the Young Irelanders', *Irish Historical Studies* III.9 (1942): 23–26.

Clyde, Tom. *Irish Literary Magazines: An Outline History and Descriptive Bibliography*. Dublin: Irish Academic Press, 2003.

Cohen, Deborah. *Household Gods: The British and their Possessions*. Newhaven: Yale University Press, 2006.

Coldrey, Barry. *The Educational Ideas of Edmund Rice and Other Essays*. Thornbury: Tamanaraik Press, 2001.

Colley, Linda. *Britons: Forging the Nation 1707–1837*. Rev. ed. London: Pimlico, 1992.

Comerford, R.V. *Ireland*. London: Hodder Arnold 2003.

Cook, S.B. *Imperial Affinities: Nineteenth Century Analogies and Exchanges between India and Ireland*. New Delhi: Sage Publications, 1993.

Coulombe, Charles A. *The Pope's Legion: The Multinational Fighting Force that Defended the Vatican*. New York: Palgrave Macmillan, 2008.

Crean, Cyril P. 'The Irish Battalion of St Patrick at the Defence of Spoleto, September 1860', *The Irish Sword*, Vol. 4 (1959–1960).

Cronin, Michael. *Translating Ireland: Translation, Languages, Cultures*. Cork: Cork University Press, 1996.

Cronin, Nessa. 'Monstrous Hybridity: Kim of the "Eye-rishti" and the Survey of India', in Tadhg Foley and Maureen O'Connor (eds), *Ireland and India: Colonies, Culture and Empire*. Dublin: Irish Academic Press, 2006, pp. 131–39.

Cronin, Nessa, Séan Crosson and John Eastlake (eds). *Anáil an Bhéil Bheo: Orality and Modern Irish Culture*. Newcastle upon Tyne: Cambridge Scholars Publishing, 2009.

Crook, William. *Ireland and the Centenary of American Methodism*. London: Hamilton, Adams and Co., 1866.

Crookshank, C.H. *A History of Methodism in Ireland*, 3 vols. London: T. Woolmer, 1885–88.

Crosbie, Barry. *Irish Imperial Networks, Migration, Social Communication and Exchange in Nineteenth-Century India*. Cambridge: Cambridge University Press, 2012.

Cryan, Mary Jane. *The Irish and English in Italy's Risorgimento*. Viterbo: Archeoares, 2011.

Cullen, L.M. *The Emergence of Modern Ireland*. London: Batsford, 1981.

Cumbers, Frank. 'The Methodist Magazine, 1778–1969', *Proceedings of the Wesleyan Historical Society* 37:3 (1969): 72–76.

Currie, Robert. *Methodism Divided: a Study of the Sociology of Ecumenicalism*. London: Faber, 1969.

Curtin, Nancy. *The United Irishmen: Popular Politics in Ulster and Dublin 1791–1798*. Oxford: Clarendon Press, 1994.

Cuthbertson, Greg. 'Pricking the "Nonconformist Conscience": Religion Against the South African War', in Donal Lowry (ed.), *The South African War Reappraised*. Manchester: Manchester University Press, 2000, pp. 169–87.

Daly, Dominic. *The Young Douglas Hyde*. Baile Átha Cliath: Irish University Press, 1974.

Daly, Mary and David Dickson (eds). *The Origins of Popular Literacy in Ireland: Language Change and Educational Development 1700–1920*. Dublin: Trinity College Dublin and University College Dublin, 1990.

Davis, Thomas. Lecture delivered to the Historical Society, *Nation*, 22 January 1848.

Davis, Thomas. *Thomas Davis: Selections from his Prose and Poetry*. T.W. Rolleston (ed.). Dublin: Talbot Press, 1914.

De h-Íde, Dubhghlas. *Mo Thurus go hAmerice: nó, Imeasg na nGaedheal ins an Oileán Úr*. Baile Átha Cliath: Oifig Díolta Foillseacháin Rialtais, 1937.

de Louvigny, Jean Bernières. *The Interior Christian: in Eight Books*, trans. Anon. Dublin: printed by Richard Cross, 1804.

Dekker, Rudolf. *Egodocuments and History: Autobiographical Writing in its Social Context since the Middle Ages*. Hilversum: Uitgeverij, 2002.

Delano-Smith, Catherine and Kain, Roger J.P. *English Maps: A History*. Toronto: Toronto University Press, 1999.

Denvir, John. *The Life Story of an Old Rebel*. Dublin: Sealy, Bryers & Walker, 1910.

Devoy, John. *Recollections of an Irish Rebel: A Personal Narrative*. New York: Chase D. Young, 1929.

Dickson, David, Justyna Pyz and Christopher Shepard (eds). *Irish Classrooms and British Empire: Imperial Contexts in the Origins of Modern Education*. Dublin: Four Courts Press, 2012.

Doherty, Gillian M. *The Irish Ordnance Survey: History, Culture and Memory*. Dublin: Four Courts Press, 2004.

Donnelly, James S. 'Propagating the Cause of the United Irishmen' *Studies: an Irish Quarterly Review* 69.273 (1980): 5–23.

Donnelly, James S. and Kerby A. Miller (eds). *Irish Popular Culture, 1650–1850*. Dublin: Irish Academic Press, 1998.

Doyle, Aidan. *A History of the Irish Language: From the Norman Conquest to Independence*. Oxford: Oxford University Press, 2015.

Doyle, Robert. 'The Pope's Irish Battalion, 1860', *History Ireland* 18.5 (2010): 26–29.

Drummond, Thomas. 'On the Means of Facilitating the Observation of Distant Objects in Geodetic Operations', *Royal Society Philosophical Transactions* Part 2 (1826): 324–37.

Duffy, Charles Gavan. *Young Ireland: a Fragment of Irish History*. London: Cassell, Petter, Galpin and Co., 1880.

Duffy, Charles Gavan. *Four Years of Irish History*. London: Cassell, Petter, Galpin and Co., 1883.

Duffy, Charles Gavan. *Thomas Davis: the Memoirs of an Irish Patriot, 1840–1846*. London, 1890.

Duffy, Charles Gavan. *The Revival of Irish Literature*. London: T. Fischer Unwin, 1894.

Dunleavy, Janet Egleson and Gareth W. Dunleavy. *Douglas Hyde: A Maker of Modern Ireland*. Berkeley: University of California Press, 1991.

Dwan, David. *The Great Community: Culture and Nationalism in Ireland*. Dublin: Field Day, 2008.

Eagleton, Terry. *Heathcliff and the Great Hunger: Studies in Irish Culture*. London: Verso, 1995.

Edney, Matthew. *Mapping an Empire: The Geographical Construction of British India, 1765–1843*. Chicago: University of Chicago Press, 1997.

Edwards, O.D. '"True Thomas": Carlyle, Young Ireland and the Legacy of Millennialism', in David Sorensen and Rodger L. Tarr (eds), *The Carlyles at Home and Abroad*. Aldershot: Ashgate, 2006, pp. 61–76.

Edwards, R. Dudley (ed.). *Ireland and the Italian Risorgimento: Three Lectures*. Dublin: Italian Institute, 1960.

Everest, George. 'On the Compensation Measuring Apparatus of the Great Trigonometrical Survey of India', *Asiatic Researches* xviii.2 (1833): 189–214.

Everest, George. *An Account of the Measurement of Two Sections of the Meridional Arc of India … conducted under the orders of the Honourable East India Company*. London: Wm. H. Allen, 1847.

Fallon, Peter K. *Printing, Literacy, and Education in Eighteenth-Century Ireland: Why the Irish Speak English*. Lewiston, NY: Edwin Mellen Press, 2005.

Fanon, Frantz. *The Wretched of the Earth*, trans. Constance Farrington. New York: Grove Press, 1963.

Fitzpatrick, Siobhán. 'The maps that keep on giving', *Royal Irish Academy*, 26 August 2016, https://www.ria.ie/news/library-blog/maps-keep-giving (accessed 25 January 2017).

Flint, Kate. *The Woman Reader 1837–1914*. Oxford: Oxford University Press, 1993.

Foucault, Michel. 'Classifying', in Michel Foucault, *The Order of Things: An Archaeology of the Human Sciences*. London: Routledge, 1994, pp. 125–65.

Fraser, T.G. 'Ireland and India', in Keith Jeffery (ed.), *'An Irish Empire?' Aspects of Ireland and the British Empire*. Manchester: Manchester University Press, 1996, pp. 77–93.

Friel, Brian. *Translations*. [1981] London: Faber and Faber, 2000.

Frucht, Richard. *Eastern Europe: an Introduction to the People, Lands, and Culture*. California: ABC-CLIO, 2005.

Furet, François and Ozouf, Jacques. *Reading and Writing: Literacy in France from Calvin to Jules Ferry*. Cambridge: Cambridge University Press, 1982.

Galton, Francis. *Finger Prints*. London: Macmillan and Co., 1892.

Garvin, Tom. *The Evolution of Irish Nationalist Politics*. Dublin: Gill and Macmillan, 1981.

Goffman, Erving. *Frame Analysis: an Essay on the Organisation of Experience*. Cambridge, MA: Harvard University Press, 1986.

Graff, Harvey J. *The Legacies of Literacy: Continuities and Contradictions in Western Culture*. Bloomington: Indiana University Press, 1987.

Graff, Harvey, J., Alison Mackinnon, Bengt Sandin and Ian Winchester (eds). *Understanding Literacy in Its Historical Contexts: Socio-cultural History and the Legacy of Egil Johansson*. Lund: Nordic Academic Press, 2009.

Grant, James. *Impressions of Ireland and the Irish, 1844*. 2 vols. London: Cunningham, 1844.

Hackel, Heidi. *Reading Material in Early Modern England: Print, Gender, and Literacy*. Cambridge: Cambridge University Press, 2005.

Hardwick, Lorna. 'Women, Translation and Empowerment', in Joan Bellamy, Anne Laurence and Gillian Perry (eds), *Women, Scholarship and Criticism: Gender and Knowledge, 1790–1900*. Manchester: Manchester University Press, 2000, pp. 180–203.

Harley, J.B. 'Maps, Knowledge, and Power', in Paul Laxton (ed.), *The New Nature of Maps: Essays in the History of Cartography*. Baltimore, MD: John Hopkins University Press, 2001.

Hayden, William. *An Introduction to the Study of the Irish Language, Based Upon the Preface to Donlevy's Catechism*. Dublin, Gill & Son, 1891.

Hayley, Barbara. 'A Reading and Thinking Nation: Periodicals as the Voice of Nineteenth-Century Ireland', in Barbara Hayley and Enda McKay (eds), *Three Hundred Years of Irish Periodicals*. Dublin: Association of Irish Learned Journals, 1987, pp. 29–47.

Hayley, Barbara and Enda McKay (eds). *Three Hundred Years of Irish Periodicals*. Dublin: Association of Irish Learned Journals, 1987.

Helmstadter, R.J. 'The Nonconformist Conscience', in Gerald Parsons (ed.), *Religion in Victorian Britain, Vol. 4 Interpretations*. Manchester: Manchester University Press, 1988, pp. 61–95.

Hempton, David. '"*The Watchman*" and "Religious Politics" in the 1830s', *Proceedings of the Wesley Historical Society* 42:1 (1979): 2–13.

Hempton, David. *Methodism and Politics in British Society, 1750–1850*. Stanford, CA: Stanford University Press, 1984.

Heron-Allen, Edward. *A Manual of Cheirosophy*. London: Ward, Lock & Co, 1885.

Hewitt, Rachel. *Map of a Nation: A Biography of the Ordnance Survey*. London: Granta, 2010.

Higgins, Roisín. 'The *Nation* Reading Rooms', in James H. Murphy (ed.), *The Oxford History of the Irish Book, Vol. IV: The Irish Book in English 1800–1891*. Oxford: Oxford University Press, 2011, pp. 262–73.

Hoey, Frances Cashel. 'Translator's Preface'. *1794, a Tale of the Terror*. Dublin: M.H. Gill & Son, 1884, pp. vi–vii.

Holmes, Andrew. 'The Experience and Understanding of Religious Revival in Ulster Presbyterianism, c.1800–1930', *Irish Historical Studies* 34:136 (2005): 361–85.

Hooper, Glenn. *Travel Writing and Ireland, 1760–1860*. Basingstoke: Palgrave Macmillan, 2005.

Hornberger, Nancy H. 'Continua of Biliteracy', *Review of Educational Research* 59.3 (1989): 271–96.

Houston, R.A. *Literacy in Early Modern Europe*. 2nd ed. London: Pearson, 2002.

Hughes, Dorothy Price. *The Life of Hugh Price Hughes*. London: Hodder and Stoughton, 1904.

Hutton, Clare. 'Publishing the Irish Cultural Revival, 1891–1922', in Clare Hutton and Patrick Walsh (eds), *The Oxford History of the Irish Book, Volume V, The Irish Book in English 1891–2000*. Oxford: Oxford University Press, 2011, pp. 17–42.

Hyde, Douglas. *A Literary History of Ireland: From Earliest Times to the Present Day*. London: T. Fisher Unwin, 1899.

Hyde, Douglas. 'The Necessity for De-Anglicising Ireland, Baile Átha Cliath: Irish National Literary Society, 25 November 1892', in Breandán Ó Conaire (ed.), *Language, Lore and Lyrics: Essays and Lectures*. Dublin: Irish Academic Press, 1986, pp. 153–71.

Insley, J.E. '"Instruments of a Very Beautiful Class": George Everest in Europe, 1825–1830', in James R. Smith (ed.), *Colonel Sir George Everest CB FRS: Proceedings of the Bicentenary Conference at the Royal Geographical Society, 8th November 1990*. London: Royal Geographical Society and Royal Institute of Chartered Surveyors, 1990, pp. 23–30.

Irving, Washington. *Astoria; or, Anecdotes of an Enterprise Beyond the Rocky Mountains*. London: Richard Bentley & Co., 1839.

Jeffrey, Keith. 'The Irish Military Tradition and the British Empire', in Keith Jeffrey (ed.), *'An Irish Empire'? Aspects of Ireland and the British Empire*. Manchester: Manchester University Press, 1996, pp. 94–122.

Johanssen, Egil. 'The History of Literacy in Sweden', in Harvey Graff (ed.), *Literacy and Social Development in the West: a Reader*. Cambridge: Cambridge University Press, 1981, pp. 151–82.

Jordan, Thomas E. 'Queen Victoria's Irish Soldiers: Quality of Life and Social Origins of the Thin "Green" Line', *Social Indicators Research* 57.1 (2002): 73–88.

Kavanagh, Robin J. 'Religion and Illustrated Periodicals in the 1830s', in James H. Murphy (ed.), *The Oxford History of the Irish book, Vol. IV: The Irish Book in English, 1800–1891*. Oxford: Oxford University Press, 2011, pp. 342–57.

Kelly, Charlotte. 'The '82 Club', *Studies: an Irish Quarterly Review*, xxxiii (1944): 257–62.

Kelly, Laura. *Irish Women in Medicine c.1880s–1920s: Origins, Education and Careers*. Manchester: Manchester University Press, 2013.

Kelly, M.J. *The Fenian Ideal and Irish Nationalism 1882–1916*. Woodbridge: Boydell & Brewer, 2006.

Kenneally, Ian. *Courage and Conflict: Forgotten Stories of the Irish at War*. Cork: Cork University Press, 2009.

Keogh, Dáire and McDonnell, Albert (eds). *The Irish College, Rome and its World*. Dublin: Four Courts Press, 2008.

Kirkham, Graeme. 'Literacy in North-West Ulster 1680–1860', in Mary Daly and David Dickson (eds), *The Origins of Popular Literacy in Ireland: Language Change and Educational Development 1700–1920*. Dublin: Trinity College Dublin and University College Dublin, 1990, pp. 73–96.

Laird, Heather. *Subversive Law in Ireland, 1879–1920: From 'Unwritten Law' to the Dáil Courts*. Dublin: Four Courts Press, 2005.

Le Bras, Hervé and Todd, Emmanuel. *L'Invention de la France: Atlas Anthropologique et Politique*. Paris: Librairie Génerale Française, 1981.

Lee, Hermione. *Biography: A Very Short Introduction*. Oxford: Oxford University Press, 2009.

Leerssen, Joep. *Hidden Ireland, Public Sphere*. Galway: Arlen House, 2002.

Legg, Marie-Louise. *Newspapers and Nationalism: The Irish Provincial Press 1850–1892*. Dublin: Four Courts Press, 1999.

Legg, Marie-Louise. 'Libraries', in James H. Murphy (ed.), *The Oxford History of the Irish Book, Vol. IV: The Irish Book in English 1800–1891*. Oxford: Oxford University Press, 2011, pp. 243–61.

Livingstone, David N. *Putting Science in Its Place: Geographies of Scientific Knowledge*. Chicago: University of Chicago Press, 2003.

Lloyd, David. *Ireland After History*. Cork: Cork University Press and Field Day, 1999.

Lloyd, David. *Irish Culture and Colonial Modernity 1800–2000: The Transformation of Oral Space*. Cambridge: Cambridge University Press, 2011.

Loeber, Rolf and Magda Loeber. 'Popular Reading Practice', in *The Oxford History of the Irish Book Vol.IV: The Irish Book in English 1800–1891*. Oxford: Oxford University Press, 2011, pp. 211–39.

Logan, John, 'Sufficient for Their Needs: Literacy and Elementary Schooling in the Nineteenth Century', in Daly and Dickson (eds), *The Origins of Popular Literacy in Ireland*, pp. 113–37.

Long, Gerard. 'Institutional Libraries and Private Collections', in James H. Murphy (ed.), *The Oxford History of the Irish Book: the Irish Book in English, 1800–1891*. Oxford: Oxford University Press, 2011, pp. 281–97.

Luby, T.C. *Illustrious Irishmen*. New York: Kelly, 1878.

McBride, Lawrence W. (ed.). *Reading Irish Histories: Texts, Contexts and Memory in Modern Ireland*. Dublin: Four Courts Press, 2003.

MacCarthy, Anne. 'A Catholic Literature for Ireland: James Duffy and *Duffy's Irish Catholic Magazine*', in M.ª Luz Suárez Castiñeira, Asier Altuna García de Salazar and Olga Fernández (eds), *New Perspectives on James Joyce: Ignatius Loyola, Make Haste to Help Me!* Bilbao: Deusto University Press, 2009, pp. 65–75.

McDonough, Terrence (ed.). *Was Ireland a Colony? Economics, Politics and Culture in Nineteenth-Century Ireland*. Dublin: Irish Academic Press, 2005.

McGee, Thomas D'Arcy. *A Memoir of the Life and Conquests of Art Mac Murrogh* [*sic*] Dublin: J. Duffy, 1847.

McGuinne, Dermot. 'John O'Donovan's Edition of *The Annals of the Kingdom of Ireland by the Four Masters*', in James H. Murphy (ed.), *The Oxford History of the Irish Book, Vol. IV: The Irish Book in English, 1800–1891*. Oxford: Oxford University Press, 2011, pp. 477–83.

Mac Mathúna, Liam. *Béarla sa Ghaeilge. Cabhair Choigríche: An Códmheascadh Gaeilge/ Béarla i Litríocht na Gaeilge 1600–1900*. Baile Átha Cliath: An Clóchomhar, 2007.

Mac Mathúna, Liam. 'Promoting Irish on His American Tour, 1905–06: 54 Cities and Hyde's Two Visits to President Theodore Roosevelt in the White House', in Attrachta Halpin and Áine Mannion (eds), *Douglas Hyde: the Professor of Irish Who Became President of Ireland*. Dublin: National University of Ireland, 2016.

Maume, Patrick. 'Young Ireland, Arthur Griffith, and Republican Ideology: the Question of Continuity', *Eire-Ireland* xxxiv: 2 (1999): 155–74.

Maye, Brian. *Arthur Griffith*. Dublin: Griffith College Publications, 1997.

Meade, L.T. *The Oracle of Maddox Street*. London: Ward Locke, 1904.

Merkle, Denise, Carol O'Sullivan and Luc van Doorslaer (eds). *The Power of the Pen: Translation and Censorship in Nineteenth-Century Europe*. Berlin: LIT Verlag, 2010.

Milan, Michèle. 'Found in Translation: Franco-Irish Translation Relationships in Nineteenth-Century Ireland', in *New Voices in Translation Studies* 8 (2012): 82–98.

Milan, Michèle. 'Found in Translation: Franco-Irish Translation Relationships in Nineteenth-Century Ireland'. PhD thesis. Dublin City University, 2013. [Online], Permanent Link: http://doras.dcu.ie/17753/, 54–55.

Milan, Michèle. 'For the People, the Republic and the Nation: Translating Béranger in Nineteenth-Century Ireland', in Ben Keatinge and Mary Pierse (eds), *France and Ireland in the Public Imagination*. Oxford: Peter Lang, 2014, pp. 79–98.

Milan, Michèle. 'A Path to Perfection: Translations from French by Catholic Women Religious in Nineteenth-Century Ireland', in D. Raftery and E. Smith (eds), *Education, Identity and Women Religious, 1800–1950: Convents, Classrooms and Colleges*. London: Routledge, 2015, pp. 183–98.

Milan, Michèle. 'Mary Anne Sadlier's Trans-Atlantic Links: Migration, Religion and Translation', *Atlantic Studies* 15.3 (2018): 365–82.

Miller, D.W. 'Did Ulster Presbyterians Have a Devotional Revolution?', in J.H. Murphy (ed.), *Evangelicals and Catholics in Nineteenth Century Ireland*. Dublin: Four Courts Press, 2005, pp. 38–54.

Milton, John and Paul Bandia (eds). *Agents of Translation*. Amsterdam: John Benjamins, 2009.

Morley, Vincent. *The Popular Mind in Eighteenth-Century Ireland*. Cork: Cork University Press, 2017.

Morris, N.K. 'Predicting a "Bright and Prosperous Future": Irish Methodist Membership, 1855–1914', *Wesley and Methodist Studies* 2 (2010): 91–114.

Morrissey, John. 'A Lost Heritage: The Connaught Rangers and Multivocal Irishness', in Mark McCarthy (ed.), *Ireland's Heritages: Critical Perspectives on Memory and Identity*. Aldershot: Ashgate, 2005, pp. 71–87.

Morrow, John. 'Thomas Carlyle, "Young Ireland" and the "Condition of Ireland Question"', *The Historical Journal* LI.3 (2008): 643–67.

Murray, Peter. *George Petrie (1790–1866): The Rediscovery of Ireland's Past*. Cork: Crawford Municipal Art Gallery; Kinsale, Co. Cork: Gandon Editions, 2004.

Navarre, Joan. 'Oscar Wilde, Edward Heron-Allen, and the Palmistry Craze of the 1880s', *English Literature in Transition, 1880–1920* 54.2 (2011): 174–84.

Newell, Stephanie. *Literary Culture in Colonial Ghana: 'How to Play the Game of Life'*. Manchester: Manchester University Press, 2002.

Ní Ghearbhuigh, Ailbhe. *An Fhrainc Iathghlas? Tionchar na Fraince ar Athbheochan na Gaeilge, 1893–1922*. PhD dissertation, NUI Galway, 2013.

O'Brien, James. *The Scientific Sherlock Holmes: Cracking the Case with Science & Forensics*. Oxford: Oxford University Press, 2013.

O'Brien, Jennifer. 'Irish Public Opinion and the Risorgimento, 1859–60', *Irish Historical Studies* 34.135 (2005): 289–305.

O'Brien, William. *Recollections*. London: Macmillan, 1905.

O'Carroll, Ciarán. 'The Papal Brigade of Saint Patrick', in Dáire Keogh and Albert McDonnell (eds), *The Irish College, Rome and its World*. Dublin: Four Courts Press, 2008, pp. 167–87.

Occupation Abstract, Part I. England and Wales, 1841 H.C. 1844 XXVII.

Ó Ciosáin, Niall. *Print and Popular Culture in Ireland 1750–1850*. Basingstoke: Macmillan, 1997a.

Ó Ciosáin, Niall. *Print and Popular Culture in Ireland, 1750–1850*. New York: St Martin's Press, 1997b.

Ó Ciosáin, Niall. 'Oral Culture, Literacy and Reading, 1800–50', in James H. Murphy (ed.), *The Oxford History of the Irish Book: the Irish Book in English, 1800–1891*. Oxford: Oxford University Press, 2011, pp. 173–91.

O'Clery, Patrick Keyes. *The Making of Italy*. London, 1892.

Ó Conaire, Breandán. 'An Dírbheathaisnéis: *Genre*, Coincheap nó Cíor Thuathail? Smaointe ar Nádúr na Tuairisce Beatha', in Mícheál B. Ó Mainín (ed.), *Léann* 1. Béal Feirste: Shanway Press, 2007, p. 10.

O'Connell, Helen. *Ireland and the Fiction of Improvement*. Oxford: Oxford University Press, 2006.

O'Connor, Anne. 'Triumphant Failure: the Return of the Irish Papal Brigade', *Journal of the Cork Historical and Archaeological Society* 114 (2009): 39–50.

Ó Criomhthain, Tomás. *An t-Oileánach: Scéal a Bheathadh Féin*. [Baile Átha Cliath]: Muinntir C. S. Ó Fallamhain i gcomhar le hOifig an tSoláthair, 1929.

Ó Cuív, Brian. 'Irish Language and Literature, 1691–1845', in T.W. Moody and W.E. Vaughan (eds), *A New History of Ireland, vol. 4, Eighteenth-century Ireland, 1691–1800*. Oxford: Clarendon Press, 1876, pp. 374–423.

O'Day, Alan. *Parnell and the First Home Rule Episode, 1884–7*. Dublin: Gill and Macmillan, 1986.

Ó Glaisne, Risteárd. *Dúbhglas de h-Íde (1860–1949) ceannródaí cultúrtha 1860–1910*. Baile Átha Cliath: Conradh na Gaeilge, 1991.

Ó Grada, Cormac. *School Attendance and Literacy before the Famine: A Simple Baronial Analysis*. Dublin: UCD Centre for Economic Research Working Paper Series, 2010.

Ó Grianna, Séamus. *Rann na Feirste*. Dublin: An Press Náisiúnta, 1942.

O'Hegarty, P.S. *A History of Ireland under the Union 1801–1922*. London: Methuen, 1952.

Olden, Michael. 'Tobias Kirby (1804–1895): The Man Who Kept the Papers', in Dáire Keogh and Albert McDonnell (eds), *The Irish College, Rome and its World*. Dublin: Four Courts Press, 2008, pp. 131–48.

Oldstone-Moore, Christopher. *Hugh Price Hughes: Founder of a New Methodism, Conscience of a New Nonconformity*. Cardiff: University of Wales Press, 1999.

O'Leary, John. *Recollections of Fenians and Fenianism*. 2 vols. London: Downey & Co., 1896.

O'Leary, Philip. *The Prose Literature of the Gaelic Revival, 1881–1921: Ideology and Innovation*. Pennsylvania: Pennsylvania State University Press, 1994.

Olsen, David R. and Nancy Torrance (eds). *The Cambridge Handbook of Literacy*. Cambridge: Cambridge University Press, 2008.

O'Neill, Ciaran. *Catholics of Consequence: Transnational Education, Social Mobility and the Irish Catholic Elite, 1850–1900*. Oxford: Oxford University Press, 2014.

O'Neill, Ciaran. 'Literacy and Education', in Eugenio F. Biagini and Mary E. Daly (eds), *The Cambridge History of Modern Ireland*. Cambridge: Cambridge University Press, 2017, pp. 244–60.

O'Neill, T.P. 'The Charities and Famine in Mid-Nineteenth Century Ireland', in Jacqueline Hill and Colm Lennon (eds), *Luxury and Austerity*. Dublin: UCD Press, 1999.

Ong, Walter. *Orality and Literacy: The Technologizing of the Word*. London: Routledge, 1999.

Ó Tuathaigh, M.Á.G. *Thomas Drummond and the Government of Ireland, 1835–40*. O'Donnell Lecture. Dublin: National University of Ireland, 1977.

Pamboukian, Sylvia. '"Looking Radiant": Science, Photography and the X-Ray Craze of 1896', *Victorian Review* 27.2 (2001): 56–74.

Parsons, Cóilín. 'The Archive in Ruins', *Interventions: International Journal of Postcolonial Studies* 13.1 (2011): 464–82.

Phillimore, R.H. *Historical Records of the Survey of India, Vol. IV, George Everest (1830–43)*. Dehra Dun, India: Survey of India, 1958.

Piaget, Jean. *Jean Piaget: A Most Outrageous Deception*. New York: Nova Science Publishers, 2001.

Pope-Hennessy, J. 'What do the Irish Read?', *Nineteenth Century* XV (1884): 925–26.

Prunty, Jacinta. *Maps and Map-Making in Local History*. Dublin: Four Courts Press, 2004.

Queniart, Jean. 'De l'oral à l'écrit: les modalités d'une mutation.' *Histoire de l'Éducation* 21 (1984): 11–35.

Quinn, James. 'John Mitchel and the Rejection of the Nineteenth Century', *Éire-Ireland* xxxviii.3–4 (2003): 90–108.

Quinn, James. *Young Ireland and the Writing of Irish History*. Dublin: UCD Press, 2015.

Rains, Stephanie. '"Nauseous Tides of Seductive Debauchery": Irish Story Papers and the Anti-Vice Campaigns of the Early Twentieth Century', *Irish University Review* 45.2 (2015): 263–80.

Raj, Kapil. 'Colonial Encounters and the Forging of New Knowledge and National Identities: Great Britain and India, 1760–1850', *Osiris*, 2nd Series, 15 (2000): 119–34.

Raj, Kapil. 'When Human Travellers Become Instruments: Indo-British Exploration of Central Asia in the Nineteenth Century', in Marie-Noëlle Bourget, Christian Licoppe and H. Otto Sibum (eds), *Instruments, Travel and Science: Itineraries of Precision Form the Seventeenth to the Twentieth Century*. London and New York: Routledge, 2002, pp. 156–88.

Raponi, Danilo. *Religion and Politics in the Risorgimento: Britain and the New Italy, 1861–1875*. Basingstoke: Palgrave, 2014.

Raven, James, Helen Small and Naomi Tadmor (eds). *The Practice and Representation of Reading in England*. Cambridge: Cambridge University Press, 1996.

Report of the Commissioners Appointed to Take the Census of Ireland, for the Year 1841. Dublin: Her Majesty's Stationery Office, 1843.

Riall, Lucy. 'Garibaldi and the South', in John A. Davis (ed.), *Italy in the Nineteenth Century 1796–1900*. Oxford: Oxford University Press, 2000, pp. 132–53.

Riall, Lucy. *Garibaldi: Invention of a Hero*. New Haven, CT: Yale University Press, 2007.

Riall, Lucy. *Risorgimento: The History of Italy from Napoleon to Nation State*. Basingstoke: Palgrave, 2009.

Riall, Lucy and Patriarca, Silvana (eds). *The Risorgimento Revisited: Nationalism and Culture in Nineteenth-Century Italy*. Basingstoke: Palgrave, 2012.

Richardson, Alan. 'Literacy', in Laura Dabundo (ed.), *Encyclopedia of Romanticism: Culture in Britain, 1780s-1830s*. London: Routledge, 2010.

Roddie, Robin. 'Reporting and Recording', *Methodist Newsletter* (January 1998).

Ryder, Sean. 'Speaking of '98: Young Ireland and Republican Memory', *Éire-Ireland* xxxiv.2 (1999): 51–69.

Ryder, Sean. 'Young Ireland and the 1798 Rebellion, in L.M. Geary (ed.), *Rebellion and Remembrance in Modern Ireland*. Dublin: Four Courts Press, 2001, pp. 135–47.

Said, Edward. *Culture and Imperialism*. London: Vintage, 1994.

St Clair, William. *The Reading Nation in the Romantic Period*. Cambridge: Cambridge University Press, 2004.

Schofield, Roger. 'The Measurement of Literacy in Pre-Industrial England', in Jack Goody (ed.), *Literacy in Traditional Societies*. Cambridge: Cambridge University Press, 1969, pp. 311–25.

Schofield, Roger. 'Dimensions of Illiteracy in England, 1750–1850', in Harvey Graff (ed.), *Literacy and Social Development in the West: a Reader*. Cambridge: Cambridge University Press, 1981, pp. 201–13.

Scott, Patrick. 'Victorian Religious Periodicals: Fragments That Remain', in Derek Baker (ed.), *Sources, Methods and Material of Ecclesiastical History: Papers Read at the Twelfth Summer Meeting and the Thirteenth Winter Meeting of the Ecclesiastical History Society*. Studies in Church History, 11. Blackwell: Oxford, 1975.

Sebba, Mark. *Spelling and Society: the Culture and Politics of Orthography Around the World*. Cambridge: Cambridge University Press, 2007.

Shep, Sydney J. 'Cultures of Print: Materiality, Memory, and the Rituals of Transmission', *Journal of New Zealand Literature* 28 (2010): 183–210.

Simeoni, Daniel. 'Translating and Studying Translation: The View from the Agent', *Meta: Journal des traducteurs / Meta: Translators' Journal* 40.3 (1995): 445–60.

Simon, Sherry. *Gender in Translation: Cultural Identity and The Politics of Transmission.* London: Routledge, 1996.

Singh, Maina. 'Political Activism and the Politics of Spirituality: The Layered Identities of Sister Nivedita/Margaret Noble (1867–1911)', in Tadhg Foley and Maureen O'Connor (eds), *Ireland and India: Colonies, Culture and Empire* Dublin: Irish Academic Press, 2006, pp. 39–57.

Smith, Adam. *An Inquiry into the Nature and Causes of the Wealth of Nations.* Dublin, 1776.

Smith, James R. 'Sir George Everest, F.R.S. (1790–1866)', *Notes and Records of the Royal Society of London* 46:1 (1992): 89–102.

Smith, James R. *Everest: The Man and the Mountain.* Caithness, Scotland: Whittles Publishing Services, 1999.

Spivak, Gayatri. 'The Rani of Simur', in Francis Barker, Peter Hulme, Margaret Iversen and Diana Loxley (eds), *Europe and its Others, Vol. 1 Proceedings of the Essex Conference on the Sociology of Literature.* Colchester: University of Essex, 1985, p. 133.

Steele, Karen and Michael de Nie (eds). *Ireland and the New Journalism.* London: Palgrave Macmillan, 2014.

Stokes, William. *The Life and Labours in Art and Archaeology of George Petrie, LL.D., M.R.I.A.* London: Longmans, Green, and Co., 1868.

Stone, Lawrence. 'Literacy and Education in England, 1640–1900', *Past and Present* 42 (1969): 69–139.

Stone, Lawrence. 'Literacy and Education in England, 1640–1900', in Lawrence Stone, *The Past and Present.* London: Routledge, 1981.

Stover, Justin Dolan. 'Witness to War: Charles Ouin-la-Croix and the Irish College, Paris, 1870–71', *Etudes irlandaises* xxxvi (2011): 27–28.

Street, Brian. *Literacy in Theory and in Practice.* Cambridge: Cambridge University Press, 1984.

Sullivan, A.M. *New Ireland.* New York, 1878.

Sutcliffe, Marcella Pellegrino. 'British Red Shirts: A History of the Garibaldi Volunteers (1860)', in Nir Arielli and Bruce Collins (eds), *Transnational Soldiers: Foreign Military Enlistment in the Modern Era* (Basingstoke: Palgrave, 2013), pp. 202–18.

Swift, Roger. 'Carlyle and Ireland', in D. George Boyce and Roger Swift (eds), *Problems and Perspectives in Irish History since 1800: Essays in Honour of Patrick Buckland.* Dublin: Four Courts Press, 2004, pp. 117–46.

Taggart, N.W. *The Irish in World Methodism, 1760–1900.* London: Epworth Press, 1986.

Tilley, Elizabeth. 'Periodicals', in James H. Murphy (ed.), *The Oxford History of the Irish Book, Vol. IV: The Irish Book in English, 1800–1891.* Oxford: Oxford University Press, 2011, pp. 144–73.

Tilley, Elizabeth. 'The Royal Irish Academy and Antiquarianism', in James H. Murphy (ed.), *The Oxford History of the Irish Book, Vol. IV: The Irish Book in English, 1800–1891.* Oxford: Oxford University Press, 2011, pp. 463–76.

Townend, Paul A. '"Academies of Nationality": the Reading Room and Irish National Movements, 1838–1905', in Lawrence W. McBride (ed.), *Reading Irish Histories: Texts, Contexts and Memory in Modern Ireland.* Dublin: Four Courts Press, 2003, pp. 19–39.

Tyerman, Luke. *The Life and Times of the Rev. John Wesley, MA*, Vol. 3, 3rd ed. London: Hodder and Stoughton, 1876.

Tymoczko, Maria. *Translation in a Postcolonial Context: Early Irish Literature in English Translation*. Manchester: Jerome Publishing, 1999.

Vaschide, Nicholas. *Essai sur la Psychologie de la main*. Paris: Marcel Rivière, 1909.

Venuti, Lawrence. 'Translation As Cultural Politics: Regimes of Domestication in English', *Textual Practice* 7 (1993): 208–23.

Venuti, Lawrence. *The Translator's Invisibility: A History of Translation*. 2nd ed. London and New York: Routledge, 2008.

Vincent, David. *Literacy and Popular Culture: England 1750–1914*. Cambridge: Cambridge University Press, 1993.

Vincent, David. *The Rise of Mass Literacy: Reading and Writing in Modern Europe*. Cambridge: Polity Press, 2000.

Viswanathan, Gauri. *Masks of Conquest: Literary Study and British Rule in India*. Oxford: Oxford University Press, 1998.

Viswanathan, Gauri. 'Ireland, India, and the Poetics of Internationalism', *Journal of World History* 15.1 (2004): 7–30.

Walker, Douglas. *French Sound System*. Calgary: University of Calgary Press, 2001.

Wallington, A. 'The Arminian and Methodist Magazine: British and Irish Editions', *PWHS*, 13:1 (1921): 11–12.

Welch, Robert. *A History of Verse Translation from the Irish 1789–1897*. Gerrards Cross: Colin Smythe, 1988.

Wesley, John. *The Journal of John Wesley in Four Volumes*, Vol.4. London: Wesleyan Conference Office, 1904.

Wesleyan Methodist Church in Great Britain: Minutes of Conference, 1891. London: Methodist Church in Great Britain, 1891.

Wesleyan Methodist Church in Ireland: Minutes of Conference, 1800–1914. Dublin: Methodist Church in Ireland, 1861–1914.

Whelan, Kevin. *The Tree of Liberty: Radicalism, Catholicism and the Construction of Irish Identity 1760–1830*. Cork: Cork University Press, 1996.

Willinsky, John. *Learning to Divide the World: Education at Empire's End*. Minneapolis: University of Minnesota Press, 1998.

Winkles, A.O. '"Excuse What Difficiencies You Will Find": Methodist Women and Public Space in John Wesley's Arminian Magazine', *Eighteenth-Century Studies* 46:3 (2013): 416–17.

Wolf, Nicholas. *An Irish Speaking Island: State, Religion, Community, and the Linguistic Landscape in Ireland, 1770–1870*. London: University of Wisconsin Press, 2014.

Wright, G.N. *Ireland Illustrated*. London: H. Fisher, Son, and Jackson, 1831.

Yolland, William. *An Account of the Measurement of the Lough Foyle Base, with Its Verification and Extension by Triangulation; Together with the Various Methods of Computation Followed on the Ordnance Survey, and the Requisite Tables*. London: Palmer and Clayton, 1847.

Zakiewicz, Tomasz. 'The Cape Geodetic Standards and Their Impact on Africa', Unpublished paper, FIG Working Week 2005, Cairo, Egypt 16–21 April, https://www.fig.net/resources/proceedings/fig_proceedings/cairo/papers/wshs_03/wshs03_02_zakiewich.pdf (accessed 30 November 2016).

Index

Abyssinia and its apostle 123
Act of Union 5, 11, 55, 60, 87, 118
agriculture 95
    grain mills 95
Airy, Sir George 170
Allen, I.S. 76
Annals of the Four Masters 7, 90, 95, 96
    description 91–92
Arminian Magazine 66, 68–69
Arthur, William 75
Asiatic Researches 170
Astoria: or Anecdotes of an Enterprise Beyond the Rocky Mountains 122
Atkinson, A. 121
availability of books 26

Babbage, Charles 169
Ballad Poetry of Young Ireland 63
Barrington, Jonah 118
The Beauties of Shakespeare: Regularly Selected from Each Play 121
Belfast Telegraph 84
Berkeley, G.F.H. 127, 130, 131, 135, 136
Black, Josephine 150
Blackney, Captain James 129
Blackrock College 112
Blackwood's Magazine 88
Bolton, Henry Carrington 189
Boyle, Patrick 109, 110, 119, 125
Brooke, Charlotte 142
Bude Light 168
Bunting, Rev. Jabez 70, 74
Butt, Isaac 111

Caddell, Mary Cecilia 123
Cahill, Rev. D.W. 118
Cape Colony 174
Carr, John 122
cartography 3, 159–75
Cary, Henry 144
Catalogue of Books Contained in The People's Library...Belfast 148
Catholic Association 17, 117
Catholic Emancipation 60, 70, 87, 91, 117–18
Catholic Guardian 151
Catholic missions in Southern India to 1865 123
Catholic Penny Magazine 88
Catholic University Gazette 119
Catholic Young Men's Society 64
Cavour, Count Camillo 127
Census of Ireland
    1841 1, 7, 23
    commissioners, 1841 16
Chambers's Edinburgh Journal 88
'Cheiro' *see* William John Warner
Cheyfitz, Eric 143
Christian Advocate 10, 79, 80, 81, 83–84, 85
Christian Brothers 148, 150
Church of England 69
Cialdini, General Enrico 130
Clongowes Wood College 126
Clooney, Patrick 136
code-mixing 32
The Coiner's Cave 150

Colby, Colonel Thomas 168–70
Colby's Compensation Bars 8
Cole, Rev. Richard 84, 85
colonialism 2, 7, 9–10, 143–44, 159
Columba Bazaar 1898 184
Conan Doyle, Arthur 178
The Confederate Chieftains: a Tale of the Irish Rebellion of 1641 120
Confederation of Kilkenny 58
Confessions: Memoirs of a Modern Seer 179, 183
Confiscation of Ulster 57
Connolly, William 46
Contagious Diseases Act 77, 78
Corn Laws 117, 118
Council of Trent 114
The Count of Monte Cristo 148
Cronhelm, Theodore 73
Crook, Rev. Dr William 73
Crookshank, C.H. 70, 81, 84
Cullen, Cardinal Paul 109–10, 119
  Cullenite revolution 108
cultural nationalism 28
cultural outputs 60, 64
Curry, Eugene 96
Cyclopia Bazaar 178

Davis, Thomas 53, 54, 63, 141, 143–44
de Cobain, E.S.W. 78, 79
de Freyne, Lord 45
De La Hoyde, Albert 11, 126
  acquisition of languages 132
  attitude to Italians 133
De Martine, Alphonse 122
Denvir, John 62
detective fiction 178
Devoy, John 62, 132
Dillon, John Blake 141
Discourses on University Education: Addressed to the Catholics of Dublin 120
Dodd, William 121
Donald, Rev. Dr John 76, 77
Down Survey 165
Drummond, Thomas 168–69
  Drummond Light 168
Dublin Penny Journal 3, 6, 88
  characteristics 89
  circulation figures 87, 88, 90
  lack of patronage 100
Dublin Review 119
Dublin University Magazine 10, 88, 141, 154
Duffy, Charles Gavan 61, 63, 152
Duffy's Fire Side Magazine 149
Dumas, Alexandre 146
Duncan, Alexander 78
Dungannon Clubs 64

Earlsfort Terrace Exhibition Palace 182
Early Irish Missions: Fruits of Irish Piety in the British Church 123
East India Company 161, 166, 167, 168
education 88
  clerical 110, 111
  denial of appropriate instruction 56
  expansion 54
  in national renewal 62
  National System 54, 56, 64, 71, 77
Elgee, Jane 148
Elizabeth; or, the Exiles of Siberia: a Tale Founded on Truth 150
Emanuel II, King Victor 130
English Society for the Diffusion of Useful Knowledge (SDUK) 88, 90
Enlightenment 144, 165
Essai sur la Psychologie de la main 189
Evans, Dr Henry 77, 78, 81
Everest, George 8, 161, 169–71

Fagan, William 117
Fanon, Frantz 143
Faraday, Michael 168
Von Fellenberg, Phillip Emanuel 172
Fellenberg School 172
Fenian movement 46
The Ferryman of the Tiber: an Historical Tale 150
Fianna Éireann 64
Finger Prints 178
fingerprint technology 178

First Vatican Council 107, 120
First World War 181
Fitzpatrick, William 119
Four Lectures on the Offices and Ceremonies of Holy Week 120
Franco-Prussian War 110–11
Freeman's Journal 80
French Revolution 10, 108, 118, 146, 149
French Third Republic 107
Friel, Brian 175

Gaelic League 5, 28, 50, 107
Gaelic Revival 140
Galerie du Luxembourg 113
Galton, Francis 178
Garibaldi, Giuseppe 129, 130, 131, 134, 137
gender 8, 9, 23, 181, 186–87
  breakdown of ability 20
  female literacy 18
  and translation 142
Geodetic Survey of South Africa 170
Ghana 9
Gladstone, William 75, 76, 79
Glebe Estate *see* William Connolly
Gospel Magazine 69
Grand Orange Lodge, Belfast 79
graphology 9, 180
  definition 180
  possible use 181
  published opinions of 180
Grattan, Henry 117
'Great Arc Series' 167
Great Famine 25, 61, 72, 87, 101, 137
Great Reform Act (1832) 70
Great Trigonometrical Survey in India 160, 167
Great Trigonometrical Survey of Ireland 171
Greer, Robert 84
Greenwich Meridian 175
Gregory, Lady 142
Griffith, Arthur 63, 64
Guard, Rev. Wesley 84
Gurney, Sir Goldsmith 168

Harper's Handbook for Travellers in Europe and the East 122
Hart, James or Seamus 45–47
  death 45–46
Hay, Edward 118
Hayden, Rev. William 142
Herbertt, Mary Elizabeth 123
d'Héricault, Charles 146
Heron-Allen, Edward 178
historical memory 109
An Historical Review of the State of Ireland (1803) 56
History of the Confederation of Kilkenny 57–58
History of the Insurrection of Co. Wexford, A.D. 1798 118
History of Ireland (1758–63) 56, 63
History of Methodism in Ireland 70
A History of the Missions in Japan and Paraguay 123
History of the Volunteers of 1782 57, 58
Hoey, Frances Sarah Cashel 145, 146
Home Rule 79, 80, 81, 84, 107
House of Commons 80
Howlin, Aloysius 136
Hughes, Hugh Price 81, 82
Hyde, Arthur 40–43, 47
Hyde, Bessie 32
Hyde, Cecily 31, 50
Hyde, Douglas 5
  Abhráin Grádh Chúige Connacht or *Love Songs of Connacht* 50
  character 42, 50
  early life 28, 30–31
  family vices 48
  Frenchpark 30, 47, 48
  interests 28, 41
  Literary History of Ireland 31
  'The Necessity for De-Anglicising Ireland' 47
  writing patterns 34–37
Hyde, Oldfield 47

The Idea of a University Defined and Illustrated in Nine Discourses 120

An Impartial History of Ireland (1809–11) 56
Inghinide na hÉireann 64
Introduction to the Study of the Irish Language 142
IRA 184
Ireland Exhibited to England in a Political and Moral Survey of her Population 121
Ireland Illustrated 98, 99, 100
Ireland and the Italian Risorgimento 127
Ireland's Own 178
The Irish Battalion in the Papal Army of 1860 127
Irish Christian Advocate 66, 76, 77, 78
Irish College, Paris 10, 107
  college year 112
  membership figures 124
  nature of education 113
  Old Library 10
Irish Confederation (1847) 61, 62
Irish diaspora 63, 87
Irish Ecclesiastical Record 119, 120, 146
Irish Evangelist 66, 67, 73, 74, 76, 81, 85
Irish Examiner 144
Irish Independent 178
Irish-language texts 25
Irish Literary Society 64
Irish National Land League 63, 107
Irish Packet 178
Irish Parliamentary Party 78, 84, 111
Irish Party 76, 82
Irish Penny Journal 101
Irish Rosary 184, 187
Irish Times 178, 183, 187
Irish Volunteers 118
Irving, Washington 122
Isolde Bazaar 184

Jail Journal 59, 63
Jervis, Thomas 172
Jesuits 148
Johnston, Frank 84
Jordan, Jeremiah 78, 80, 85

Kelly, Mary Eva 141
Kildare Place Society 150
Kim 162
Kipling, Rudyard 162
Kirby, Tobias 128

Laboratory of Pathological Psychology of the School of Higher Study in Paris 189
Lady of the House 180
Lady's Pictorial 184
Lalor, James Fintan 61
Lambton, Colonel William 166, 171
Land War 76
The Language of the Hand 179, 188
Larcom, Thomas 96
'The Last Crusade' 128
Lawrence, Henry Montgomery 171
  early life 171
Lectures on the Principal Doctrines and Practices of the Catholic Church 120
Legends, Lyrics and Hymns 120
A Letter Addressed to his Grace the Duke of Norfolk on Account of Mr. Gladstone's Recent Expostulation 120
Lettres d'Irlande 109
Lewis, Samuel 122
'Library of Ireland' 57, 59, 61, 62
Life and Times of Aodh O'Neill, Prince of Ulster 57
Life and Times of Daniel O'Connell 116–17
Life and Times of Daniel O'Connell with Sketches of his Contemporaries 116
literacy
  as a driver of rebellion 16
  as a path to employment 176–77
  denominational breakdown 22, 23
  historiography 15, 24
  measurement 15, 19, 24, 176
  regional variations 15, 18, 23
  skills 109
London Gaelic League 132
Lord's Cricket Ground 169, 170
Louis XIV 110
Luby, Thomas Clarke 62

McArthur, William Alexander 76
Macauley, Thomas Babbington 172

McCutcheon, Rev. Dr 84
McGee, Thomas D'Arcy 60
MacGeoghegan, James 56
MacHale, Archbishop John 140
Maclear, Sir Thomas 170
MacMurrough, Art 60
McNamara, Thomas 113, 115
MacNevin, Thomas 57
Mangan, James Clarence 96
Meade, L.T. 188
Meagher, Thomas Francis 61
Mechanics' Institutes 88
Meehan, Fr C.P. 57
Mentana, Battle of 131
Mentana Letter *see* George Berkeley
Methodism
  literacy levels 67
Methodist publications
  Methodist Magazine 69, 74
  Methodist Recorder 66, 74, 75, 76
  Methodist Times 66, 76, 80, 81, 82, 83
Mitchel, John 57, 58–59, 61, 63
monster meetings 56
Montgomery, Robert 172
Moran, Patrick 123
Moriarty, Bishop of Kerry 115
motivation to learn 7
Musée du Luxembourg 113

Napoleon 110, 116
Napoleonic Wars 110, 121
Nation 5, 6, 10, 53, 92, 130, 134, 136, 140, 141, 143, 144, 145, 149, 151–53
'A Nation Once Again' 58
national identity 11
National Library of Ireland 5, 28, 40
National Literary Society 47
National Museum of Ireland 90
new literacies 3
New Testament 37
Newman, John Henry 120
Nine Years' War 58

O'Brien, William 62
O'Brien, William Smith 73, 141
O'Byrne, Patrick 149
O'Carroll, Richard A. 133, 136
O'Connell, Daniel 55, 56, 57, 60, 61, 71, 116
O'Connell, John 116
Ó Críomhthain, Tomás 47
O'Donovan, John 92, 95, 96
t-Oileánach, An 47
O'Keeffe, C.M. 116
Old Testament 114
O'Neill, Hugh 59
O'Neill, Owen Roe 59
oral history 31
Orangemen 55
Ordnance Survey of Ireland 6, 96, 160–61, 165–66, 170, 175
  Dublin 8
O'Reilly, Major Myles 130
orthography 4
Otway, Caesar 89

Palais des Beaux Arts 113
Pall Mall Gazette 76
palmistery 180–81
  court proceedings 185
  criticism of 184
  dissemination of 181
  practitioners of 182
Papal Army 129
  De Lamorciere, General Louis Christophe 129
  Papal Battalion of St Patrick 11, 126, 130, 131, 133–34, 135, 136, 138
Papal Zouaves 11, 131, 132, 134, 137, 138
Parnell, Charles Stuart 76, 81, 82, 183
  fall of 82–83
Penny Magazine 88
Petrie, George 6, 7, 89, 90, 91, 92, 95, 99, 100, 101
Petty, William 165
Phoenix Park 96
Pictures of the First French Revolution, being Episodes from the History of the Girondists 148
Pictures of Missionary Life in the Nineteenth Century Western World, on the Shelves of the College Library 123

Pigott forgeries 81
plays by Shakespeare 121
Plowden, Francis 56
The Poetical Works of Lord Byron 120
Pontifical Irish College Rome 128
Pope Leo XIII 183
Pope Pius IX 11, 128, 136, 137
Potter, Thomas 120
printers and publishers
  Cross, Richard 10, 147, 154
  Duffy, James 10, 147, 148–49, 151
  Folds, John S. 98
  Gill, M.H. and Sons 10, 146, 147, 148, 149, 150
  Gúm, An 47
  Hodges, Smith & Co 147
  Napper, Robert 69
  roles of 147
  Simms and McIntyre 147
  Wesleyan Methodist Newspaper Company 70
Protestant Irish Penny Magazine 88

Rambler 119
Rasputin, 183
Rebellion of 1798 119
Redemptorists 148
Reform Act (1867) 75
Reformation 75
Registration Act 1863 17
Repeal Association 55, 56, 61
Repeal Campaign 144
The Rise and Fall of the Irish Nation 118
Roentgen, Wilhelm 177
Royal Commission 1854 115
Royal Dublin Showgrounds 182
Royal Irish Academy 7, 31, 88, 90, 91, 95
Royal Society Philosophical Transactions 169

Sadlier, Mary Anne 120
St Denis 113
St Germain 113
Sand, George 152
Sarsfield, Patrick 59
Saunderson, Major Edward 78
scientific discoveries 177
Select Speeches 116
The select speeches of the right Hon. Henry Grattan 117
'The Sham Squire' and the Informers of 1798 119
Shamrock 178
Shillington, Thomas 78, 84
The Sign of Four 178
Smith, Adam 16
Smith, Michael 136
Speeches of the Right Hon. Richard Lalor Shiel 117
The Spirit of the Nation 60
The Stranger in Ireland or a Tour in the Southern and Western Parts of that Country 122
Sullivan, A.M. 63, 64, 130
Sullivan, T.D. 63
Survey of India 172, 174

Taaffe, Denis 56
The Tablet 109
Tale of Terror 146
Teagask Creestye, An 25
Temperance movement 145
The Times 79
Tobias, Matthew 80–81
A Topographical Dictionary of Ireland 122
traits of a good cleric 115
Translations 175
Travels in the Holy Land or a Visit to the Scene of our Redeemer's Life 122
Trinity College Dublin 31, 95
Troughton & Simms 169, 170
Twain, Mark 183
Twelve Lectures on the Connection between Science and Revealed Religion 120

Ulster Convention (1892) 84
Ulster Covenant 85
Ulster Revival 67, 72, 73
United Irishmen 5, 57, 61, 118
University College Dublin 5, 28

Vaschide, Nicholas 189
Versailles 113
Vincennes 113
Volunteers of 1782 61

Warner, William John 179, 183
Washington, George 116
Watchman 66, 70, 71, 72, 74, 75, 76, 79
Weekly Irish Times 142
Wesley, John 68
Wesleyan Methodist Relief Fund 72
Wild Geese 59
Wilde, Oscar 179
Wiseman, Nicholas 120
Witchcraft Act 1735
World's Fair Waxworks 182
Wright, G.N. 96

Young Ireland 5, 6, 53, 54–55, 57, 59, 60, 61, 62, 63, 64, 72, 92, 101, 140, 144, 148, 149
Young Irelanders *see* Young Ireland